To My friend
Dick Pritchard
Best Wishes

Maurice Zolar

MENSCH

BIOGRAPHY AND WRITINGS OF MANFRED ERIC SWARSENSKY

Marvin Zolot, M.D

Edgewood College Press

Edgewood College Press
1000 Edgewood College Dr.
Madison, WI 53711
608-257-4861
www.edgewood.edu

First published by AuthorHouse 4/15/2009
2nd Edition - June 2009

ISBN: 978-1-4389-7545-0 (hc)
ISBN: 978-1-4389-7546-7 (sc)

Library of Congress Control Number: 2009903418

Printed in the United States of America
Stevens Point, Wisconsin

This book is printed on acid-free paper.

DEDICATION

FOR

MY BELOVED WIFE

DIANE RACHEL

&

MY DAUGHTER

MADELINE EVE

OF

BLESSED MEMORY

Publication of this book is made possible through a grant from the Evjue Foundation, Inc., as well as contributions from private donors.

Published by Edgewood College Press

Acknowledgements

The following individuals have in some way contributed to the book, lending time, knowledge, and encouragement through personal interviews, research material or information.

First and foremost, I owe a great debt to Jean Loeb Lettofsky for information garnered from 12 hours of Interviews with Rabbi in 1980, which she taped. These proved to be an enormous well of knowledge about Rabbi's life. These interviews were done as part of the State Historical Society of Wisconsin Project of Wisconsin Holocaust Survivors sadly never published due to inadequate funding.

Second, my wonderful and patient editor, Sister Mary Ellen Gevelinger. OP, EdD

First Congregational Church
John Toussaint

Edgewood College
Bill Emmon
Sister Loretta Dornisch, OP
Sister Sarah Naughton, OP
John Uselman
Elizabeth McGowan

Rotary
Carol Toussaint
Pat Jenkins

State Historical Society of Wisconsin
Harry Miller
Andy Krauschaar

Capital Times
Jacob Stockinger

Wisconsin State Journal
Bill Wineke

Bethel Church
Larry Kelliher

First Unitarian Society
Reverend Max Gaebler

Heritage Congregational Church
Reverend Richard Pritchard

Beth Israel Center; Madison
Anita Parks

Temple Emanu-El – Waukesha
Riva and Bill Merkow

Beth El Temple – Either by membership or association

Larry Kohn	Swarsensky Family
Shirley Sweet	Professor Is Fine
Joe Silverberg	Jeanne Silverberg
Hal Blotner	Eva Deutschkron
Hilde Adler	Professor Sam Jones
Hannah Rosenthal	Phil Sinykin

Miscellaneous

Erv Baumgart	John Tortorice
Lowell Mays	

TABLE OF CONTENTS

INTRODUCTION

Manfred Swarsensky was there for me from the beginning as he was for so many. He spoke movingly at my installation as pastor of the First Unitarian Society in 1952. He occupies a very special place in the lives of thousands of people on both sides of the Atlantic. A recognized scholar and leader of the Berlin Jewish community while still a young man in Germany, he managed to escape the Nazi terror at the very last moment. He soon settled as founding Rabbi of what was then a modest Reform congregation in Madison, and quickly became one of the city's most valuable citizens. For decades he was a central figure not only in Temple Beth El but also in the Madison community and the State of Wisconsin.

He was recognized as an outstanding ecumenical figure in the Christian-Jewish dialogue. No one in Madison's history has received such universal recognition, as did Manfred Swarsensky. Yet it is not the recognition that really counts; it is the up-beat, ecumenical, intelligent and always reassuring presence that Rabbi Swarsensky brought to every occasion and every group in which he participated. He was small in physical stature, but a giant in his influence on this remarkable city that was privileged to be his home for so many years.

It is most appropriate, I believe, to retrieve an excerpt from a radio talk I gave on November 21, 1981, soon after Rabbi's death, as a befitting introduction.

In the course of any given year many human lives come to end, some peacefully in the fullness of time, others violently and prematurely. In the ultimate economy of the universe each life counts;

none is finally and completely in vain. The reason—if any be need-ed—why I have singled out the life of Rabbi Manfred Swarsensky as the subject of my talk has nothing to do with the scope of his con-tributions, which were enormous, or the range of his talents, which were many, or the dramatic quality of his life experience, which was certainly unusual if not quite unique. It is, rather, completely per-sonal; it is because he meant so much to me personally that I want to give voice in some small way to my own gratitude for having known him well over many years, and to my sense of loss at his departure from us.

It was one of Manfred Swarsensky's rare gifts that he managed—as one of our colleagues put it the other day—to make almost ev-eryone feel very special in his presence. One always had the sense that somehow one's own relationship to him was something unique, something to be treasured.

I know it was so with me. He was already a veteran of a dozen years as spiritual leader of Congregation Beth El when I arrived in Madison many years ago, and there were far more than personal rea-sons for my regarding him as my closest professional colleague from that day to this. For one thing, when he came here in 1940 as the first rabbi to serve Madison's then newly organized Reform Jewish congregation, they met for some time in the old Unitarian Church located just off the Square on the site now occupied by Manchester's pigeon-hole parking. In a way, this represented repayment of an old debt; for our First Unitarian Society, from the time of its orga-nization in 1879, met for several years in what was then called the Madison Hebrew Synagogue, the building now known as the "Gates of Heaven" in its new location in James Madison Park.

Manfred Swarsensky had a long and rich ministry not only to Congregation Beth El but also to this whole community. He has been called a "bridge builder"—between Jew and Christian, between town and gown, between old and young—indeed, between all the varied segments of what he called "the wonderful City of Madison with its symphony of nature and culture."

He was profoundly Jewish, deeply committed to the central loyalties and values of that great heritage. Yet the heart of that heritage itself, as he understood it and exemplified it, was an inclusiveness that reached out to all and left no one out. He was profoundly and authentically Jewish, too, in his marvelous combination of realism about the frailty of our human nature with a wonderful humor that enabled him to accept it all without despairing. How many times we emerged together from a meeting where foolish or parochial or even insidious ideas had been voiced! Manfred would say, "I tell you, Max, I don't know what the world is coming to." Then he would laugh and take my arm.

Another thing we had in common was our German ancestry. My paternal forebears left the old country during the disillusionment following the collapse of the liberal revolution of 1848. Manfred Swarsensky came himself in his mature years, finding his way from Germany to America almost miraculously at the very last moment. This escape always seemed to him a gift of grace, a second chance. In a 1976 interview with the <u>Capital Times</u> he recalled: "I was in a concentration camp, but I got out, fortunately. So the last thirty-six years have been a very special bonus. I could have belonged to the six million just as well. I have always said to myself that because life was given to me a second time, you have to make up for it."

That was a typical understatement. The fact was that he exemplified this grateful rejoicing in the gift of life in unusual degree. One of the foundations of Jewish religious life—and of Christianity at its best as well—is the assurance contained in the last verse of the first chapter of Genesis: "And God saw everything that he had made, and behold, it was very good." The creation is flawed—no doubt about that. All we need to do is to look inside ourselves in order to recognize the extent of our stupidity, our self-righteousness, and our envy—all the familiar weaknesses of human nature. And there is more than enough sorrow and suffering and bad luck to go around. But despite all of that, in spite of life's burdens and hardships, it is still good. It is a marvelous gift for which we should give thanks every day of our living.

That is the traditional Jewish view. Over and over again in Jewish history, ever—or perhaps especially—at times of great danger and persecution, there have arisen within the Jewish community spontaneous reassertions of this basic joy in life itself, however hard and however perilous it may be.

That is "the Jewish feeling of the appreciation of life" that Manfred Swarsensky reflected so profoundly. No one was more sensitive than he to the sham, the posturing, and the downright hypocrisy that is all too evident in human affairs. No one knew better than he that the world is full of fair-weather friends who cannot be counted on when the going gets really tough. He had experienced it firsthand in Germany, and he had no illusions that people anywhere else are really any better. That is a major reason he always supported the State of Israel so strongly. Yet despite all that, he truly loved life. He gave his utmost to it and took from it every ounce of satisfaction he could find. Both his gifts and his satisfactions were enormous.

I have spoken of his German heritage. He loved the German language all his life; many a time a German Sprichwort or aphorism would come automatically in his conversation. He once said to my wife, "I always say my prayers in German."

Perhaps the most revealing measure of the largeness of his spirit has been his attitude toward his native Germany in the wake of Holocaust. To forget what happened then, he insisted, would be "a sin against the memory of the dead." Nevertheless, despite his personal sufferings at the hands of the Nazis, he also insisted that today's post-war generation of Germans should not be held accountable for the sins of their parents. And he was too realistic in his understanding of human nature not to perceive that what happened among the Germans might well have happened elsewhere. Few of us are absolutely immune even to such heinous perversions of the human spirit as Nazism revealed. Yet even this did not lead him to despair or cynicism. Again and again his ultimate faith in the goodness of creation came through.

So it was that when the city of Berlin invited him to return as its guest in 1970 to share in the reopening of the synagogue in which he had begun his rabbinate, he accepted. "Twenty-five years ago I would have said 'Never again shall I set foot on that cursed soil,'" he told the Capital Times in an interview at the time. "But twenty-five years ago, no one would have invited me."

I have spoken of Manfred Swarsensky several times as having a "realistic" view of human nature and the whole human situation. He sensed the indispensable importance of those central institutions that bind us together in community and that undergird social stability and continuity in times of trouble. He supported the University of Wisconsin at the time when it was under serious attack from those who wanted to "close it down." And he supported churches and synagogues and hospitals and service clubs and the United Way—all those institutions that bind us together in community.

This same realism carried over into his views on social and political issues. In the last sermon he gave at our Meeting House, he sounded this note. "To live by principals of pure, abstract morality is possible for an individual," he said; but "for nations it is absolutely impossible.... When the President of the United States takes office, he swears that he will defend his nation against its enemies, foreign and domestics. If he were to apply the privatist ethics in international relations, i.e., if he, so to speak, would turn our nation's other cheek, advocate not resisting the evil of aggression and abandon our defense establishment, he would be declared insane and be impeached. Would that all this were not so; would that human beings were amenable to moral suasion and that the world's leaders would rally to the invitation: 'Come, let us reason together, said the Lord.' Would that all the billions that are being expended for lethal weapons because of man's unreasonableness, moral immaturity, and primitively could be used for peaceful purposes.... But alas, so long as the Kingdom of God is not here, mankind will need codes of laws for the adjudication of differences, police forces to check criminals, and armies to ward off the aggressor."

Rabbi Swarsensky preached from our pulpit a number of times, and he shared most of our moments of high celebration. He participated in my installation as minister here in 1952, and he contributed to the celebration of the twenty-fifth anniversary of that occasion. He ended that latter greeting with a Latin salutation, "Ad multos annos, Max!" I would end this brief personal tribute on a similar note: "Ad pacem aeternam, Manfred!"

Much can be learned from his life and work and I am pleased and honored to have the privilege of introducing this book of his biography and writings.

Max Gaebler

Pastor Emeritus, First Unitarian Society, Madison

Fall, 2008

PROLOGUE

"In our tradition, a Mensch is a complete person, both human and humane."

Manfred Swarsensky

While haunting my local library several months ago, I came across two slim volumes by Manfred Swarsensky, esteemed founding Rabbi of Temple Beth El in Madison, Wisconsin. The first volume was *From Generation to Generation* published in 1955, an excerpt of which appears in the Writings. It was inspired by the celebration of the 300th anniversary of the first Jews coming to what would become the United States, an important milestone in the 4000-year history of the Jewish people. This book told the story of the Madison Jewish Communities first hundred years.

The second book was a collection of Rabbi's Writings, published by the Edgewood Press in 1981 shortly before his death, entitled *Intimates and Ultimates*. I went online to access his biography, but although there was some biographic data available, there was no biography.

In the next month repeatedly my thoughts turned to Rabbi; what he was, that what he stood for and what he had accomplished might be lost to future generations. It was true that a Chair in Religious Studies had been named for him at Edgewood College where he taught for many years; that the chapel at Meriter Hospital where he served on the board for more than a quarter century is named in his honor; and that his fellow Rotarians had established the Manfred Swarsensky humanitarian award given annually to a person who exemplified the principles which Manfred Swarsensky represented;

and in addition Temple Beth El, the congregation he served as Rabbi for 36 years had honored his memory with an annual weekend lectureship, the so called "Swarsensky Weekend". Madison Magazine named him one of the most influential individuals of the 20th Century.

It came to me that the only way to further memorialize Rabbi Swarsensky was by writing a biography. I vowed that since no one else had done it, that I would take up the task.

How to convey to those who did not know him that Manfred Swarsensky was truly unique and represented to many the most significant, dynamic, humane moral and ethical force in mid America in the last half of the 20th century was a significant challenge. This may seem to be hyperbole; it is not. He was at the forefront of "building bridges" and never refused a hand outstretched in friendship.

He was much more than that, however. He lived his life as his beloved mentor Leo Baeck had prescribed, "let your greatest sermon be the way you have lived your life". You, the reader, are about to find out about this remarkable man; this eloquent force of nature, this legend, this phenomenon, Manfred Swarsensky.

In my preparation for writing this book and in reading Rabbi's correspondence, sermons and other writings as well as reviewing material in his personal papers and archives and in interviews with family, friends, acquaintances, educators, ministers, and government officials, I have been enriched, inspired, and am in awe of his life and accomplishments.

Marvin Zolot, MD
December, 2008

PART I – GERMANY

CHAPTER 1 –
FAMILY AND EARLY LIFE

"This Little Jewish Peasant from Pomerania"

In the tumultuous geo-political hotbed that was 19th century Prussia and situated between eastern and western Europe on the border between Germany and Poland was the Prussian Province of Pomerania, its northern border on the Baltic Sea. Near the major city of Posnan was the village of Swarsense. It was here that the Rabbi's family was first established many centuries ago. As was the custom, the family Swarsensky took its name from that village. Before Manfred's great-great grandfather's time, the family relocated to Marienfleis, a village of fewer than one thousand in Pomerania in Eastern Prussia, now situated in Poland. In the same modest home where the Swarsensky family lived since the time of his great-great grandparents Manfred Eric Swarsensky was born on October 22, 1906. His father Jakob was born in the same village in 1860, as had his grandfather Moses been in 1832. Manfred was named after him. His traditional Jewish name was Moshe, in English translated as Moses, a name both appropriate and prophetic, given the outstanding leader he became.

His mother was Louise Lewinsky Swarsensky, born in 1876 in Bad Polzin, a city known for its therapeutic baths. Manfred's maternal grandparents were Ascher and Rosalie (Lewin) Lewinski of Bad Polzin. His paternal grandmother was Fredericka Swarsensky. His father's father died before Manfred was born, but his father's mother

3

Fredericka lived with them. Manfred had one brother, Herbert who was born in 1908.

Manfred related that his father was a very kindly and honest man who was deeply religious and prayed twice every day, as well as saying grace after meals. Jakob had large farms where various grains and potatoes were raised. He was also a grain dealer. Manfred's mother raised her own flax which she wove into linen. She had a large garden and was remembered for being an accomplished gardener. She raised chickens, ducks, and geese and the long winter evenings were sometimes spent with neighbor ladies plucking down for bedding and pillows.

There was no electricity, no indoor plumbing, and the light was by kerosene lantern. Water was drawn from the well and an outhouse served the family's needs. The little village of Marienflies with so few people had no other Jewish families. Manfred's mother kept a kosher home and he was impressed that she was very compulsive on keeping the "cleanest home in Pomerania". She was constantly cleaning. The home was relatively primitive as were most of the local dwellings.

The first school that Manfred attended was a one-room school with both boys and girls. This was the only co-educational school he attended throughout his life. The teacher was described as a "horrible man" who was extremely rigid and who beat the children unmercifully for minor infractions. His name was Herr Nightingale. At the end of World War II when the Russians captured the village and burned it to the ground his "dearly beloved" teacher was hanged from a tree. Every year Manfred's father gave Herr Nightingale a box of excellent cigars, which seemed to mitigate the teacher's ardor for physical punishment toward Manfred and his brother.

In this rural school, as was the custom in all schools in Germany, religion was part of the traditional curriculum. It was taught four hours per week. Manfred and his brother were the only Jews among the primarily Lutheran students in the school, so the only religion taught was Lutheran. In other parts of Germany there were a significant number of Catholics, but none lived in much of northern

Germany and Prussia, and Manfred never met a Catholic until he was in his teens. Strong anti-Catholic feelings were conveyed in his Christian Lutheran teachings. The teacher made frequent references to those horrible people across the Alps, the Popes. Although anti-Semitism was virtually absent in Marienflies, it was ever present in the vehement anti-Semitic writings of Martin Luther. In the five years Manfred attended this school he received a thorough grounding in the New Testament and Christian theology, which was to serve him well throughout his life in his relationships with many Christian clergy and also in his writings.

Although the elementary school continued until the eighth grade his parents had high aspirations for him, and he was sent at the tender age of ten to the gymnasium in Stargard, a much larger city, where he boarded with a Jewish family. A gymnasium is the equivalent of a high school in the United States. It was a very large school according to Manfred, with thousands of students and a few, perhaps three or four Jewish students, but enough of them to have a Jewish teacher for religious instruction. The local cantor named Wilman did the teaching. He came to the school and taught the prescribed four hours of religion per week, standard throughout Germany. It was also in Stargard that Manfred studied for his bar mitzvah with Doctor Emil Silberstein, the Rabbi of the local liberal synagogue. The gymnasium was said to have a very long and complicated German common name, which Manfred did not divulge.

There were two types of gymnasiums in Germany. One was the humanistic gymnasium and the other was science and technology orientated. The science and technology gymnasium included courses such as chemistry, physics, and math, of which Manfred knew nothing. This was the gymnasium his brother Herbert, who became a surgeon, attended. Manfred attended an all boys humanistic gymnasium, which stressed the humanities, the classics, multiple languages including Latin and Greek, and literature, both prose and poetry. He studied Latin and Greek for six years and also studied French and English.

German educational institutions were syntonic with the Germanic characteristics of rigidity and the unquestioned authority of the teachers. The atmosphere at all levels was totally different from the atmosphere at American learning institutions. In the latter, the questioning of authority was pervasive and welcomed, and a much more casual attitude was tolerated as compared with the very formal, competitive, humorless German model. This was to be a revelation when Manfred came to America. In addressing students, the appellation of "Herr" which is translated into the English mister, was applied to all, and not just the teachers. The atmosphere was often dismal and humorless although the natural obstreperousness of young boys occasionally tried the patience of the teachers, with the consequences of swift corporal punishment.

By all accounts Manfred was an outstanding student. He loved all his studies in the gymnasium, and was an educational sponge, absorbing every bit of knowledge offered. He was very unlike his younger brother Herbert who was a superb athlete in any sport he undertook. In contrast, Manfred was totally uninterested in sports. He was a bookworm; today we would call him a "nerd".

He returned home frequently and especially for the Jewish holidays. His father was a traditionalist and eschewed the liberal synagogue in Stargard for a small traditional synagogue in a town near their village, Freienwaldes. Since driving their horse drawn conveyance was against Jewish law on Sabbath and holidays, a driver was employed to take the family to the traditional services. The cacophony and seemingly disorganized and uninspiring services were in contrast to the more sedate services, along with an organ and choir in Stargard. Rabbi felt these elements were uplifting and came to appreciate them as he grew older. His father was well regarded in this tiny synagogue in Freienwaldes and each Yom Kippur he was awarded the honor of reading the Maftir Jonah, a prophetic tale, a very instructive lesson for the "Day of Atonement". It was in this tiny orthodox synagogue in 1927 that Manfred gave his first sermon, while a rabbinical student in Berlin.

Rabbi flowered at the gymnasium in Stargard. In 1980 Rabbi received an invitation to the celebration of the 350th anniversary of the establishment of his beloved gymnasium. However he was unable to attend, as his health was failing.

Very little is known of Manfred's association with other students and teachers and the family with which he boarded in Stargard. We have no knowledge of his personal life either in the gymnasium or the colleges he attended. He seemed to be totally engrossed in the educational life to the exclusion of the private. If he had any close friends we do not know. He appeared to have little contact with the opposite sex with the exception of his mother and other female relatives.

We know that Manfred wanted to become a Rabbi from the time he studied for his Bar Mitzvah with his revered mentor, Rabbi Emil Silberstein. He was Manfred's primary source in preparing him for his Bar Mitzvah and served as an early role model. The aura of the liberal synagogue in Stargard, while a very small and modest place, celebrated its orderly solemn service enhanced with a professional choir and organ. This was a revelation to Manfred, in stark contrast to the traditional "shul" he attended with his family. Whether or not his training in the liberal tradition was of concern to his very orthodox father, we do not know. He could not however have been Bar Mitzvahed in the liberal tradition without the acquiescence of his father, whose authority was unquestioned in the Jewish family. It appears that the family may have been so impressed by Manfred's outstanding mind and his zeal for learning that his father did not want to dampen his son's ardor by imposing his traditional ways on his son. He appeared to trust his son's judgment in this area.

When asked why he chose to become a Rabbi, Manfred became very thoughtful and circumspect in thought. He had thought about this many times in the past. He noted that there were no rabbinical predecessors in his family to serve as model. It both fascinated him and troubled him that as a Jew he was so different from his contemporaries. He wanted to find out why he was so different from others and what made him different. He was extremely curious as to what it meant to be a tiny member of a tiny minority surrounded by a vast and powerful majority of citizens, some of whom had markedly negative feelings about Jews. He always felt for lack of a better word, *spiritually internally driven*, which he discerned was an absolute necessity for one who was to become a Rabbi. His associations later with rabbis in Germany impressed him that most of them were outstanding individuals who possessed this internal spirituality. His associations with rabbis in America will be seen as much less positive. This was perhaps because they disagreed with him on many aspects of the practice of Judaism and the stringent traditional ways of living a Jewish life, practiced by his co-religionists. It is interesting to note that as a rabbinical student Rabbi also returned to the Stargard synagogue where he was Bar Mitzvahed. It was here that he made some of his first attempts at sermonizing.

CHAPTER 2 -- THE BERLIN YEARS

Seminary

Although there were other theological seminaries in Germany, Rabbi chose to matriculate to the Hochscule Für Die Wissenschaft Des Judentum, in Berlin. This is translated as the Academy of the Science of Judaism. Here he was also required, as were the other students at the seminary, to simultaneously pursue a doctorate in Semitic studies at a university of his choice. He chose the University of Würzburg, attending both institutions from 1925 to 1932 and he received his ordination as Rabbi and his PhD at the same time. The seminary was the same one which had been attended by his beloved tutor, Rabbi Silberstein. Martin Buber, Abraham Joshua Heschel and Leo Beack were outstanding theologians who were also associated with the seminary. The course of study was extremely rigorous and demanding. Almost super human effort was needed to be devoted to studies at the seminary and the university concurrently.

Fortunately the two institutions were in walking distance of each other. According to Manfred, you tried by "hook or by crook" to arrange your programs to dovetail with each other. The work at the university was somewhat neglected in deference to the seminary work, which was more appealing to him. The classes at the seminary were very small six, eight, ten or twelve students at the most, with much direct contact with the professors. At the university, in contrast, the atmosphere was completely depersonalized. There was no contact at all between students and professors, "the classes were large, you obtained a book on the subject, attended the lecture with myriads of others, and once a year there was an examination to see if you had absorbed enough to pass the course", he observed. Attendance was not mandatory, the gold standard was the one and only yearly examination, and students were totally on their own. Occasionally there were teachers at the University who took an interest in students but this was rare.

At the seminary with other co-religionists the atmosphere in the classes lent itself to close personal contacts with teachers and students. Manfred revered Doctor Abraham Geiger, the Rabbi who started the liberal seminary he attended. He was the individual who set the almost impossibly high standards maintained by the seminary, including the requirement that students simultaneously pursue a doctorate at one of the many Berlin Universities.

Since Berlin was the academic Mecca, the level demanded was very high. Although there were Harvards and Princetons, there were also Wisconsins where the standards were not so impossibly hard to meet. This appellation of second line but still outstanding applied to the University Rabbi chose, Würzburg. This was the university alma mater of Wilhelm Roentgen who gave the world x-ray. Würzburg was a 400-year-old Catholic University, first established in its eponymous Bavarian city with its magnificent medieval castle. Before Manfred's time it established a presence in Berlin. This was Rabbi's first contact with Catholics with whom inexplicably he formed close bonds in later years. Years later he formed a special bond with several prominent Catholic theologians in Madison.

When Rabbi came closer to the final exam, the orals for his PhD , he was suddenly told that in order to complete the course requirements he would also have to study Arabic and Persian, also known as Farsi, as well as the other European languages he had previously known about. He especially hated this "horrible Persian". He had to learn it in a hurry. He felt it was terribly difficult. He described it as a European language but written in Arabic letters. In the final examination the professor chose a Persian text, which he had to decipher and with which Manfred acquitted himself well. One of the professors was a Catholic priest and is remembered as asking reasonable questions to which Manfred felt he could give intelligent answers. Some of the other examiners were not so gracious. He passed his exams, "Thank God" and also had to write a doctoral dissertation. He used the knowledge he received at the seminary to dovetail into a dissertation on Semitics, which was acceptable at the university. There was a renowned semiticist at Würzburg who accepted the subject of the thesis and ultimately the complete document was approved. Manfred received his PhD contemporaneously with his ordination at the seminary.

Leo Baeck

It was at the Berlin seminary that Manfred was to meet the man that had the most profound effect on him both personally and professionally; Leo Baeck was his mentor, par excellence. Baeck was a Rabbi and was memorialized in a talk Manfred gave to the Madison Literary Club in 1978. This club was one of his most prized associations. It is a prestigious 100+ year-old group with a sophisticated membership. The following reminiscences of Leo Baeck were published in *Intimates and Ultimates*. It is rather extraordinary to consider that in quoting from his talk, where Rabbi tells about the many positive attributes of Leo Baeck, one can almost feel that the Rabbi is talking about himself, since he came to have many of these characteristics as his "modus operandi". In the way he lived his life, Rabbi may have even exceeded the very high standards that his beloved mentor set. The following quotations are taken from that talk. In referring to Leo Baeck he said,

Our age is reluctant to attribute divine qualities to flesh and blood and yet saintliness need not be understood as a gift of supernatural grace. Saintliness is consistency of character that unifies the life of an individual with his ideals. Saintliness is a way of life in which every thought and deed is a projection of the spiritual ideal. It is a way of life in which biography and philosophy fuse into a mystic unity. The artist enriches the world with his art, the scholar with his research, the prophet with his words, with his moral passion, and the saint with his personality.

His life is the supreme contribution to mankind.

Rabbi compared Leo Baeck favorably with other outstanding individuals of the 20th century who exemplified this ideal. Mahatma Ghandi, Albert Schweitzer, Pope John XXIII, and Martin Buber were the personages who achieved the highest standards that Leo Baeck prescribed. Rabbi Manfred Swarsensky achieved these standards in the minds of many thoughtful persons and perhaps in some ways surpassed them.

The one deficiency that Leo Baeck had was that he was not a silver-tongued orator. Rabbi Swarsensky, in contrast, was a most engaging and inspiring speaker. The content of Baeck's sermons and writings was exemplary, but the delivery left much to be desired. "His intellect was of titanic scope, his knowledge encyclopedic," according to Rabbi Swarsensky.

Endowed with a remarkable memory, Baeck read and retained the original in whatever language. He never used a single note when he gave a lecture, even at age 81, and he admonished his charges, "know your subject thoroughly and then you will have no need for written speeches." Rabbi Swarsensky never used notes in Germany but began using them after coming to America, a defect that would have appalled his mentor.

"An orderly mind," Baeck once said to his students, "is not a matter of intellect but of character; the search for truth is rooted in man's innermost impulses." Manfred related that Baeck arose every morning at five am and began the day with physical exercise, prayer and two hours of studying. He was blessed with boundless energy and was a paragon of punctuality. Baeck proclaimed, "He who is not disciplined is not educated." It was not just knowledge he imparted but wisdom. He despised unctuous pomposity and he cautioned against the temptation to speak in superlatives. His most profound pronouncement was the watchword by which Manfred Swarsensky lived his life. "The greatest message one can preach is the way one lives one's life." Manfred was an apt pupil.

Manfred Swarsensky further recorded "many times in later years, yes, even today, when struggling for clarity of thought and expression or for the proper attitude in a difficult issue I would ask myself, what would Baeck have said? What would he have done? Here indeed was a master in whose light one could see light." In recent years Christians would echo the sentiments expressed above by the phrase "what would Jesus do?" Manfred noted that Baeck wrote his magnum opus, *Das Wesendes Jedemtums, The Essence of Judaism* in German, originally based on a series of lectures given at the turn of the century by protestant theologian Adolf Van Harnack on the subject on the essence of Christianity. Baeck's work has been translated into many languages including English and Japanese.

Manfred was intrigued by the author's description of Judaism as a unique phenomenon in religious history and Jews as a HAPAX-LEGOMENOM OF HISTORY, a linguistic term meaning a word occurring in literature only once. He was referring to Jews and Judaism entering the world of the spirit as a revolution, by introducing into a pagan world a distinct new world view of God, man, and life. Baeck pointed out that Judaism has a two -fold history, the history of the Jewish people and the history of the Jewish spirit, which has come to permeate the world. It is dedicated to the prophetic task of building the world into a Kingdom of God, tikkum olam, translated as *healing the world*, with the special characteristic of monotheism and the commandment of Leviticus "love your neighbor as yourself."

Besides his *Essence of Judaism*, Baeck was a prolific author of 400 publications. During the dark days of national socialism, dominated by the Hitler regime in the 1930's until 1945, Baeck was a tireless critic of the government, working constantly to arrange passage out of Germany for his coreligionists, especially the children. Baeck was arrested by the Gestapo and ultimately released five times. In 1943, the sixth time, he was sent by cattle car in inhuman conditions to the collection depot for Jews all over Europe. This was Thereisenstadt in Czechoslovakia, the antechamber to the crematoria. In Auschwitz he was harnessed to a wagon and assigned to the daily task of drawing garbage. This was supposed to be the ultimate humiliation, foreshadowing death for the saintly man. Prior to being sent to the concentration camp he was offered multiple opportunities to leave the country. However, he insisted on staying in Germany to strengthen the morale of his despondent fellow Jews. His multiple arrests and persecution did not go unnoticed by his Christian colleagues throughout the world, but their vociferous protests fell on deaf ears, as the propaganda machine that was assiduously programmed by Goebbels and his cohorts was immune to any criticism. Although many protested, many were silent. To their everlasting discredit many in Europe and the rest of the world were silently applauding at the systematic dehumanization and eradication of the Jews of Europe, as the "final solution" to the "Jewish Question" was put into operation in the gas chambers and crematoria in the concentration camps throughout Europe.

Leo Baeck was an outstanding example of the insanity of this plan, a personage so saintly that he can be reasonably compared to biblical figures such as a Job in the Hebrew Bible and Jesus in the New Testament.

In the dark of the night when his captors were concerned with carousing and getting drunk, Baeck went from barracks to barracks in an attempt to strengthen the spirit of his congregation of the doomed. His very presence in the midst of indescribable misery and dread gave the desperate souls an example of quiet heroism. He brought cheer to the sick but also occasionally from his gleaning of the garbage, he brought a bit of bread or sausage to nourish them. Leo Baeck was in Thereisenstadt for over two years as the population of the camp dwindled from 50,000 to 700 due to extermination and disease, yet he was spared. Another Rabbi with a similar name was murdered in his stead. One night a storm trooper, accompanied by the Obberführer Adolf Eichman, discovered the error and came to Baeck's barracks to inform him that he would die at dawn.

He sat down to write his farewell letter to his widowed daughter in London but in the morning, instead of Eichman's henchmen, a Russian officer announced the liberation of the camp. After 28 months in a veritable inferno his life was saved by a miracle. When the Russian soldiers turned their guns on the few remaining German soldiers in the camp Baeck interceded, quoting from the Bible he exclaimed "vengeance is mine saith the Lord," vengeance is reserved for God alone. Baeck did not believe in vengeance; he could not hate. When asked if he could ever forgive the German nation for what it had wrought against the Jewish people, he stated it is for the Germans to forgive themselves.

When released from the camp he found his way to London, through a network of those who knew him and his work. During the final ten years of his life, half the year he resided in London and resumed the presidency of a religious organization he had previously led, the World Union of Progressive Judaism. The other half of the year he spent in the United States and taught yet another generation of future spiritual leaders at the Hebrew Union College Jewish Institute of Religion in Cincinnati.

Many honors were bestowed on Leo Baeck. He was received by the Archbishop of Canterbury, welcomed at the White House by President Truman, invited as the only foreign clergyman to give the invocation to congress, and the German government issued a stamp bearing his likeness and attesting to the regard in which he was held throughout the world. Perhaps one of his most outstanding accomplishments was his part in building the life and character of Manfred Swarsensky. He and Rabbi Swarsensky stayed in constant touch after he escaped. To quote Rabbi Swarsensky, "This saintly man was my teacher and friend; I treasure him as one of the greatest blessings of my life". Honoring his life and work, Leo Baeck Institutes have been established in New York, in Frankfurt Germany, and in Jerusalem.

Religion in Germany

Religious activities and organization was very different in the 19th and first half of the 20th century in Germany. There was no separation between church and state. The state was responsible for the funding and maintenance of religious institutions, Lutheran, Catholic, and Jewish. These religious community organizations were democratically composed of the most outstanding members of their respective co-religionists. They were not only responsible for the building, support, and maintenance of their churches and synagogues, but also for a myriad of ancillary religiously oriented institutions and organizations including old age homes, hospitals, and schools for those who wished to attend such institutions.

Citizens were required to register with the police as to their religious affiliations within a few days of moving into an area. Regrettably, this made it simple for the Gestapo to identify the Jews during the Nazi years. The religious institutions were funded by a surcharge of 10% of the taxes that a citizen was assessed and this was for the support of the religious groups. The money was transferred to leaders of the three religious communities and was dispersed by them for general support of all within their purview. This made it unnecessary for the groups to constantly raise money for their support, and the Rabbis, in the case of the Jewish community, were concerned mainly with teaching and conducting religious services, and life cycle aspects such as baby naming, marriages, and burials. In addition, in the case of liberal Jews, confirmation and bar mitzvah were also the concern of rabbis. Bat mitzvah, the female equivalent of the male Bar Mitzvah, did not exist at that time. Manfred described his duties as Rabbi in his tongue in cheek fashion as "hatching, matching, and dispatching".

The liberal tradition in Germany and throughout Europe was very different from the so-called Reform or liberal branch of Judaism in the United States. Although liberal Judaism began in 19th century Germany, it changed radically when it crossed the Atlantic. In Germany, services were held on Saturday morning, and except for sermons, which were preached in the vernacular, the service was mostly in Hebrew. The men and women sat in separate areas, with women in the balcony. There was only one synagogue in Berlin in which the men and women sat together. The men wore traditional skullcaps and prayer shawls, tallisem.

In contradistinction in America, the services were held mainly on Friday night in deference to the necessity to work on Saturday. In some extremely liberal congregations such as the Emanuel in New York and the Chicago Sinai Congregation, they were held on Sunday morning as they were traditionally in the Christian community. Sunday became the Sabbath for these Reform Jews. The service and sermon were mostly in English, and skullcaps and prayer shawls were eschewed and frowned upon. As a Rabbinical student Rabbi Swarsensky conducted Sabbath and high holidays in smaller communities near Berlin, speaking from the pulpit of his father's traditional synagogue, and also in the liberal synagogue in which he was Bar Mitzvahed in Stargard. For three years he officiated in the Weisbaden liberal synagogue. He also participated in overflow services during the high holidays in Berlin.

The liberal synagogues in Berlin were extremely large and very beautiful and tastefully designed. Their capacity was enormous; between 2000 and 4000 worshipers could attend the services at one time. Large professional choirs and impressive organs enhanced the beauty of the services. In the Prinzregenten Strasse Synagogue the men and the women sat together. The synagogues usually were named for streets on which they were built.

As a Rabbinical student, Manfred Swarsensky attracted a large following with his interesting, informative and inspiring sermons, enhanced by an outstanding delivery, which was to serve him well throughout his life in all his talks and sermons. He became famous for his sermons. Because of his many attributes, the leaders of the Jewish community in Berlin took the unprecedented step of appointing him as one of the dozen or so Rabbis who served the Jewish community of approximately 150,000, as soon as he was ordained at age 26. This pleased the little man with a big booming voice and was a huge ego booster. He admonished himself not to be too pleased, but in reality he was the youngest Rabbi ever appointed to the Berlin Jewish community. His modest parents were understandably "kvelling," bursting with pride, extremely proud that their son had been ordained as Rabbi and also was appointed to the Rabbinate in Berlin. This was the big leagues among German Jewry. Manfred was especially honored to be among Rabbis he felt reflected the highest aspirations of Judaism.

Manfred tried not to let this degree of success go to his head, as this would not be in keeping with the demeanor and teachings of his mentor, Leo Baeck. He did not disappoint those who chose him. His sermons continued to engage and enthrall those who heard them. Hannah Rosenthal, the daughter of a younger rabbinical student Rabbi who attended the Breslau traditional seminary, Frank Rosenthal, ordained in 1937, tells this story. Since travel on the Sabbath was forbidden to traditional Jews, rabbinical students all over Germany used to travel to Berlin in order to get there before nightfall on Friday, so they could hear Manfred Swarsensky preach to overflow crowds on Saturday morning.

Hitler's Germany

For Swarsensky, the joy of ministering to the Jewish community of Berlin was short lived when Hitler came to power in 1933. The halcyon days were over soon after his ordination and the obtaining of his doctorate. The national socialist movement of the Austrian paperhanger Adolf Hitler was on the march, usurping control of Germany and ultimately most of Europe, and initiating the blood bath that was World War II, and along with it the unspeakable horror of the Holocaust.

How the fascists came to power can be understood considering that the Germany of post World War I was fertile ground for development of the national socialist movement. The punishing reparations demanded of Germany by the allies after World War I helped to impoverish the German nation. Its industrial foundation was in ruins. There was extremely high unemployment, and rampant inflation followed, making the deutschmark virtually worthless and casting a depressing pall over the German nation. Several national governments came to power with promises of better days and one by one in quick succession failed miserably.

National Socialism, with its vision of a superior German nation idealized by the beautiful blonde blue eyed Aryan and the myth of its destiny to control the world, became attractive to many. This was a nation which achieved the highest cultural and intellectual levels, and Hitler and his cohorts promised that they would and should take their proper place as the *master race*. The myth was irresistible to the downtrodden and defeated nation. The Nazi movement gave the deutschvolk something they severely lacked, hope.

This vision was enhanced by the traditional Lutheran inspired vehement anti-Semitic statements with which Germans were imbued from their earliest years. An evil internal Jewish conspiracy inspired by this cursed nation of Christ killers, was responsible for all the woes of the German nation. Paul Joseph Goebbels, Reich minister of Public Enlightenment and Propoganda in Nazi Germany, was responsible for the very successful propaganda campaign waged by the Nazis and said "if the Jews did not exist we would have to invent them". They were the perfect scapegoat. Anti-Semitism could unite the Germans in their latent bigotry, always just below the surface of a highly cultured and sophisticated society. The Jews were the perfect foil.

It was during his early Rabbinate in 1932 that Manfred became familiar with a family who would play a significant role in the early years of the Nazi regime and many years later in Madison, the Mosse family. There are many stories told of the relationship of Hans Lachmann Mosse, head of the Mosse family in 20th century Germany, and the Nazis. Prior to his ascendency to chancellery in January 1933, Hitler repeatedly referred to the Mosse family, a very prominent and extremely wealthy Jewish family, in his inspiring political speeches. He spoke against Lachmann Mosse as a classical example of the nefarious liberal conspiracy against the German Nation on more than a dozen separate occasions. The most authoritative account is in his son George Mosse's biography, *Confronting History*.

The Mosse family had roots in Germany from the 13th century. Rudolf Mosse, George Mosse's grandfather, established what would become the largest publishing and advertising conglomerate in pre

WWII Germany, Mosse Verlag, including the *Berliner Tageblatt*. It was the most widely read and influential newspaper in Germany. The paper espoused a liberal tradition and vociferously opposed Hitler and his National Socialist Fascist Movement.

The head of the Mosse family in 1933 was Hans Lachmann Mosse. Rudolf's daughter, Felicia, had married Hans Lachmann, son of another prominent Jewish family. Hans changed his name to Lachmann Mosse when he succeeded his father-in-law as the head of Mosse Verlag.

One of the first acts of the Nazis when they came to power was to confiscate the Tageblatt and dismiss all Jewish employees. The Mosse family fled to France in March 1933. In a complete turnabout, thinking it would be to their advantage to enlist Herr Mosse in the enormous propaganda campaign for the hearts and minds of the German population, the second in command field Marshal Hermann Goerring, sent for Hans Lachmann Mosse, in exile in Paris. He was guaranteed safe passage to return to Berlin for discussions. Goerring offered Herr Mosse a very high level position in the government. As an inducement he is said to have offered Mosse *Aryanization,* that it would be erased from all records that the family had Jewish roots, if he would accept the position. The meeting occurred on April 28, 1933. After prolonged discussions with Goerring and other officials, perhaps even Hitler himself, he returned to Paris to confer with his wife. Mosse was accompanied by the Head of the Gestapo Secret Police, Rudolf Diels. He ultimately refused the insulting offer.

Since Hitler came to power in early 1933 Rabbi Swarsensky did his work chiefly under Hitler. Unbeknownst initially to Manfred, at each and every religious service over which he presided there were plain clothed representatives of the Gestapo. Rabbi repeatedly and heatedly spoke out against the regime. Ultimately was called to the Gestapo headquarters on several occasions and repeatedly warned to desist his blasphemy of the government. He refused and continued to give hope that this abnormal and abhorrent government would soon be over. Rapidly after Hitler came to power, the demeaning anti-Semitic laws he had promised were promulgated.

It is almost impossible, looking back from the 21st century as Americans, to understand the pervasive self deception of German Jews during most of the 1930's. They felt 100% German, with a minor quirk of being a different religion than their neighbors. They responded to the occasional occurrences of anti-Semitism with vociferous articles in the Jewish press, but they mostly considered these merely cracks in the sidewalk. When those in power persisted in their increasingly dehumanizing and ghettoizing pronouncements, the Jews continued to cling to this self-delusion. The self-created dream world of the Jews was that this new radical government would be a thing of the past in a short period of time, as numerous other governments before them had been. They assuaged themselves with the delusion of another week, another month, another year; soon their nightmare would be over.

The German Jews, along with their Christian German neighbors, were imbued with certain Teutonic characteristics, which encouraged the ascendency of the fascist regime. They were mostly disinterested in politics, but they were taught to obey, obey and not question authority. Targeting of Jews in various ways, restricting travel on public conveyances, hours which they could shop, places in which they could shop, theaters, concerts, even schools that they could attend, followed one after the other. Soon restrictions from holding jobs in any public or governmental agency including the armed forces, then university and large industrial firms followed one after the other. Confiscation of Jewish businesses including shops, department stores, newspaper and other publications, manufacturing facilities, farms, galleries, and theaters quickly multiplied.

The dictum that the Star of David must be worn by every Jew on the outside of their clothing was a demeaning public display of anti-Semitism. Rumors that concentration camps were being built were only too true. Initially they were established to receive mainly Christians, primarily intellectuals who spoke against the regime. Christian clergyman, gypsies, and homosexuals, as well as Jews, were targeted. The concentration camps became a dreadful reality. Given this reality why did the Jews not resist? Some have questioned why. How to resist? With what? Given the ever-present threat of beatings, public humiliation, and deportation to concentration camps and ultimately death, resistance was fruitless and impossible. Given the complete control over all aspects of the German nation exercised by the fascist government it was fruitless. Resistance was a recipe for disaster. Some answered with their feet. Immigration was easily available to the German Jews in the early 30's but became increasingly difficult after the horrible conflagration that was Kristalnacht, in November of 1938.

Kristalnacht

Under the pretext of retaliation for the killing of a Nazi by a Jewish youth on the night of November 9/10, 1938, Hitler's SS guards smashed every window of shops owned by Jews all over Germany. In the Rabbi's own words from his most famous sermon "You Can't Go Home Again" a phrase first used by Thomas Wolfe,

"I remember the horrible indescribable shock of being awakened from my sleep at 2 am in the morning following the night of November 10 when the telephone rang and the resident custodian at the Prinzregenten Strasse synagogue, where I served, shouted in a tearful shocked voice, our synagogue is burning. I arose and ran to the building. I pulled my hat way down on my face so I would not be recognized and saw the horrible things I shall never forget. I saw that Hitler's henchmen were pouring gasoline over the inside and outside of the majestic cupola and walls and they turned the building into a sea of flames.

Police were standing idly by and the firemen were pouring water on adjoining buildings to protect them from the heat of the flames.

There were huge frenzied mobs around shouting 'heil Hitler, death to the Jews.' Then, toward morning I stood there petrified, not knowing what to do, but there was nothing to do. Then I ran toward the Fasanen Strasse Synagogue not too far away, where I saw the same picture. Three huge domes and the fire rising from the pews up to the cupola. A horrible site. The synagogue was completely demolished, only the skeleton remained."

Following Kristalnacht, finally there came the total realization of what it meant, and the greatest feeling of depression overcame the entire Jewish community. No one knew what to do. Everything was disrupted and even communication among the Jews was virtually impossible. During the chaos a few righteous gentiles performed acts of loving-kindness. A prominent staunch Lutheran pastor, Paul Kahl and his wife, on the next morning went out deliberately to sweep up some of the debris as an act of defiance and solidarity with their Jewish neighbors. In the wake of Kristalnacht, unbelievably, a fine of several million marks was imposed on the Jewish citizens to pay for the clean up of the debris. In addition, the Nazi government collected from insurance companies for the fires. By the morning of November 11 close to 200 synagogues had been burned to the ground all over Germany. During the day, mass arrest of Jews took place, filling concentration camps. Some 10,000 adults were rounded up in Berlin alone, with many thousands more all over the country, all taken in huge police trucks to concentration camps. Among them was Rabbi Swarsensky.

Soon after Kristalnacht, Rabbi received word from concerned friends that the Gestapo were looking for him, as they were for thousands of other Jews all over Germany. Indeed they soon came and pounded at the door of the tiny apartment he shared with his aging parents. And thus began the most horrible chapter of his life, which he repeatedly related in later years in his writings and in the many talks he gave to concerned groups. Interestingly, most of these groups were Christian who seemed to have a great interest in the Holocaust experience. It was to Rabbi's consternation and puzzlement that Jewish individuals and groups seemed to have much less interest in the Holocaust, especially in the first 20 years of his ministry in Madison, Wisconsin. The reason for this apparent lack of interest is unclear; perhaps it was in some way denial. The full impact of the holocaust in all its horror gradually came to light over many years following the downfall of the third Reich.

Sachsenhausen, the concentration camp to which Rabbi was taken, located only 40 miles from Berlin, was a world away. Soon after arrival the brutality began. He was given flimsy shoes and a coarse striped uniform attired with a large Star of David prominently displayed, and all of his hair was shorn. The inmates were then set upon by the horrendous S.S. guards like a pack of wild beasts, shouting obscenities as they inflicted random beatings and required the poor creatures to stand at attention for countless hours. Some of the prisoners were required to shed all their clothing in the bitter cold, while the guards played degrading overtly sexual games with their prey. Endless days of being awakened before dawn followed, and hard labor ensued for all the prisoners daily. One project that Rabbi related was that they were required to carry heavy bricks from one part of the camp to the other, and when that was done, haul them back to their original place. The obnoxious guards took extreme delight in increasingly severe measures of torture. During this all the inmates were required to sing hour upon hour of militaristic martial music and pornographic songs.

The prisoners were housed in flimsy huge barracks without basic facilities and only buckets for urine and feces, so the stench was unbearable. They were forced to sleep on pallets and bunks several levels high. They were grudgingly given only watery soup and a slice of bread as their sustenance once per day. Constantly the prisoners were required to assemble very quickly for no reason, only so the guards could repeatedly check the roster to be sure no one had tried to escape. The thin clothing and the unheated barracks were little help in protecting these pitiful creatures from the unremitting cold. The best assignment was the garbage detail. Besides emptying the human waste from the barracks, it was on this assignment that a prisoner might convey leftovers from the S.S. mess, and an occasional bit of bread or sausage could be salvaged. Rabbi recalls that a prisoner he knew on the garbage detail gave him a bit of German wurst. He thought this was manna from heaven; he could not believe his luck. Jews were also chosen for tasks as guards, which involved other inmates, or so called Kapos. In these favored positions sometimes these coreligionist exhibited cruelty in enforcing their duties. They could not say no to the S.S. guards, otherwise they themselves would be beaten unmercifully. One day a guard who was a Jew perceived that the Rabbi was not straight enough in line or fast enough in performing a task and was about to beat Rabbi. It was difficult to recognize one prisoner from another because everyone was bereft of all hair. Suddenly the guard exclaimed "Herr Swarsensky doctor" upon recognizing Rabbi, and he started to sob.

He was a young man whom Rabbi had previously confirmed, and he was appalled that he had stooped so low as to contemplate beating his revered Rabbi. These were the methods of "Internal Torture, Incredible, Inconceivable", according to the Rabbi. Another pitiful example cited was that two sons were required to brutally beat their beloved aged father under immediate threat of death. Such cruelty! Rabbi remembers them crying bitterly as they performed their task under the watchful eye of their gleeful captors.

Numerous times in desperation some prisoners tried to escape through the underground sewer system. They were invariably caught and placed on a block in the middle of the exercise field where they were tied up and brutally beaten again and again and again. Many of the bestial S.S. Guards participated in the beatings and appeared to take extreme delight in inflicting severe pain. The victim was then left nude in the December and January bone chilling cold. All the while the other prisoners were required to stand at attention and watch while singing the repulsive songs previously mentioned. In addition, the guards would pour ice-cold water at the end of their sub human performance, and then through the night these pitiful examples of resistance would mercifully die of their wounds or freeze to death.

The rations were totally inadequate. Diseases such as typhus, intractable diarrhea and other infections were rampant. Prisoners died daily and the dead bodies were hauled on a cart to a local dump. But through it all after dark, while the guards were busy getting drunk and not watching the bunk houses closely, Rabbi, like his mentor Leo Baeck, would stealthily go from barracks to barracks, trying to give a measure of spirituality and hope to the hopeless. Another story told by the Rabbi was how desperate he became when his flimsy shoes fell apart and he had no shoes. Shoelessness predicted an early death, so one time in the night he saw a dead Jew lying on a pallet. He made sure that the poor man had breathed his last and then Rabbi said the appropriate prayers for the deceased and went on to steal the shoes from his feet. He put them on and they were good sturdy shoes. The only trouble was that they were much too large. He stuffed the shoes with grass and paper in order to walk in them. But soon these ill fitting shoes caused multiple areas of blisters and bleeding, constantly rubbing against his skin. He was afraid he would get blood poisoning and die, but mercifully he did not. The extremely poor diet caused multiple vitamin deficiencies, diseases which in modern man with a decent diet are virtually unknown. Rabbi developed a life long heart condition when he was in the camp. He probably had Beriberi, a vitamin deficiency that causes severe heart problems.

After five months, Manfred was called to the commandant's office. Rabbi was afraid he was fated for death but instead was offered release from the camp, freedom! He felt it was a miracle. Then due to some type of complete madness, he refused to leave, in order to minister to others in the camp. When the offer was repeated a few weeks later, he came to his senses and in desperation, he accepted. He was told he would have to leave Germany as soon as possible, as apparently the authorities felt that his continued presence was a threat to the Nazi Government.

After release, he returned to Berlin. At first he made a half-hearted attempt to emigrate. Every two weeks on Friday, he had to appear at the S.S. Headquarters with a written report about his efforts to leave the country. With each visit their threats to Rabbi became more and more immediate.

It was during this period of several months that he performed an increasing number of funerals for Jews who died during their incarceration at the concentration camps. It was first a trickle but soon became a flood of deaths. He recalls that he was soon performing 3 to 4 funerals a day when the number of deaths increased markedly in the first death factory, Buchenwald. Families were forced to pay 10 marks in order to retrieve the remains of their loved ones; first in sealed coffins and later in small containers of their cremated remains. Ultimately two thirds of the Jews of Berlin died in the Holocaust.

It was only after receiving the blessing of Leo Baeck and the Jewish community leader Henry Stehl, that he redoubled his efforts to leave. After Kristalnacht the Jewish community was totally disenfranchised by the Nazi government, having withdrawn both recognition and all financial support. When Rabbi returned from the concentration camp everyone now knew and understood very well the nefarious plans of the Hitler government. By early 1939 everyone was running for shelter, sending cables to long lost relatives around the world, but especially to America, seeking affidavits of support if they were allowed to emigrate. They were approaching every possible Jewish organization that might aid them in any way in their efforts to seek safe harbor. The Palestine office was inundated with those trying to find out how to get to the Holy Land. Kristalnacht and the concentration camp experience had convinced even Swarsensky that the situation was hopeless.

It was in 1940 that his parents were forced to move from the tiny apartment he shared with them prior to his immigration to even more cramped quarters in a designated "Jewish" building where many people were squeezed into inadequate space. His parents had the difficult task after Manfred left Germany to find accommodations in one of these ghettoized buildings. They were crowded together and during the process his aged, beloved, and gentle father, age 81 died of heart attack. His mother, who was considerably younger, had to get out of Germany. Otherwise she too ultimately would perish in the final solution death camps. He had left his parents behind when he fled Germany, with much trepidation concerning their welfare. They were not sent to a concentration camp, as in the early years perceived enemies of the state were chosen mainly for incarceration. Old Jews without an antigovernment agenda were not targeted initially.

Manfred was required to leave his parents behind with the promise that arrangements would be made for her to join him and his brother Herbert, as advanced provisions were already in the works. He was ultimately able to bring her to America as promised, but only after unforeseen interminable delays.

Manfred finally arrived in New York Harbor in July of 1939 through the efforts of his brother Herbert who saw the writing on the wall and emigrated to America significantly earlier than Manfred. He was able to obtain an affidavit of support from a long established and respected Jewish friend attesting that he would not become an economic burden to the community. In addition a three-year contract as assistant Rabbi to Temple Sholom, a large prestigious Reform congregation on the north side of Chicago was tendered Manfred. Under a special exemption to the stringent US immigration rules, he was allowed to come to America. The exception to this policy applied to outstanding scientists, intellectuals, educators, and clergymen, including rabbis. During this period this was a welcome exception to the overtly anti-Semitic policies of the U.S. State Department, which was then riddled with important officials who had strong anti-Jewish feelings.

His travel to the US was very circuitous. He initially was welcomed to Holland under a transit visa obtained by some individuals whom Rabbi had met at a visit to Holland some years before. The Netherlands was not yet under the domination of the Nazi government in 1939. Then he flew to London, sponsored by a rabbinic acquaintance he had stayed with on a previous trip to England. A program initiated by the British government overseen by the chief Rabbi of Great Britain made this possible. The plan provided temporary asylum to certain individuals using similar criteria to the US exemptions.

He finally embarked to the United States on the USS Washington. Prior to his departure from Southampton, as an honored visitor he was allowed to conduct religious services for German immigrants in London. The liberal Jews of England were kindly disposed to the escapees from Nazi terror. The services were conducted in German and many of the attendees were thrilled to see their former revered Rabbi from Berlin.

While in London, Rabbi was honored by an invitation to a very prestigious Jewish organization for a social evening. Red Lodge Thirty was in a very impressive, very British castle- like edifice where guests were required to wear a top hat and tuxedo. Ironically, in the midst of fleeing the terror of Nazi Germany and by now impoverished, he was required to wear formal dress to this dinner in his honor. He was lucky to have a substantial coat and hat and a serviceable pair of shoes; a top hat and tuxedo were out of the question. Another expatriate from Berlin who had been in England for a long time, loaned him his tuxedo and top hat, although the benefactor was a significantly larger man. As in the past Manfred made do. He was fortunate to have the loan of the tuxedo as he had no money to rent formal dress and certainly not to buy. He recalled this as a pleasant interlude and since this was prewar England before rationing, the food was a wonderful change for this undernourished immigrant.

He boarded the US ship SS Washington, having purchased a ticket with the last of his meager funds. He described the royal treatment on board, "They gave us excellent food served from a special kosher menu, good living quarters, and kindly and efficient service." This luxury was experienced only a few months after being reduced to the nothingness and inhumanity of the concentration camps. During the voyage there was a celebratory dinner in honor of Independence Day from which he retained the menu. This helps to date the voyage to July of 1939.

Upon arrival in the US on the Sabbath day the immigration officer did not believe that Manfred was a Rabbi since he did not have a long beard and the traditional orthodox dress of a long black frock coat and caftan. The officer accused him of trying to enter the US under false pretenses. He was relegated to the jail, a detention center on Ellis Island, until he could receive a hearing from an immigration judge. This confinement was like a summer resort compared with what he had experienced in Germany.

In this detention center there were hundreds, if not thousands of people interned for various reasons. This was the first time Rabbi had ever laid eyes on individuals from Asia and Africa, persons of different skin color. It seems impossible that so sophisticated and educated a man had never mixed with other races but such was the situation in the 20th century Germany. Although never seeing a black person until he came to America, he later was at the forefront of the civil rights movement in the 1960's. Up until this time everyone in his world had been white. All nationalities, both men and women, were interned in this prison.

The fear in everyone was the same, "what if they send me back?" Rabbi passed the time as best he could. He did a great deal of reading. The wait was very difficult. He was put into a kosher section which he requested, since he had always kept the kosher dietary habits of his forefathers. In this area they inexplicably served a menu of white bread of the American variety, which tasted to him like cotton. They also had what they called peanut butter which was completely new to Rabbi, and which he never countenanced at that time. He didn't like it then and avoided it throughout his life. He ate white bread, peanut butter, pieces of cheese, and tremendous slices of onions. He had never seen or eaten such big onions. This was the introduction to American kosher cuisine, soft white bread, peanut butter, cheese, and onions, oy vay. The sleeping was not in barracks but in huge clean and well-kept halls like at Waupun prison, he later noted. Everyone got a mattress and a real bed. After several excruciating days he appeared before the immigration judge who is remembered as stern, to the point, but friendly. He asked all kinds of questions about his Rabbinical training and fortunately believed Rabbi's credentials, was not put off by his unorthodox dress and cleared him for immigration. Since Manfred was adequately paid as a Rabbi of the Jewish community in Berlin in the early years of Nazi rule, he had enough money for flights to Amsterdam, London, and steam ship passage on the USS Washington. He finally arrived in July of 1939 at Chicago into the waiting arms of his brother Herbert. He had four dollars left in his pocket. Like so many before him, he was a poor immigrant hoping to start a new life in the new world.

The enormity of his experience in Nazi Germany can only be understood by including his entire talk "You Can't Go Home Again" first published in *Intimates and Ultimates,* by the Edgewood College Press. Ironically the publication was shortly before the Rabbi's death in the early morning hours of November 10, 1981, the 43rd anniversary of Kristalnacht. I have a personal memory of the night Rabbi gave his most famous speech.

After an absence of thirty years, Manfred Swarsensky returned to Berlin in 1970 with his wife Ida, his daughter Sharon, and his son Gerald. The mayor, the senate, and the State of Berlin, invited him as guest, along with only a dozen or so former leading Jewish residents of Berlin. These individuals were considered the most important surviving Jewish personages of prewar Berlin. They were invited to celebrate the 25th anniversary of the reestablishment of the Jewish community in Berlin. After receiving the invitation, Rabbi did much soul searching before he finally decided to return to his beloved city. He had previous sworn never to return "to the cursed soil" that was Germany.

The talk upon his return from Berlin was given at Beth El Temple on Arbor Drive in Madison, Wisconsin, of which he was founding rabbi 30 years earlier. It was Christmas night, December 25, 1970. The weather was mild for that time of year. It was one of those beautiful still winter evenings and a light snow was falling. The temple was crowded as never before with several hundred congregants and many from the community who were anxious to hear his experiences in a situation so complicated and filled with angst. This talk was given extemporaneously and represented the zenith of his speaking abilities and his intellectual powers. The contents reflected his attaining a level of morality and forgiveness exemplified by his lifetime watchword *Building Bridges, You Can't Go Home Again.* See Writings

PART II –

AMERICA – REBIRTH

CHAPTER 3 -- CHICAGO TO MADISON – THE EARLY YEARS

As previously noted, Manfred's admission to the US was paved by an affidavit of support from his brother Herbert and a three year contract from Temple Sholom in Chicago as assistant Rabbi with full support of its long time revered Rabbi Louis Binstock, at a salary of $100 per month plus full maintenance. Even in today's dollars this salary was at a bare subsistence level. The full maintenance was a tiny furnished apartment on 52nd street, in the Hyde Park section of Chicago's south side. The temple was a magnificent limestone structure ideally situated on Lake Shore Drive on the shores of Lake Michigan about four miles from downtown Chicago. This was an affluent neighborhood on the north side well populated with a significant percentage of Jews, many of western European background. The interior of the synagogue was clothed in a very dark wood paneling, which proved a disappointing contrast to the impressive exterior. However it was heaven and represented a new life to Manfred.

We know very little about Manfred's six months in Chicago. It was from the onset viewed as a way station because to be an assistant Rabbi was not Manfred's desire. We know only that the ladies in the congregation were anxious to entertain this eligible and attractive Rabbi, in order to showcase their daughters. Their usually lavish meals were in direct contrast to Manfred's customary fare of a drugstore lunch counter meal, where soup was hearty and tasty and was only five cents rather than the ten cents charged at most places. It was always served with a slice of dark bread, not white, and butter sometimes. While in Chicago he was asked to perform the marriage of a young German immigrant couple. The bride was related to Herbert's wife. They were named Winkler and they were to become the parents of Henry Winkler who later became Fonzie of the "Happy Days" television program. The Winklers remained in contact with Rabbi for many years as did their son Henry.

During his six months in Chicago, despite his strong German accent, his unfamiliarity with the colloquialism of the language, and his immigrant's status, he was approached by numerous congregations in the Midwest seeking a spiritual leader. He was asked to speak in Madison, Wisconsin, as some of his reputation as an outstanding speaker had followed him to the United States. Upon arrival in Madison he was very impressed, and reacted very favorably to the geographic beauty of the lakes and the verdant hills of the small city. The exciting intellectual atmosphere of the University of Wisconsin and the smaller Catholic Edgewood College, and the center of the Wisconsin State government all contributed to his positive impression of the community. Heavy lobbying led by Joseph Rothschild and his fine Cuban cigars, convinced Manfred to come to Madison as founding rabbi of a liberal congregation, Temple Beth El. Swarsensky had been a prominent Rabbi in the large metropolitan city of Berlin with its population of several millions, among them 150,000 Jews. His new position was founding Rabbi of a fledging congregation in a college town of 67,000 with less than 2,000 Jews. Madison was soon to learn how fortunate it had become. For Rabbi Swarsensky, the challenge was too hard to resist.

At the onset, the synagogue consisted of only a dozen or so families of prominent Jewish members of the community of both eastern and western European origins. The temple had no building of its own in the early years. As founding Rabbi of Temple Beth El of Madison, Rabbi later learned that the Jewish community in Madison had been established for more than 100 years but it had never had a liberal synagogue. At the University prior to World War II, there was a very small faculty presence but a very large Jewish student body and there were a number of liberal minded Jews in the Madison community. The Jews were served, however, by both orthodox and conservative shuls. This was fertile ground for a Reform temple. Rabbi accepted the pulpit of this neophyte congregation. "I went to Madison like biblical Abraham, completely on faith, though I don't want to compare myself with the patriarch," he later remarked. It turned out to be more positive experience than anyone could have imagined, for both the Jewish and the Christian community of the City and the State as well.

In Chicago he was very surprised and amazed that the temples in the USA were so different than the congregations in which he served in Berlin. He thought the American synagogues were more like social clubs, where one could choose to belong or not. This was in contradistinction to the previously noted situation in Germany where every Catholic, Protestant, or Jew was required to register and be taxed to support their respective communities.

He absolutely couldn't believe that as part of the synagogue there was invariably a social hall and a kitchen where various entertainment and enrichment programs were presented and meals were served. The absence of the prayer shawl, the yarmulke or skull cap, services on Friday night or in some temples on Sunday morning rather than Saturday morning, along with a notable lack of Hebrew in the service and without the traditional cantorial accompaniment were in sharp contrast to German services, and very difficult to accept at first.

Two of the most difficult challenges for the new Rabbi in Madison dealt with membership and fundraising. In beginning a new temple, the necessity of convincing people to become members of the new venture required all the gifts of Rabbi's charismatic personality. The additional onerous task of raising funds was foreign to Rabbi's experience and sensibilities. Throughout his life he never felt comfortable with these roles. He perceived that one was expected to be deferential to the more affluent donors, even if they had personality and characteristics which made them unappealing to Rabbi's sense of morality. Throughout his life this aspect bothered him. In a rare display of pique some years later, he described having to deal with some of these phonies, so full of themselves they actually thought that because they had money that they could call the shots. This was always a great problem throughout his life in America. It didn't occur very often that he found persons like this but when they appeared he did his best to conceal his dislike in public. In private he did vent his concerns to those close to him. It also struck Rabbi as very unfortunate and disappointing that many American Jews knowledge and appreciation of Judaism was wanting. Poor attendance at synagogue, except at high holidays, reflected this indifference.

He also had concerns that his activities in America, including sermons and talks about his horrendous experience in Germany, might negatively impact his efforts to bring his mother to America, or worse, that she might be targeted for abuse. Initially, since he was convinced that the Gestapo had agents or sympathizers in his audience here as in Germany, he asked that his true identity not be revealed and he spoke under the pseudonym of "Doctor Baum".

Manfred's initial arrival in Madison was inauspicious. He arrived to the train station on a snowy cold February day in 1940. Two ladies, wives of the founding members of what was to become Temple Beth El, met him at the station. They were Leah Rothschild, wife of Joseph and Rose Silberberg, wife of Sam.

Besides the Rothschilds and Silberbergs, the families who figured prominently in the early days of the temple included Joseph Tobias, Jay Jesse Hyman, David Novick, Sam Stein, Harry Epstein, Sam Woldenberg, Max Weinstein, Louis Milan, Robert Levine, Robert and Erwin Goodman, and Maurice Pasch. In 1940 there was a significant shortage of housing in Madison with the nation heading inexorably toward war. However, after a brief stay at the Lorraine Hotel, Joseph Rothschild was able to obtain a small spartan room for Rabbi at the University Club on the UW campus.

Rabbi's initial salary of $125 went much further in the student oriented community and he took many of his meals at the reasonably priced Club when he was not being hosted to home cooked meals by the ladies of the congregation. Rabbi remembered that he enjoyed the atmosphere at the University Club which housed mostly newly arrived young bachelor professors representing many disciplines, who taught at the University of Wisconsin.

The first venue the traveling congregation was to have during its first ten years of existence without its own building was at Barons' Tea Room. Joseph Rothschild ran a department store called Barons, fronting on the beautiful Capital Square. Barons contained a tearoom used daily for ladies light lunches for those who chose to shop at the store, and Rothschild was willing to offer it to the tiny nascent congregation for its Friday night services. For its first few years of existence the services were enhanced by the tea room organ which reminded Manfred of the services he had conducted as Rabbi in Berlin, although the volunteer organist is remembered as lacking in expertise.

Rabbi worked assiduously to shed his immigrant status. His English continued to improve but his thick Teutonic accent seemed to be impervious to change dramatically. Although a recent arrival, Rabbi's perceptions were very acute noting numerous aspects of the conduct of the Jewish community and the community at large, which he voiced in his sermons and privately. Swarsensky was not shy in speaking about what he perceived as areas that needed improvement.

Although Rabbi inexplicably claimed to be a shy person, he exclaimed, "Would you believe it?" His demeanor may have been an overreaction to his well-hidden secret. When specifically asked about his closest friends, he candidly stated that although he had close relationships with many, he truly felt the lack of very close friends with whom he could share his innermost thoughts and aspirations.

Of the individuals who were very important to Rabbi, the most important was his erstwhile teacher and mentor Leo Baeck. After his release from the concentration camp, Leo Baeck spent half the year in America and half in England. The last ten years of his life in exile from his beloved homeland, he taught six months in America in Cincinnati, at the Hebrew Union Institute Seminary for Reform rabbinical students and half the year in London, performing his administrative duties as head of the World Union of Progressive Judaism. Frequent communication was important and nurturing to Manfred and the relationship was mainly sustained by letter and occasionally by phone calls and always in their native language, German.

Concerns about his widowed mother's well being and safety continued to plague Manfred and his brother Herbert. With support provided by the brothers' combined meager funds, they began the task of bringing their mother, Louise, to America. It became impossible to bring Manfred's mother directly to America, so he and Herbert first paid for visas and passage to Shanghai. When this fell through then they arranged for passage and entry into Cuba. Visas to Cuba, they later discovered, were invariably forged. This arrangement and the money expended also came to naught.

Finally, a well established and respected Chicagoan and a German Jew who knew the family, issued an affidavit of support and used his influence to obtain a visa for Louise Swarsensky. Luckily, passage was obtained on the last boat ever to leave Spain with immigrants. The brothers obtained transportation for their mother to Spain, where ultimately she boarded a filthy, overcrowded, unseaworthy vessel, sleeping with others in the hold of the ship. She predictably became ill, and always frail and thin, she lost a significant amount of weight. It took seven to nine weeks for this ancient tub to get to the US, and when approaching land, the captain cabled for more money as ransom to deliver Louise Swarsensky. The captain refused to land until he had extracted more funds from the Swarsensky brothers. Finally the boat docked in New York and both Herbert and Manfred were there to welcome her with loving arms. Manfred recalled, "I didn't recognize her; she was only skin and bones and she was completely brown. Her skin was sallow and she looked pitiful and unwell but she was finally in the USA". She was able, with nurturing, to return to health and to live many years with Manfred in Madison.

CHAPTER 4 -- NEW FRIENDS

The next development met with the Rabbi's disbelief, consternation, and wonderment. Had he really come to the golden city where the arrival of the Messiah after almost 4,000 years of Jewish history was soon to arrive? Soon after his arrival in Madison and to his amazement the hand of friendship was extended by numerous Christian clergymen, including Reverend Kennedy of the First Presbyterian Church, later known as Christ Presbyterian, as well as others. In Germany the three religious groups were funded by the central government and there was absolutely no interaction on any level between Jew and Christian. Rabbi was soon asked to join the Madison Ministerial Association and formed lasting friendships with Reverend Alfred Swan of the 2,000 member First Congregational Church. Reverend Swan was one of the first to welcome him. Reverend Swan was known as the dean of theologians in Madison, and when Rabbi was asked to preach to his congregation at the First Congregational Church, early in his Rabbinate in Madison, Manfred exclaimed that he had "died and gone to heaven." This was the first of an almost constant stream of requests over the next forty years for Rabbi to preach and teach at most of the Christian institutions throughout the Madison area and many throughout the State.

His first talk to his beloved Rotary, which he joined some years later, occurred only a few months after his arrival in Madison. Outside of his full time duties as Rabbi at Temple Beth El his other full time occupation was of *apostle to the gentiles* and his frequently repeated appellation as *the finest Christian in Madison* soon followed. During the 1950's and 1960's, close friendships with Reverend Lee

Moorehead of the First Methodist Church of Christ on Wisconsin Avenue developed. Reverend Moorehead was later to write the most beautiful, perceptive and profound tribute to Rabbi after his death in 1981. Friendships with Reverend Richard Pritchard of the Westminster Presbyterian Church and Reverend Max Gaebler of the First Unitarian Society were established. He exchanged pulpits with these men many times and he considered them close associates.

With Pope John XXIII's leadership in calling Vatican Council II, the Catholic Church began to modernize its practices and attitudes. One document of the Vatican Council II was the encyclical *Nostra Aetate*, Declaration on the Relationship of the Church to Non-Christian Religions, stressing Christianity's Judaic roots. In the years before he became Pope John XXIII, Monsignor Angelo Roncalli played a pivotal role in saving the lives of thousands of Jews during World War II, when he served as the papal legate to Turkey. Roncalli referred to the death of European Jews as "six million crucifixions." The impetus created by *Nostra Aetate* sought to repair the relationships damaged by centuries of mutual hostility between Christians and Jews. It radically changed the Catholic Church's perceptions and teachings relative to the Jews, and created many positive initiatives.

It was in this context that Rabbi met his theological soul mate in Sister Marie Stephen *Stevie* Reges, OP, Chair of the Religious Studies Department at Edgewood College. It was a match made in heaven. Sister Stevie, as she was affectionately known, a Dominican Sister of Sinsinawa, remains a legend at Edgewood and is revered to this day at Edgewood and throughout Wisconsin.

As noted above, one of the first clergymen in Madison to extend his hand in friendship was the much revered and recognized Dean of Protestant clergyman, Alfred Swan of the very large and prestigious First Congregation Church of Christ on University Avenue and Breese Terrace. Reverend Swan was senior to Manfred, having been born in 1897 and a descendent of several generations of pastors of the Congregational Church, church of the original pilgrims. Reverend Swan was of a very formal demeanor, a very tall imposing man who was righteous and lived his life as a true Christian. Besides his stirring and engaging sermons he was known for involving himself as a champion of many causes in his 35 years as head of the Madison church. He embraced unpopular causes with fervor, sometimes to the disapproval of his parishioners. He shepherded Rabbi and oriented him to the many worthwhile organizations and activities in Wisconsin, while advising Rabbi as to organizations to which he should lend his support. He survived Rabbi and died in 1991.

With the approach of the 1950's Rabbi found himself as the third of the triumvirate of Protestant, Catholic, and Jewish clergy when invocations or speeches were necessary at state, university, or large social functions. When they needed a Jew, Rabbi was invariably asked, and he never refused a worthwhile invitation, according to his wife, Ida, and his long time secretary, Shirley Sweet. It was therefore natural that Rabbi Swarsensky was asked to speak at the installation of many of the new Protestant clergyman who assumed pulpits in Madison, and several of these became very important to Rabbi Swarsensky.

Reverend Lee Moorehead of the First United Methodist Church on Wisconsin Avenue was junior to Rabbi by more than ten years. He had a great interest in the holocaust and enlisted Rabbi's help in trying to understand this horrific period. Moorehead was very involved in the civil rights struggle in which Rabbi also took part as well. Reverend Moorehead was an accomplished speaker and his tribute to Manfred Swarsensky on the occasion of Rabbi's death, as he spoke to his flock was one of the most profound and beautiful offered as eulogy. His sermon is included else where in the book. Reverend Moorehead offered his pulpit as a forum for oratory on many occasions to Rabbi Swarsensky. Reverend Moorehead survived Rabbi by more than 20 years, dying in 2003.

Richard Pritchard, very much the opposite of Rabbi, was very conservative in theological and political matters. Rabbi was asked to speak at his installation at the Westminster Presbyterian Church. Initially a small congregation on West Lawn Avenue off of Monroe

Street, the church, under Reverend Pritchard's tutelage, ultimately became a very large congregation in its new home on Nakoma Road. Regrettably, after a number of years a rift developed in the congregation. He left Westminster and founded the Heritage Congregational Church. Many parishioners followed him and for several months before they built their own church, they held services at Rabbi's Temple on Arbor Drive.

Though an archconservative, Reverend Pritchard was involved with Rabbi in many humanitarian causes in the 50's and 60's, including civil rights and in efforts to quell the severe unrest which tore the Madison community apart during protests against the Vietnam War. Still outspoken and feisty at 94, although his eyesight and memory are failing at the time of this writing, Reverend Pritchard related, "I've never met a finer man than Manfred Swarsensky." He remembers that Manfred first used the phrase that it was, "his mission to comfort the afflicted and afflict the comfortable." Reverend Pritchard was from the very strict Calvinist background and grew up with the Anti-Semitic teachings espoused by Martin Luther. He had very little contact with Jews prior to Rabbi, and learned that the earlier Anti-Semitic teachings were not true. His sense of humor is sustained to this day; during the interview for this book, he remarked, "I can still play for the Packers any day."

Another person to arrive in Madison who became one of Manfred Swarsensky's closest confidants was the outstanding theologian and head of the First Unitarian Society for many years, Max Gaebler. A graduate of Harvard University and Divinity School and steeped in Yankee tradition, Max hit it off with Manfred immediately, when he came to the area in 1952. Again, Rabbi gave the welcoming address at his installation. Their relationship blossomed, as they were both liberal, theologically, and politically. They formed a mutual admiration society and worked on many projects and causes together. The Unitarian Society was small with only 200 families prior to reverend Gaebler's arrival, but grew very large as he led it for 35 years. The Society's magnificent home is the Frank Lloyd Wright designed Meeting house on University Bay Drive in Shorewood.

Max, too, was omnipresent in community affairs and was revered by parishioners and non-parishioners alike. He was junior to Rabbi and has been enjoying his retirement since 1987. At this writing he lives with his wife Carolyn, in Madison.

Another theologian who came to Madison in the early 60's was Robert Borgwardt, born in 1922. Although no stranger to Madison, having previously served at the Trinity Lutheran Church after his ordination in 1947, it was not until 1963 that he returned from Sioux Falls, South Dakota, to become the new pastor of the Bethel Lutheran Church on Wisconsin Avenue. The church was slated to become one of the largest Lutheran Churches in America, enhanced immeasurably by his ministry and outreach. His influence was augmented first by radio broadcast; subsequently a venerable morning television program brought the Bethel services to a wider audience which included Rabbi Swarsensky, watching assiduously to see what the competition was up to every Sunday morning. Several Bethel services were necessary because the congregation ultimately grew to 7,000 members. According to Wisconsin State Journal columnist, Bill Wineke, "Reverend Bob" was not an orator to be compared with Manfred or Alfred Swan, but his influence was enormous in the range of his activities throughout the community and beyond. His training and seminary was rather strict and although theologically conservative, socially he was an activist. He was there on Mifflin Street, a hotbed of student activism, and on the UW campus, meeting and talking with demonstrators and activists during the anti-Vietnam riots; many nights in the late 60's he was shoulder to shoulder with other clergyman including Rabbi Swarsensky, trying to calm the crowd and prevent damage to individuals and property, and avert threatened anarchy.

Borgwardt and Rabbi were brother Rotarians, mixing and schmoozing with other clergyman and those from business, professions, university professors, legislators, and government officials at the weekly Rotarian luncheons. Pastor Bob was an engaging conversationalist and along with Alfred Swan of the First Congregational Church, considered the Dean of Madison's Ministers, Pastor Bob was a close second. Although Rabbi was never asked to speak from the pulpit of Bethel Church he was asked to teach in the educational programs offered by the Bethel Church. Reverend Bob served Bethel for 28 years, retiring in 1991. Although backgrounds and life experiences were very different, Manfred and Pastor Bob found much in common and formed a solid friendship. He died in 2003 at the age of 80.

Finally, Rabbi's only female compatriot was Sister Marie Stephen Reges, OP, whom everyone called "Stevie". She is described as wonderful person and equal both as a teacher and humanitarian to Manfred, and an outstanding Chair of the Department of Religious Studies at the Catholic liberal arts college of Edgewood in Madison. She was a serious scholar of religious and biblical matters. By all accounts she was the antithesis of the often derided, humorless, stern, teacher/nun, both feared and revered by former students and memorialized in literature. Stevie is said to have had a heart as big as all outdoors. We are told that on Saint Patrick's Day after a bit too much of the grape, she was known to do a table top jig to the delight of those present. She idolized Rabbi and by all accounts the feelings were mutual. Much more about Rabbi's Edgewood association will be found later in the text.

CHAPTER 5 -- WHO'S MINDING THE STORE?

Rabbi was definitely a one man band, especially in the early years of Temple Beth El, as Rabbi, teacher, cantor, janitor, sexton, advisor, membership chairman, head of the Sunday school. Outreach to the community was a major activity from the beginning. He was still a bachelor for the first dozen years in Madison.

Beside those imposed by his immigrant status in a new land, his first difficult challenge was the Joseph Rothschild affair, which Rabbi related as one of the most onerous of his early years. Joesph Rothschild was instrumental in bringing Rabbi to Madison, wining and dining him and plying him with excellent cigars until he yielded and accepted the position of founding Rabbi of Temple Beth El. But there was another side to Mr. Rothschild. As head of Barons Department Store, he was accustomed to being in charge, and by all accounts he was a difficult man. Initially, in his newcomer status, Rabbi was reticent to speak out about his feelings, but with Mr. Rothschild's increasing demands to erase all traditional signs of Judaism from the religious service and observances, it became too much for Rabbi. Joseph Rothschild's stated purpose was to make the services and atmosphere so much like Christian services that his friends would feel at home if they attended. A power struggle ensued, with Rabbi emerging as the victor. There were bad feelings on both sides. Joseph Rothschild kicked the small congregation out of their temporary home at Barons Tea Room, and in return they kicked Joseph Rothschild out of the temple. Rabbi remembers this period as very difficult. Although involved in many worthwhile causes, he was not one who was comfortable making waves either politically or socially.

In the early years in Madison, especially prior to his mother's arrival, he felt totally alone in his bachelor status. Numerous members of his congregation were aware of this and did whatever they could to help make Rabbi welcome. While he was living at the University Club it was conscripted by the V12 program of the United States Government, in an attempt to accelerate the training of personnel needed for the anticipated war effort. Manfred then obtained housing in a dismal, drafty apartment on Frances Street. But all that was important to Rabbi was that he was a free man in a free country. He followed the dictum that an immigrant who was not married should get an American girlfriend, so he would quickly learn the language and not have to pay for lessons, or he could get a radio. Rabbi got a radio.

He especially remembers the kindness shown to him by the gracious Sarah Sinaiko, acknowledged dowager of the large Sinaiko clan. She was well known as very active in the community in the Women's Club and all kinds of worthwhile civic enterprises, and she had "real feelings for all human beings irrespective of their religion or race", according to Rabbi. She was one of the finest, most sincere ladies it was ever Manfred's privilege to meet. She showed Manfred many kindnesses and fed him delicious food exclaiming, "you remind me of my son Russell", who at the time was overseas in the war and later a prominent Madison surgeon.

Another of the Sinaiko clan was Arle. He was the surgeon who removed Rabbi's appendix in an emergency operation, and refused to charge a fee. Rabbi is remembered to have convalesced in the Silverberg home, lovingly attended by Rose. During his recovery Rabbi stayed in the Silverberg's young son, Joe's room. The room was adorned with sports memorabilia including baseball bats, which had to be temporarily removed, as they reminded Rabbi of the instruments used by the SS troops in bludgeoning concentration camp prisoners, and this caused nightmares for Rabbi.

Rabbi subsequently moved a few doors away on Gilman Street to a much more commodious apartment over the newspaper distributing offices of Joseph Tobias, one of the original organizers of the temple, who made sure the rent was very reasonable. It was there that Rabbi welcomed his beloved mother, Louise, in 1941. She lived with Manfred until his marriage in 1953 and spent many happy years in Madison before dying in 1968 at the age of 92. Rabbi relates that after coming to Madison, she went to MATC to take English classes. Rabbi exclaimed, "would you believe it" in telling the story. Slowly, methodically, Louise learned the language because she didn't want to miss anything, even initially preferring to speak English at home. She was ever present with her son, at temple services and during shopping excursions. Both she and Manfred liked to stop at Sam Stein's Bakery on University Avenue for a delicious pastry and a cup of coffee or tea. It was here on one especially bitterly cold night that Rabbi was seen at the bakery without a coat or hat. Several sources have related that when queried why he was not wearing winter clothing, Manfred simply said, "I met a man who did not have a coat and hat and he needed it much more than I. I can get another."

Rabbi was never his own advocate when it came to his compensation. He watched the temple expenses very carefully, in order that the dues should not be a burden to the young families in the temple. He refused salary raises on more than one occasion when offered, in order to keep temple overhead low.

True to their heritage as wanderers before having their own facility, the Beth El family held services and other functions at many places after being ejected from Barons' Tea Room. They were known to assemble at the Ester Vilas Hall at the YWCA; at the Women's Club on Gilman Street; at the old Saint Andrews Episcopal Church on Stockton Court; the old Unitarian Church on University Avenue; and at the Workman's Circle on Mills Street down the block from the Italian Working Men's club. The last facilities were in the Greenbush, a blue collar enclave between Regent Street and Monona Bay near what was then the Madison General Hospital, now Meriter. In this neighborhood Jews, Italians, and Blacks lived in harmony, until city redevelopment usurped the "Bush" in the 50's and 60's. The Greenbush is still remembered fondly by many Madison residents. No matter where the congregation met, Rabbi was ubiquitous, as always. He was responsible for turning on the lights, arranging the chairs, tidying up, turning off the lights, and locking up, as no one else was employed for these duties.

Besides trying to arrange for places of worship and for religious school, Manfred's days as an itinerant Rabbi began as well. Early on, he was contacted by representatives of several families in Waukesha, Wisconsin, members of the newly formed Temple Emanu-El, as to whether Rabbi would serve as part-time spiritual leader for this tiny embryonic congregation, also without its own home. Initially his thick German accent was hard to understand, and ultimately his accent faded somewhat, but his words were always glorious, according to several members of the congregation. He continued to service Temple Emanu-El for over 30 years. Although he occasionally drove with family members or Beth El congregants accompanying him, most often he rode the bus on Sunday to perform services in the evening for this struggling congregation. During the 65 mile trip each way, he got to know the bus drivers and a few other Sunday night regulars. In the beginning he was paid $12.50 plus bus fare. This was all that the tiny group could afford. The money was obviously not an incentive, but performing a mitzvah was.

Mitzvah is variously defined as commandment, blessing, or good deed, interchangeably. Through the years the congregation grew and now has its own home and full-time Rabbi, but many congregants have never forgotten the selfless service he rendered. Rosalind Merkow, a long time member of the Temple Emanu-El, is effusive in her praise, "we still always remember Rabbi Swarsensky gratefully with love and respect." The temple hosted a gala dinner honoring him in 1977 to celebrate his many years as a Rabbi. It was held at the grand ballroom of the Marriott Inn in Brookfield, Wisconsin, attended by members of the congregation and area officials. In 2006, a posthumous honor was also bestowed, as the chapel of the

Temple Emanu-El was named in his honor; the Manfred Swarsen-sky Sanctuary.

The ultimate home of Temple Beth El came to be built as their wanderings in the late 40's made it more and more difficult to function without their own permanent home. The effort to build the new temple was helped immeasurably by some of the younger members of the congregation, including Laurence Weinstein, and Bob and Irwin Goodman. Property off Monroe Street at the corner of Arbor Drive and Knickerbocker, fronting on the University of Wisconsin Arboretum, and the shores of Lake Wingra was obtained. The cornerstone was laid in 1949 and a very tasteful prairie-type limestone structure was built. It contained a sanctuary, chapel, classrooms, administrative offices, social hall, and kitchen. A beautiful monolith, its outstanding architectural feature was a carved traditional seven branched menorah on its summit. The menorah distinguishes the Temple building to this day. The first services were celebrated in the new temple during the Holy Days in the fall of 1950. Temple Beth El became affiliated with the Union of American Hebrew Congregations, the central organization for American Reform Jews.

The mostly successful liberal German Jews who came to America in the early and mid 19th century shunned their Eastern European blue-collar co-religionists from the shtetl, the ghetto like villages in Eastern Europe, consisting entirely of Jews. These Eastern European Jews clung to traditional ways and were orthodox in their practices. The German Jews who organized the Union of American Hebrew Congregations named their organization Hebrew rather than Jewish, because they felt that the term Hebrew had a softer and more biblical ring than the harsher sounding Jewish, which in many quarters was met with derision among their Christian neighbors. It is interesting that only recently in the 21st century the Reformed Jews felt confident enough in their own skin to change the name to the more appropriate Union for Reform Judaism.

There were many individuals in the early years, while building the congregation from a dozen or so families to 500 families at the time of Rabbi's retirement, who worked very hard in numerous activities for the temple. Today, Temple Beth El is the spiritual home to more than 700 hundred families. These early devoted congregants deserve recognition as they were very important to Rabbi. First among these was Shirley Sweet, a diminutive dynamo who became Rabbi's secretary. For many years Rabbi did without secretarial support. Then a congregant, Sue Blotner worked as a volunteer for Rabbi a few hours a week. Finally Shirley appeared on the scene and was Rabbi's devoted secretary for 25 years, until his death. She recalls that Rabbi always addressed her formally as Mrs. Sweet, always wore a suit and a tie, and often would give her scraps of paper with some of his thoughts; after three or four or five drafts these thoughts would evolve into a sermon or one of his many talks he gave to the community.

She recalls that when he became frustrated or angry he swore to himself in German, so she never knew what he said. She recalls that Rabbi was not a well man for much of his life, suffering from ever worsening angina, which is heart pain from lack of blood on effort. Because of his escalating severe angina pectoris over the years, he used increasing amounts of nitroglycerin tablets which he would surreptitiously slip under his tongue to relieve the discomfort. Finally, after many years he had quadruple bypass performed at the University Wisconsin Hospital in 1977 by Doctor Donald Kahn, who is reputed to have invented this procedure. Rabbi's venerable secretary, Shirley, is smiling and outgoing at the time of this writing, and seemingly robust as ever, walking several miles a day at age 90. She still works at the temple two mornings a week.

Jess Dizon was an impeccably turned out bachelor haberdasher who was responsible for helping Rabbi clothe himself, in addition to the many tasks he performed for the temple. Jess had a men's store in Madison, and as a single man, he had many things in common with Rabbi; this included being the recipient of many invitations to dinner from mothers of yet unmarried daughters, in the hopes that their offspring might catch the fancy of one the bachelors. Jess was a very exact soft spoken unassuming man who involved himself in many activities in the temple for many years.

In contrast to the self-effacing quiet demeanor of Jess Dizon was Rosetta. Most people did not know her last name, Glaeden. She was the long time wunderkind of the kitchen. The principal caterer to the temple, she ruled the non-kosher kitchen with an iron hand. Most people would agree that Rosetta was a real original. Rosetta was given to wide mood swings which dictated her reactions. Her food was not only beautifully prepared; it was invariably delicious. She was sought after for temple sponsored affairs as well as weddings, bat and bar mitzvahs and a host of other affairs by both members of the temple and by many persons of the community at large. She was not Jewish.

If she had one weakness, *it was Rabbi*. Anything he said or did was perceived as wonderful; she was like a blushing teenage girl around him and Rabbi would twist her around his little finger with a wink, a word or a story. She always had great respect for Rabbi and his position in the community. When she served her food at any affair, large or small, she came out from the kitchen to observe people's reaction to her efforts and comments from the guests. Rosetta also had another weak spot, as she was partial to doctors, any doctor, but especially long time Madison internists Hy Parks and Roy Rotter. She would often corner physicians at any of these affairs and regale them with her many real or imagined symptoms or illnesses. But woe to you if she took a disliking to you! Inexplicably she either loved you or hated you and treated you according to her whims. If she catered for you, you were expected to be effusive with praise of her food. Often her bill was dictated by how she felt about you, but always very reasonable. One often had to treat her with obsequious deference; otherwise you could be on her persona-non-grata list. She had a good heart, and her somewhat menacing countenance dissolved into a smile that could light up the room, when she became amused. She often enjoyed a good laugh, brought on especially with a story told by Rabbi. She was a character and a fixture at Temple Beth El for many years. When Rosetta died, Rabbi was present at her memorial service at the Gunderson Funeral Home, where he paid a beautiful tribute to his long time friend Rosetta, before family, friends, and many admirers.

Finally, after more than 20 years as Rabbi, a parish house was built for Manfred and his family. He had always rented small apartments, as more commodious residences were not affordable on his salary. By all accounts, Rabbi's compensation was a salary not commensurate with his worth. It finally occurred to some in the congregation and on the temple board that as a token of the high esteem with which he was held, a parish house should be provided. This occurred more than 11 years after he married. Manfred had long known that most of his Christian contemporaries had homes provided by their churches, but he did not pursue the matter. The inadequate space that the rental apartments provided became unsuitable for Rabbi and his growing family's needs, but he never complained. A beautiful one-story prairie style residence was built on Plymouth Court, near his friend and fellow expatriate George Mosse. It was one mile from the Temple in a lovely wooded neighborhood, off Glenway and Mineral Point Road. This was provided for the Rabbi and his family, for as long as they wished to occupy it. As of this writing, Ida continues to reside in the residence because Rabbi warned her before he died, "don't let anyone move you out after I go", and she hasn't.

Friday night weekly religious services attracted an increasingly large crowd, and the chapel where the services were held became too small. On the occasion of the 25th anniversary of the construction of the Temple, major construction, adding a much larger chapel, more classrooms, administrative space, and a much larger office for Rabbi, was accomplished. The weekly service was usually 45 minutes long; however Rabbi's sermons were usually 30, 45, or even an hour in length in addition. It had been said after Rabbi used his homiletic prowess that there was not a *dry seat in the house*. There is some truth to this; however his sermons were always interesting, informative, and well received, even if occasionally lengthy.

CHAPTER 6 IDA: "WE MET IN BED"

It was only after the congregation had its own spiritual home on Arbor Drive that Manfred gave serious thought to building his own family and fulfilling the biblical admonition to be fruitful and multiply. It was also during this time that Rabbi started his self imposed duties as a perpetual visitor to area hospitals, and also places of incarceration, and his self involvement grew and grew. Soon, seven days a week, he could be found at Madison General Hospital, now Meriter, St Mary's, Methodist, University Hospital and the Madison VA Hospital and as chaplain of the United States Army Air Force at Truax Field on Madison's east side. He also often visited St. Coletta's, a Catholic home for mentally impaired near Milwaukee.

He tried to give a measure of encouragement to the patients and he was even known to go to the VA Hospital in Tomah, WI two hours away, to visit the one or two Jewish veterans in the hospital there. His visits were mostly welcomed, and always peppered with his insatiable humor. Some who knew him characterized him as a little leprechaun with his frequent exclamation of "by golly," one of his favorite phrases. This term fit his elfish personality perfectly. On one occasion he insisted on carrying on a Passover Seder at the Waupun prison for its one Jewish inmate. According to Shirley Sweet, he dragged his volunteer cantor, Morey Schwartz, and his long suffering secretary Shirley, who was a long time choir member, to accompany him. Waupun had only one Jewish prisoner; however, the Seder was attended by more than 50 temporary converts as the several cups of sacramental wine were an integral part of the service.

This was a welcome change to the boredom of prison life and was much appreciated by those who attended.

It was while haunting the halls of the University of Wisconsin Hospital that he met a patient named Ida Weiner. Ida Weiner, born on January 22, 1918, grew up to become a very statuesque 5'8", considered very tall in her generation. She was also very beautiful. She was raised in a traditional Jewish home in Chicago and spoke Yiddish, what Rabbi referred to as Judeo-German at home. Her father was an exceptional lady's tailor, who not only did alterations but made fine suits of clothing and dresses for women. Judaism was very important and pervasive in their kosher home and was also very important to Ida. She became a self described "school marm", educated at the Chicago Teachers College which had been organized by the city of Chicago to produce teachers for the massive school system. Tuition was free but admission was very competitive by exhaustive examinations; admission could be expedited, as could most things in the City of Chicago, by political pull exercised by the local ward committeeman who exerted much influence in the affairs of the city. Ida was brilliant; she did not ask for nor did she need any political favors. She obtained admission with the highest marks on her examinations.

She loved books and loved her studies. She admits that as the youngest of four girls in the family she was very spoiled. She was the valedictorian of her large graduating class at John Marshall High School on the city's *Great Vest Side,* the home of a great number of eastern European Ashkenazi Jews. She first taught at the elementary level after graduation. Further college studies resulted in a master's degree, and thereafter she taught at Harrison High School. She always lived at home and had numerous suitors but none of them measured up to her high standards of mind and devotion to Judaism.

Her mother suffered from rheumatism and one summer she went to Florida to a kosher hotel to bathe in the warm waters of the Atlantic, which she found therapeutic. Ida decided to go to beautiful Madison, Wisconsin to study advanced French literature and language at the University of Wisconsin. On one of the first mornings in Madison she was expected at a university office very early in the morning, and since it was still dark, she engaged a taxicab. She states that the driver took her on a wild ride, and went through a red light. The cab was involved in an auto accident. Ida was shaken up very badly, though not apparently suffering from serious injury, and she was taken to the student infirmary at the University Wisconsin Hospital and admitted as an inpatient. It was while convalescing from her injuries, having filled out her admission card with Jewish as her religious preference, that Manfred walked into her life.

By all accounts, Manfred was *smitten*. After meeting her he could not wait to return daily to discuss many things of mutual interest and to gaze on the lovely Ida. He found her level of knowledge and her mind outstanding and her appearance was "not too bad". For her part, she remembered Manfred's "gorgeous blue eyes". Soon he was spending more and more time in her hospital room and another Jewish patient wondered aloud to Ida, "he only visits me once a week, how come he comes to see you every day?" On the day Ida was discharged, Rabbi met her in the lobby of the hospital with a bouquet of roses and took her to lunch. It was beshert in Yiddish, which indicates it was meant to be. When asked recently whether the fact the she was so tall and he was a short man was ever a concern she responded, "it's what's in your mind and in your heart and not the length of your legs that's important." Rabbi said after meeting her and getting to know her, "I did her the honor of marrying her." The wedding was a small family affair at Ida's home in Chicago, with her older sister baking the wedding cake, and an all too brief honeymoon at the Guion Paradise Hotel, a kosher hotel in Chicago for honeymooners. They were married on October 26, 1952; he was 46 and she was 34. He had finally given up his bachelor status; tears were shed from Janesville to Superior by the hopeful mothers all over Wisconsin, their dreams that their daughter might marry this paragon were dashed. When Ida and Manfred arrived in Madison a large reception at the Temple welcomed them.

Ida and Manfred had two children. Their daughter Sharon was born just a year later in 1953 and their son Gerald was born in 1956. Sharon is very much her mother's daughter in stature and appearance and like her mother, Rabbi complained, always late. She is however outgoing and outspoken, and is very bright. She obtained a BA at the University of Wisconsin, in Madison and her law degree at Northwestern University. She practiced law as a litigator in Chicago for many years and married a physician, well-regarded radiologist Paul Bilow. She lives in Highland Park, Illinois. Sharon and Paul have two children, a daughter and a son.

Rabbi and Ida's son Gerald earned a BA in accounting and a law degree from the University Wisconsin, Madison. He favors his father in so many ways, although much taller than his dad. He resembles him in stature and face, and has inherited many of Manfred's positive personality traits. As a young man he taught at the religious school at Beth El and was very well regarded by his students. His students and supervisor considered him the best teacher in the religious school. He now teaches business law as an assistant professor at the University of Wisconsin, Stout, in Menomonie, Wisconsin. He devotes himself at the Jewish Community Center in St. Paul, Minnesota, coordinating meals for the homeless. The fact that both children chose law was a matter of pride in their achievement to Rabbi, but also a matter of some consternation in their chosen profession. Both children are very devoted to their mother Ida, age 89 at this writing, who still lives in the family home. Gerald drives his 1999 Ford Escort approaching 250,000 miles on the odometer, the 288 miles from his home to Madison almost every weekend to be with his mother and to see she is well cared for. He remains a bachelor but Ida has not given up hope.

For eleven years the family lived in small apartments as the parish house was not built until 1963. Family life in the early days was influenced by the fact that Ida did not drive, so only one car was available and Rabbi's salary would not allow for more than one anyway. This required Rabbi to do the grocery shopping which he enjoyed, going to several markets to get the best values, and he did the usual duties of schlepping the children to all their activities. This was extra time he could spend with Sharon and Gerald and was very precious to Manfred, as his other activities kept him away from the family much of the time. Some say that Rabbi was not a good driver but this is disputed by the family. He never got into an accident, but since he was a multi-tasker his attention was sometimes diverted from his driving and this may have been responsible for his reputation. The children recall some things about the family life including that they were never able to listen to their favorite radio programs on the weekends. On Saturday the Metropolitan Opera was blaring all afternoon, to the delight of Ida and Manfred and to the dismay of Sharon and Gerald. At the crack of dawn on Sunday until it was time to go to Sunday school at 10 o'clock, Rabbi would assiduously listen to every local church sermon on radio and later watch them on TV so he could hear and see what the competition was up to.

For her part, Ida concerned herself with the details of keeping a kosher home and devoting herself completely to her children and her beautiful blue-eyed husband. She loved music and books and read assiduously and frequently late into the night. Since her intellectual passion was books, for many years she was in great demand by numerous groups in the Madison community as an outstanding book reviewer. She was a regular at the choir and was a prime mover of the temple sisterhood. Otherwise she concerned herself with the affairs of the Jewish community, all the while basking in the reflective glory of the accomplishments of her husband and children. She had a few close friends and to this day is respected and revered by many.

When Ida was criticized in the early years for not regularly attending Friday night services by a self righteous congregant, as their budget would not allow for a babysitter, she quipped, "I've got more than enough holiness at home, thank you." Though we know of few vacations that the Swarsenskys took, we do know that Rabbi and his family went to Germany twice in 1970 and 1979, and to Israel twice as well. Although an ardent Zionist, he never felt that the ingathering of all the Jews to Israel was necessary or even wise. With so many voracious and ferocious enemies, he felt that if all Jews were in Israel, it would make too attractive a target for attempts at genocide. Much of Manfred Swarsensky's feeling about his family is expressed in his sermon on the occasion of Gerald's bar mitzvah. It is titled *A Father's Ethical Will*, see Writings.

Through the years in Madison, Manfred established relationships with many holocaust survivors throughout the Midwest. Many were in the category of DP's, displaced persons, unfortunate survivors of the camps had very deep scars from their experiences. Most of them could not or would not return to what was left of their prewar homes and lives, many immigrated to the newly established State of Israel. Many also found their way to the United States and some of these came to Madison. They arrived via HIAS, the Hebrew Immigrant Aid Society, and Rabbi willingly served as unofficial welfare director. He was one of the most welcoming members of the community, helping to find housing, temporary economic support, employment, and most important, friendship. These newcomers often needed small loans to start their own business and Rabbi co-signed many of their loan requests to local banks. The loans were always repaid in a timely fashion and this did not represent a burden for Rabbi. Some of these DP's were so depressed and disheartened that they had great difficulties adjusting to life in the United States and Madison in particular. Many of these had lost their entire family, some of them wanted nothing to do whatsoever with the local Jewish community and religion, in any form, but this made no difference to Rabbi in the help he so willing rendered.

There was a network of survivors who found out about each other in the Middle West and also in the East. He kept in close touch with his mentor Leo Baeck. One of the people in his network of survivors was Rabbi Frank Rosenthal, one of the young students who traveled great distances in Germany to hear Rabbi Swarsensky speak. Through the years they developed a close relationship. Rabbi Rosenthal, originally orthodox in Germany, became a Reform Jewish Rabbi, and one of the most prominent and respected in Chicago and the Midwest.

Chapter 7 -- Rabbi to Wisconsin
– Building Bridges

In 1955, three young professors who were to become important to Rabbi came to the University of Wisconsin; an American from Oklahoma, Sam Jones, a German from Berlin, George Mosse, and an Egyptian from Alexandria, Menachem Mansoor, a singer, an historian, and a biblical scholar. With the building of the Temple on Arbor Drive in 1950, the services were enhanced by organ music and a volunteer choir. However, the quality of the choir and the organist left much to be desired, so Laurence Weinstein, always selflessly involved in Temple affairs, prevailed upon the newly arrived and well regarded professor of music, Sam Jones, to act as cantor and music director. He had moved to Madison from Texas. Sam was widely known and admired for his magnificent voice. He had an extremely wide tonal range and although a baritone bass, he was able to sing in the mostly cantorial range of tenor when required. He had previous experience in the cantorial repertory as cantor for a liberal synagogue in Dallas, his previous home. The much improved quality of the music at Beth El became well known. Although of the Welsh background, for some reason Sam was drawn to German culture, language, and people. He and Rabbi became very close, and their frequent conversations were usually in German. After divorce from his first wife, Sam went on sabbatical to Argentina and gave up his post as cantor after ten years. Thereafter, the cantorial position was ably filled by volunteer Morey Schwartz, a local jeweler. Though not a professional, Morey did a credible job for many years as cantor.

Sam and Rabbi remained friends after Sam went to Argentina and Manfred was thrilled to hear that Sam had met a German fraulein, Eva, studying in South America and made her his second wife. When they arrived in Madison, Rabbi gifted Eva with a dozen roses at the train station. She was bright and blonde and beautiful, and she and Rabbi got along famously. She, Sam, and Rabbi got together frequently for interesting discussions and social evenings along with Ida. The Jones' home was completely German, where the language was spoken by Sam, his wife, and his children. Eva and Sam remain very happy in their beautiful modern home in a neighborhood fairly close to the Swarsensky residence.

The second to accept a professorship at the University of Wisconsin, Madison was George Mosse, a European history scholar. He was born Gerhard Lachman Mosse in Berlin in 1918. Rabbi knew the family well as devoted members of the Jewish Community. George's father, Hans Lachman Mosse was the head of Mosse Verlag, referred to earlier in the book. The Mosse family fled Germany immediately after Hitler came to power, as there was no room for liberals in Germany any longer, and certainly not those of Jewish background. The family fled to Paris soon after Hitler came to power. They had significant holdings throughout Europe, so they were able to sustain their lifestyle. After their Paris exile they moved to London, where the Mosse children attended the finest private schools.

George matriculated at Cambridge in England, and completed his undergraduate education at Haverford College, when the family came to the United States. At the graduation ceremony, George received his Bachelors Degree from the hand of President Herbert Hoover. A PhD from Harvard University followed, and for a number of years, George taught at the University of Iowa in Iowa City before coming to his most important academic home at the University of Wisconsin, Madison. George retained a copy of the recommendation from his senior professor at the University of Iowa to the head of the History Department at the University of Wisconsin as a reminder of the attitude of many academics toward Jews at that time.

It read, "I highly recommend George Mosse to you even though he is a Jew". During his academic career, George taught literally all over the world and became a world famous historian. As an ardent Zionist he was very devoted to the Hebrew University in Jerusalem, where he taught several months annually for many years. He published 25 books including *The Crisis of German Ideolog*, his seminal work. The book is highly regarded to this day. George became one of the world's foremost authorities because of the many titles he published on the Nazis, National Socialism and fascism. His classes were always over-subscribed with hundreds in attendance, as he was an absorbing and fascinating lecturer. His books were some of the most important published on National Socialism, and widely read in academic and lay circles even today.

Mosse lived for many years in a modern, aluminum clad wooden home close in proximity to Rabbi's residence on Plymouth Circle. In their profound commitments both to education and Israel they formed a common bond. He and Rabbi were close, spending endless hours discussing the broad range of subjects of mutual interest, always speaking in their beloved German.

After German unification, George sought and received very substantial reparation for the properties seized by the Nazi government. The appearance of an academic monastic existence, surrounded by books with the ever-present Dunhill pipe protruding from his mouth and spewing ashes over himself, was a picture familiar to many Madisonians who knew George. However, he had a very active social life and was involved in the affairs of his students, his academic children. He died a wealthy man in 1999, leaving the bulk of his estate to be administered by his partner, John Tortorice. He left the estate to the University History and Semitics departments. The funds are being used for an exchange program between the University of Wisconsin and the Hebrew University in Jerusalem. The large and imposing and architecturally controversial Mosse Humanities Building on the University Wisconsin, Madison campus is named in his honor. His legacy is also his close association with many students who went on to become outstanding historians and academicians. His fascinating life journey is recorded in his autobiography, *Confronting History,* published by the University of Wisconsin Press.

The last of the 1955 arrivals was Menachem Mansoor, born in Alexandria, Egypt in 1912. He came to the University Wisconsin to help the newly organized department of Hebrew and Semitic studies, one of the first departments of Hebrew and Semitic studies at a secular University in the United States. Semitic, in its modern usage, refers to both Jews and Arabs. In the classic sense it also refers to other Middle Eastern cultures such as Babylonian and Syrian. All were considered the purview of the newly organized department.

As a young man, Menachem took a job at the British embassy in Israel and was put in charge of the English athletes who came to participate in the Maccabiah Games, the Jewish Olympics. Among the athletes was a young women javelin competitor, a very attractive woman named Claire, who was to become his wife. Claire was the perfect companion to Menachem. She managed all the details of their home and social life, leaving the somewhat absent-minded scholar to completely devote himself to academic pursuits. Although in some ways inscrutable, he is described by those who knew him as a very warm and outgoing individual. Clashes with his fellow academic, George Mosse, in the history department, were inevitable as both sought to defend their respective academic territory. Menachem had a rather formal demeanor and was considered courtly, always dressed in suit and tie, and highly regarded and loved by his colleagues and students. The story is told of him that once a young woman was threatened with an incomplete on her course of Hebrew studies because she had to leave early for her wedding. Menachem asked her to bring her a katubah, the traditional marriage contract, for him to examine. He asked her to translate the contents and upon completion he declared that she had passed the course.

For many years Menachem conducted tours of Israel each year for members of the Madison community under the aegis of Edgewood College, where he taught for many years as well. The annual trips were well attended by Catholics, Protestants, and Jews; being led by one of the foremost biblical scholars of his generation, they were thoroughly enjoyable and educationally rewarding. He referred to attendees as "Mansoor's pilgrims." Menachem was also an accomplished chanter of Torah, the hand written parchment scrolls of the Hebrew bible, a task which he fulfilled for many years at the Temple Beth El. He was very close to Rabbi both academically, socially and spiritually. Manfred also taught at the UW, and for many years at Edgewood College, and with Sister Stevie, they formed a triumvirate of scholarly teaching and deep friendship. Doctor Monsoor died in Madison at age 90 in 2002.

Though not part of Rabbi's world until several years later, in the 1960's Sister Marie Stephen Reges, OP, *Sister Stevie*, was perhaps Manfred's most important friend and associate in the last 20 years of his life. Nine years younger than Manfred, she was born in 1915 in Washington DC; initially a mathematician, and a Catholic sister, theirs might seem to be an unlikely friendship. With a BA in Math and Physics *cum laude* from Trinity College in Washington, DC in 1937 and three masters degrees, a masters degree in Math from the Catholic University of America in Washington, DC , a masters degree in Religious Studies from Providence College in Providence, Rhode Island in 1952, and finally a masters degree in Hebrew and Semitic studies from University of Wisconsin Madison in 1970, Sister Stevie became a widely respected theologian, biblical and ecumenical scholar. She was a female counterpart to Rabbi, everywhere at once in the community teaching, lecturing and in her advocacy of worthwhile causes. She was a tireless worker in interreligious understanding and appreciation, and along with Manfred and Menachem was a devoted Rotarian.

Although in its strictest sense, ecumenism refers to the relationship between various Christian sects, it is used here in the unauthorized common usage of also referring to Jewish and Muslim relationships to Christianity, and in this area Sister Stevie was a champion. Although initially she came to Edgewood College in Madison as a mathematician, her interest morphed into the religious realm and she ultimately became the Chair of the Department of Religious Studies. She had a profound interest in Judaism, often attending

Friday night services at Temple Beth El and was known to spend all of Yom Kippur at services at the Temple on Arbor Drive. She basked in the light of Rabbi's religiosity. His sermons were often the intellectual highlight of her week. She was so often at the temple that Rabbi gave her a key to the building, so she could pray in the sanctuary any time she wished.

Both she and Rabbi shared a sense of humor that was a bit off beat and the story is told about something that Rabbi said to her that would only be humorous to another theologian. He met Sister Stevie one day carrying the Catholic version of the Hebrew Bible, The Old Testament, and said to her, "would you show me where the Ten Commandments are?" Inexplicably they both thought this was hysterically funny, and they dissolved in laughter. They loved to share theological discussions. Ida welcomed Sister into their home as a family member. She was very highly regarded at Edgewood by the staff and students and she was instrumental in bringing Rabbi and Menachem as professors to Edgewood. She was also responsible for initiating efforts which resulted in Rabbi being awarded only the second honorary doctorate given by the venerable Edgewood College. Sister Stevie was the impetus behind memorializing Rabbi with the establishment of the Manfred Swarsensky Chair of Jewish Life and Thought at Edgewood, as well as being instrumental in publishing a collection of Rabbi's talks and sermons. *Intimates and Ultimates* was published by the Edgewood College Press in 1981, several months prior to Rabbi's death. She died in 1997.

PART III: THE FINEST CHRISTIAN IN MADISON

CHAPTER 8 -- CONTROVERSIES, DIFFICULTIES, AND VIGNETTES OF JOY

After 20 years in Madison the man who came to this mid size midwestern city as an impoverished immigrant, and an escapee from the horror of Hitler's Germany, became an outstanding member of the community, universally admired, respected and revered. However it was the next 20 years, the 60's and 70's which were to represent the greatest challenges, difficulties, and ultimately the greatest rewards for Manfred Swarsensky. A contemporary of Jesus and a Jewish sage, Hillel said "never separate yourself from the life of your community." This served as an anthem on which Rabbi based his life and he adhered to it.

Manfred Swarsensky achieved the greatest accomplishments of his career in building bridges. If there was a worthwhile organization to which Manfred did not lend his support, it was unknown to him. He was the ultimate joiner. How he found time for all his commitments is a mystery. If a request came, a meeting was arranged, even at 11 p.m. Besides the Madison Ministerial Association, he attended a weekly 7 a.m. Ministers Breakfast at the Bethel church. He served on the boards of the Madison General Hospital, now Meriter, Boy Scouts of America, Dane County Mental Health Association, Rotary, United Way, Red Cross, and the Madison Jewish Community Council. He served on the ecumenical committee of the Ministerial Association and was a member of the Governor's Equal Rights Commission. In 1971 he represented Wisconsin by attending the White House Conference on Aging as a member of the Wisconsin delegation. He was a member of the Wisconsin State Historical Society, the Wisconsin Society for Jewish Learning, the Madison Literary Society, and served as Chaplain to all area hospitals, Truax Field, Tomah VA Hospital, St. Coletta's, and various prisons. Early on he taught Hebrew at the University of Wisconsin, prior to the establishment of the Department of Hebrew and Semitic studies, and he taught in that department as well. He was an integral part of the Religious Studies Department at Edgewood College. Besides sermonizing all over the State, he taught in the educational programs of many Wisconsin churches. His often repeated mission was that besides building bridges, "I was saved so that I could be a *messenger from the dead to the living.*"

One of Rabbi's most enriching and rewarding associations was the Madison Downtown Rotary. Rotary club members are business and professional leaders who volunteer in their communities and promote world understanding and peace. There are 31,000 rotary clubs in more than 165 countries and these clubs encourage high ethical standards and carry out humanitarian projects to address such issues as poverty, health, hunger, education, and the environment. This group was tailor-made for Rabbi Swarsensky. The Downtown Rotary to which he belonged was one of the largest Rotary clubs in the nation, with over 500 members. He spoke at downtown Rotary only a few months after his arrival in Madison in 1940, and innumerable times through the years, and at Westside Rotary and many other community groups as well. It was not until 1960 that Rabbi could afford to join, and was able to adjust his schedule to conform to the weekly compulsory lunches. He loved Rotary and found that associations with many of the prominent citizens of Madison added another dimension and life experience for him. Attendees included a large contingent from the theological community; his buddies Menachem, Sister Stevie, Max Gaebler, Bishop Cletus O'Donnell and Pastor Bob from Bethel were in attendance, as well as several other prominent clergymen, including Alfred Swan. It is said that one of Rabbi's most prized possessions was a plasticized parking permit for St. Raphael's Cathedral parking lot, across from the Lorraine Hotel where the Rotary luncheons were held, a gift of the bishop, and a boon to the Rabbi, as parking in downtown Madison was always a challenge.

The Madison Club Affair

In 1965, a major event that precipitated opening the doors of all institutions to Jews and other minorities was the refusal of the Madison Club to admit Jewish members. It was well known to Madison Jews but perhaps not widely known to the Christian community, that certain institutions in the area were closed to them. It is true that prior to the Second World War, there were only a handful of Jews on the faculty of the University Wisconsin, Madison, although the University had a large contingent of Jewish students and, without imposed quotas, was very welcoming to them. However this barrier to faculty participation of Jews rapidly fell after 1945, and in the 60's and 70's the number of Jewish faculty members was in the hundreds. To quote Rabbi when he spoke in the late 60's, "there are between 150 and 200 Jewish faculty members and this number is rapidly increasing." The institutions which denied memberships to Jews were the Madison Club, some of the local country clubs, while certain local medical clinics and law firms did not welcome Jewish doctors and attorneys.

Although not overtly concerned with this affair, and true to his policy of *not making waves* with his Christian neighbors, it is reasonable to assume that Rabbi was involved behind the scenes. According to the recollections of some who knew Manfred, those involved being denied membership were congregants who doubtless sought Rabbi's advice. At any rate, the effect on Rabbi and his flock was to be significant.

The Madison Club was and is basically a longtime social and business venue in downtown Madison to which many of the prominent local citizens belong. It was the policy for the Club to offer a complimentary membership to all members of the State Supreme Court, until Myron Gordon, a Jew, was elected to the court. Although all the other judges were offered complimentary member-ship, Judge Gordon was not. Since the judges held working lunches at the club, Myron Gordon, noting the outrageous slight, refused to attend these lunches. Gordon Sinykin, prominent head of the local prestigious law firm of LaFollette, Sinykin, and an active member of Rabbi's temple, was approached by Colin Ferris, the president of a local bank with a significant number of Jewish clients. Mr. Ferris asked permission to submit applications to the Club for Mr. Sinykin and Judge Gordon, in an effort to break the barrier to membership. They agreed, knowing full well that the chances of acceptance were slim. The Club had archaic membership standards which allowed a tiny minority of board members to blackball any membership. Pre-dictably, membership was refused to Sinykin and Gordon.

When the matter became publicly known, several prominent members of the club resigned in protest, including University of Wisconsin President Fred Harvey Harrington. Then all hell broke loose, with relentless local newspaper and media coverage. Exclusion was not the image most people had of Madison. The City Council passed resolution after resolution and threatened to revoke the Club's liquor license. The local equal opportunities commission launched an investigation. The frenzy elicited by the affair created a great deal of embarrassment for the Club and many of its members were very unhappy. Finally the Club relented; the rules for membership were changed to approval by a democratic majority. The Club asked Gor-don and Sinykin respectfully to resubmit their applications, and they were approved and invited to join; they did. This was a pivotal event in Madison and soon other barriers fell as well. Today in Madison there are no discernable impediments based on race, religion, sex or national origin to membership of all institutions. This was a real vic-tory for the American way.

Rabbinical Association Action

One of the saddest chapters in Rabbi's life in America was the reaction of fellow Rabbis to Manfred Swarsensky's completely open policy on mixed marriages. He would and did travel anywhere in the State to perform a Jewish ceremony for couples of mixed religious backgrounds who requested it. At the time this was very unusual as most Reform Rabbis, in concert with their orthodox and conservative counterparts, flatly refused to perform marriages of couples, one of whom was Jewish and the other was not. A few Reform Rabbis would perform these marriages, but they required conversion of the non-Jewish spouse, and many other caveats and barriers were erected as well. Rabbi would have none of it. He felt if he did not marry these couples, they and their children would be lost to Judaism forever. He felt this was essential for the survival of Judaism and he said to his intimates, "I do it for the Jewish mothers." Recent information has come to light which seems to vindicate Rabbi Swarsensky's position. New data suggests that 2/3 of couples, one of whom is of another religion, when married by a rabbi, adopt Judaism as the preferred religion in which to raise their children. This is so, even if the non-Jewish partner does not convert. In addition to not performing mixed marriages, all branches of Judaism did not welcome converts.

Outreach and conversion are stated primary purposes in many Christian denominations. Judaism, in contradistinction, erected many difficult barriers to those wishing conversion. In the mid 20th Century, all sorts of road blocks were still present when individuals expressed the desire to convert to Judaism. However, it was in the 60's and 70's that there began a series of stirrings and attempts at being more inclusive, primarily by Reform Jews relative to all types of women's issues: equality, acceptance of female Rabbis and cantors, and even bat mitzvah, the female equivalence of bar mitzvah. In addition, acceptance of alternative lifestyles and families, although part of the liberal tradition now, was not even considered by Reform Rabbis prior to the 1980's.

The Wisconsin Association of Rabbis, to which Rabbi Swarensky belonged, was a group from all branches of Judaism: Orthodox, Conservative, Reconstructionist, and Reform. Their meetings, according to Manfred, were lengthy and boring and often concerned with the minutiae of halachah, following all the strict laws of traditional Judaism, and not often touching on the critical issues of concern to modern Jews. According to Manfred, the spiritually driven force so important to Rabbi seemed to be lacking in a number of the members, especially those critical of his liberal policies. Rabbi discerned that many of their policies and concerns were irrelevant to the modern world, and he was not shy about expressing his feelings. It was no secret that Manfred was held in very high regard by most, and jealousy may have played a part. The Rabbis, to their everlasting embarrassment and shame, rescinded Swarsenky's membership in the group.

It seems almost impossible for us to conceive that these men, and in those days they were all *men*, were so narrow minded that they "kicked me out of the group, mostly for performing intermarriage," Rabbi recounted. That arguably, the greatest rabbinical mind in Wisconsin, whose life and deeds were considered by many above reproach, should be kicked out of this group is almost outrageous to conceive, looking back today. Rabbi did not go quietly into the night and vehemently expressed his displeasure and disgust. He said he was not embarrassed that he was summarily dismissed. He said he was terribly embarrassed for the group and for their action. Although not primarily ego driven, still at some level it must have hurt.

Parenthetically it should be noted that today, although great progress has been made in all aspects of women's issues, intermarriage, welcoming conversions, and becoming much more inclusive relative to homosexuals and alternative life styles, many Rabbis still refuse to perform intermarriage, except with numerous barriers and caveats.

Manfred had a welcoming, fraternal, and kind association with other local Rabbis, although he did not form close relationships as he had with several local Christian theologians. These included Rabbis at the Hillel Foundation and the conservative congregation on Mound Street, Beth Israel, none of them Reform. The local Rabbis worked on many projects of mutual concern together. The Madison Club affair and the Wisconsin Rabbis actions, although not truly comparable, do bring to mind Groucho Marx's famous quip, "I wouldn't want to join any club that would have me as a member!"

Letter From a Second Grader

The next two vignettes are on a much more positive note; a letter from a second grader and the Gates of Heaven, on the move. In the January 1974 monthly Bulletin of Temple Beth El a letter from a second grader was published, along with Rabbi's immediate reply. The letter, although remarkable in content, reflects the lack of spelling acumen of a seven year old. There are no misprints in the following copy of that letter. In Rabbi's reply the spelling is somewhat better (torah may be spelled with or without the terminal h).

Dear Rabbi Swarzensky,

I think you are one of the best rabbis I have ever saw. You tack very nisly and you don't show off and you read very well from the tora. I am the son of Julees Alder. Remember when you tacked to my dads father and mother and father? I remember it very well. I also remember the serves that you gave last Friday. You did very well at that there shood be no superstishes. Not that I've said ALL this I wood like to ack you afyou questions. The first questing is that HOW did you get to be a member of the templ and be a rabbi of the temple. My sekent questing is when you were a little boy did you go to reelijes school and study very hard? Or did you stay at home and study yourself. My third questunis is the first time you saw the tora wer you very interested in it ore you just din't think it was so important. My third qusttion is in the oden days was the tora inventitied yet ore did it get invetied a little bit later. My forth questunis is when

75

the tora was invented did thay have all thos things that decorate the tora lick the brest plante and the ponter? My fith questing is when the sawyer started too rite the tora what was the longtest time it tock for him to rite the toraand what was the shortest time it tock for him too rite the tora. My sicth questing is when the heebroo langwij was just invented how did that persen spred the heebroo lagwij arong? Pleese rite back.

Your frend

David Adler

Under the letterhead of Temple Beth El, Rabbi Swarsensky responded immediately with the following letter:

October 23, 1973

Dear David,

I was so delighted receiving your letter that I am dropping everything else in order to answer your questions:

I became a rabbi of the Temple because there was no rabbi here and the leaders of the congregation heard about me while I was in Chicago. This was in 1940. I had just arrived from Germany, the same country in which your grandparents lived at one time.

When I was a little boy I did not stay at home and study myself but I went to Religious School and studied very hard. It is good that we have public schools and religious schools at which teachers can teach us. It we stayed at home and studied, we would never be able to learn as much. Of course, we must also study at home by doing the homework our teachers assign to us.

I still remember the first time I ever saw the Tora. I was very excited and interested because I noticed it was written on parchment, that is sheepskin, which I had never seen. I was also surprised to hear from my teacher that the Tora was written by hand with a quill by a man who is called a Torah Scribe.

The Tora is very old, probably more than three thousand years old. It took many centuries before the Jewish people actually put all the stories of the Tora together. Before they did that, one generation would tell the next one what was in the Tora, namely the stories of their forefathers and the laws by which they were supposed to live.

At the very beginning the Tora was just a scroll without cover and decoration such as the crown, the pointer, and the breastplate. It was many centuries later in what people call the Middle Ages that they added the decoration.

I really could not tell you how much time it took and still takes to write the Tora. It takes longer for some people than for others to write the Tora. No doubt, if a person is more skilled, he can complete the Tora in much shorter time than others. In either case, it is a difficult job which takes a long time.

7. When the Ten Commandments or other laws were first given, people would write them on stone which was the original material upon which men wrote. Can you imagine how difficult that was! However, the way in which the knowledge of the laws was spread was through teaching and preaching. It is still the purpose of education in the Temple and of sermons in the service to spread the knowledge of the Jewish religion.

I hope that I answered your questions. However, if I did not make myself clear enough if you have more questions, please write to me again – I love to hear from you – or come into my office, when you are here at the Temple.

It was kind of you to tell me that you like me. I like you, too.

It was good to have seen your grandparents. Please give them my best regard. With all good wishes to your parents, Jean and you, I am

Your friend,

(signed) Manfred Swarsensky

David's parents Hilde and Julius both escaped Germany in 1939 and met and married in the United States. Julius is a retired biochemist at the University of Wisconsin and Hilde is trained as a librarian. As many young couples do, they only joined the temple when it came time to educate their children in the Jewish tradition. David and his sister Jean were both remembered as very bright pupils at the religious school at Beth El.

Being escaped German Jews, they formed a close relationship with their lanceman, Manfred. Today David is an accomplished freelance musician currently living in Madison and his sister is married and living in Hawaii.

Rabbi accorded immediacy and feigned importance in his response to the young boy's letter. The alacrity and seriousness of this reply, along with a twinge of playfulness and humor, illustrates significant aspects of who Rabbi was and what made him universally highly regarded. To respond immediately to simple inquiries from a child and to inform those in the Beth El family on the matter with publication of the child's letter and Manfred's reply shows profound consideration of a youth looking toward the world for answers. It illustrates that Rabbi's responses to all, young, old, simple souls, as well as prominent personages were the same according to their needs.

When befriending and comforting Displaced Persons and those individuals lost in the turbulence of the modern world, Rabbi was there for them. To movers, shakers, rich, poor, governors, mayors, students, academics, intellectuals, anarchists, bishops, and young children there was ever present warmth, concern and love, as if one were the only person in the world who mattered at the moment Manfred was giving help, counsel, and solace to those who sought him. He could always be depended upon. He was a friend to all. This was the measure of a great man, a mensch.

Gates of Heaven, on the Move

There were only a few Jews in Madison when they banded together to form the first synagogue, Shaare Shomaim, translated as the Gates of Heaven, in 1856. The tiny congregation built the first Jewish house of worship in Madison in 1863 at 214 West Washington, one block from the Capital Square near the much larger and imposingly beautiful Grace Episcopal Church. The structure was used as a synagogue only for 20 years, as the number of congregants dwindled and several left town due to adverse economic conditions. It was, however, a jewel of a building, built of a light colored sandstone; both architecturally and esthetically pleasing, with its classical gothic structure. With a capacity of at most 100 persons, it included a customary balcony for the women. After being sold, throughout the years it was used as a church by several different denominations including the Unitarians and the Christian Scientists, as law offices, as a storage area for the State of Wisconsin, and finally in 1960 it was used as a dental office.

The threat of demolition in the late 60's came to the attention of a number of the members of the community, both Jew and Gentile, who felt that because of its unique history and its architectural features, it should be preserved as a tribute to Madison's past. In addition, research revealed that it was the third oldest synagogue still standing in the United States. After its significance was realized, an application was made to have it placed on the National Register of Historic Places and it was declared a National Landmark in 1970. Prominent early supporters were Lois and Norton Stoler. When Miles McMillian, editor of the Capital Times, learned of the project, he, in conjunction with writer Frank Custer, prominently featured the project with almost daily articles in the newspaper. This helped to gain widespread community support.

Many felt the building should be saved from the wrecking ball as an enormous building was planned for the site by the United Bank. What to do? Build around it? The innovative answer soon came. Whether or not it was the idea of the City Housing Director,

Sol Levin or not is uncertain, but after a careful engineering survey it was determined that the building was structurally sound and could be moved. The Planning Commission was offered the option of placing the structure at the western edge of the tiny James Madison Park on Gorham Street on the shore of Lake Mendota. It was a beautiful and a very prominent site.

At first Rabbi was lukewarm and uninvolved in the project as the building had been used as a temple for only a few years, but as time passed he saw the symbolic and practical perspective of the plan. He came onboard giving it his considerable support, and even helping with the onerous task of fundraising to complete the project. The board of directors of one of the oldest Wisconsin synagogues, Temple Emmanuel B'nai Jeshurun in Milwaukee was approached by a committee of Madisonians, including then Mayor Bill Dyke and Rabbi Swarsensky, concerning an unused, magnificent and delicately carved oak ark built in 1858. It was generously and gladly donated to the worthwhile cause of the restoration of the Gates of Heaven. The name of the artist who carved the beautiful ark is lost to memory. The ark is a traditional repository for the Torah. It is the Ark of the Covenant. The Torah is painstakingly hand written on parchment scrolls by a torah scribe. The ark was crated and very carefully shipped to its new Gorham Street home and when installed, it lent a beautiful artistic centerpiece to the otherwise very stark interior of the building. The whole community was energized by the project and thousands of bystanders viewed the temple's slow progress in its move to the beautiful new site.

After considerable work on a new foundation, and renovation done by a volunteer crew including city fireman, office workers, and other members of the community, with contributions for construction from the John Aihl and the Orville Madsen Construction Company as well as members of the community, the Gates of Heaven was rededicated on August 5, 1971 to a crowd of over 500 people. Richard Buirne, a well-known reconstructionist, oversaw the restoration.

The tiny synagogue stands today in its beautiful setting almost 40 years later, as a symbol of love for our heritage and represents the cooperation of people of many walks of life, in preserving a historic past. In its new location the Gates of Heaven is not just a monumental symbol, it is used almost daily for weddings, Bat and Bar Mitzvahs, community meetings and lectures, and church services of various denominations. Every year, using a *martyred torah* recovered from a concentration camp, Hannah Rosenthal, daughter of Rabbi Frank Rosenthal who helped obtain the torah, conducts Rosh Hashanah and Yom Kippur services for many members of the community. Musical accompaniment is always provided by famous jazz pianist Ben Sidran with chanting provided by Lynette Margules. The moving and the restoration of the Gates of Heaven was a real mitzvah, a blessing, for all of Madison and Wisconsin.

Vietnam Riots

Rabbi had experienced riots and he knew about the threat of anarchy ever present in post World War I Germany, but he never thought that the experience would be repeated in his beloved America. The most horrendous, divisive and the bleakest chapter in Rabbi's over 40 years in Madison resulted from the Vietnam War, and growing resistance to it. There is an enormous literature relative to the war, its aftermath and the gradually increasing resistance to it. It is not my intention to repeat information available from many other sources but as a background to the developments in Madison, I wish to give some framework to the events as they developed. Opposition to the American involvement in the Vietnam War began slowly and sporadically on several college campuses. Prominent among these was the University of California at Berkeley and the University of Wisconsin, Madison. This was during a period of unprecedented student activism. All types of individuals became involved. Though initially protests began in the liberal leaning students and professors, it rapidly spread throughout all ethnic, political, and religious groups. The tidal wave of vociferous protests threatened anarchy, especially on the nation's campuses. In addition, new federal legislation allowed uncensored information to be freely available about the Vietnam War, as compared to limited and guarded news in previous conflicts. Repetitive, relentless, gory, television and press coverage of the carnage enraged the American public. A public draft conscription, which granted deferments to the wealthy, the middle, and upper classes and those attending college, resulted in inducting a disproportionate number of minorities and poor working class men and boys into the military. The deaths mounted inexorably. The unfairness of the situation fanned the flames of the already incendiary situation. The overwhelming feeling of the American people was that this was an unjust war. As casualties mounted and the war on the ground showed no end in sight, public opinion polls revealed a majority of Americans were opposed to the war and wanted it to end.

At the 1968 Democratic Convention in Chicago, there occurred a pitiful over-reaction to war protestors by police, with beatings of the demonstrators ordered by long time Mayor Richard Daley. In Madison, the so called "Dow Riots" on the University of Wisconsin campus occurred when recruiters for the company, known for making war materials, came to the campus. Increasingly ferocious demonstrations and serious forms of sabotage followed. What has been come to known as the Radical New Years Eve Gang brought sabotage to a new level. Only one of the members of the gang was a student at the University of Wisconsin, while the others were part-time students or hangers-on. The gang started by firebombing the *Old Red Gym*, then unsuccessfully bombed the Badger Ordinance works in Baraboo from the air, and bombed the University primate lab in an ill directed attempt at the Selective Service Office housed in the building.

Sterling Hall on the University of Wisconsin Campus, which housed the Physics and Astronomy Departments and also the Army Mathematics Research Center, was the target of a home made bomb so powerful that when detonated at 3:42 AM on August 24, 1970, from a van in the driveway of the building, it killed a young physics researcher working during the night, Robert Fassnacht. It injured six others, did damaged to 26 buildings on campus and the blast was so enormous it could be heard as far as 30 miles away. With the help of the FBI, three of the four perpetrators who immediately fled to Canada were caught and imprisoned. The brothers Carlton and Dwight Armstrong and David Fine were arrested, tried, convicted and imprisoned. Only Leo Burt was never found. Although only one was a Jew, the perception in the community was that all the protestors were student agitators from the east, the euphemism for Jews. With continued demonstrations, firebombings, broken windows, etc. confusion and paranoia in the community was widespread, as was fear of anarchy. Although admittedly there were a significant number of protestors who were Jews, including several of the leaders, the overwhelming majority were Christian Wisconsinites, protesting rightfully what they felt was an unjust inhuman war.

It was Fred Harrington, the President of the University, always a voice of reason, who said that the explosion was a violent response to overreaction and excessive repression by authorities against the protestors. He said protesting, even vigorous protesting, should not be met with overwhelming repressive measures. The uses of repressive measures were not only bad, they were counter-productive, just as the bombings were counter-productive.

In addition, after the killing of student protesters at Kent State in Ohio, things were spiraling out of control as of May of 1970, when frightened unsophisticated national guardsmen overreacted in deadly fashion. It was the Sterling Hall bombing in August 1970 that signaled to all that both repression and protest had gotten completely out of control. During this terrible period, Rabbi, who along with other community leaders comprised the so called "committee of 30," were everywhere, every night, trying to quell the burgeoning violent protests on the University campus and the adjacent Mifflin Street, a hot bed for radical protests. Rabbi sometimes rode around all night with police and alighted from patrol cars to help as a mitigating force of reason and love. Rabbi was known and recognized and admired, and tried to convey that the community as a whole shared the demonstrators frustrations; by all accounts, he along with others, was able to dampen the ardor of those bent on destruction and to demonstrate a vociferous disapproval of government policies, which had become counter to the wishes and feelings of the great majority of Americans.

Robert Fassnacht, the victim of the Sterling Hall bombing, 33 years old, was married to Stephanie, and had twin girls and a son. Although Robert was not a Jew, Rabbi Swarsensky was asked to give the eulogy at his memorial service at the Fitch Lawrence Funeral Parlor on University Avenue. The eulogy for Robert Fassnacht is included in the Writings. At the service there were family, colleagues, representatives of University, city, state and federal government. The service was nationally televised.

CHAPTER 9 -- RABBI SPEAKS OUT

Although not generally known outside the Jewish community, Rabbi had very negative feelings about a number of subjects. His stated policy was not to make waves but his intimates knew his deep feelings, especially about the attitudes of many theologians and most specifically the Vatican toward the Nazi regime and the Holocaust. Most authorities now agree that the Vatican did not speak out and made little or no effort to ameliorate the situation and indeed at some levels, worked with the Nazi regime. Many Christian protestant theologians reacted similiarly, although some righteous Christians expressed their horror. Rabbi occasionally spoke of this, generally only to co-religionists. Another matter of concern and supreme disappointment to Rabbi was the state of Jewish education, and the widespread disinterest of American Jews in their religion. Although Zionism and support of Israel was pervasive in the Jewish community, many American Jews were unschooled, ignorant and indifferent to their religion, a religion which gave the world the concept of monotheism and an ancient code of morality and conduct, ultimately universally adopted by Christians and Muslims.

Belonging to a synagogue was more of a social function for many with attendance only for the high holidays of Rosh Hashanah and Yom Kippur, life cycle events of Bat and Bar Mitzvah, and weddings and funerals. The spirituality of Judaism was lost to many, and a lack in this area was one of Rabbi Swarsensky's profound disappointments. He did, however, perceive that during his tenure there was a significant return to these basic Judeo-Christian tenants, though not as great as Rabbi would have hoped.

Another matter which Rabbi felt passionately about was Christianity's attitudes and teachings relative to the Jews, which had caused untold suffering in the nearly 2000 years since the birth of Jesus and the establishment of Christianity. However, rarely when Rabbi was provoked, he did speak out.

The first occasion was in December 1965 in an article published in the Wisconsin Jewish Chronicle titled "Season of Ill Will." See Writings. In this article, Rabbi shared his strong feelings of discrimination toward Jews during the Christmas season. The second time Rabbi spoke out was in a local Madison paper, the Wisconsin State Journal, July, 1977, in an article titled "Lutheran Writer Rapped by Rabbi." In this column, Rabbi challenged the President of Northwestern Lutheran College whose position was that "the highest love Christians can show Jews is to convert them." See Writings. Both pronouncements are cogent and poignant, and speak to both Christian and Jew.

CHAPTER 10 -- HONORS

Manfred Swarsensky's sojourn in America extended from July 1939 until his death in November of 1981, at the age of 75. As a very young Rabbi, he was one of the most important figures in the Jewish community of Germany in the 1930's. He was reduced to the status of an impoverished immigrant by the Nazis, but was to go on to become one of the most important humane, moral, and ethical forces in mid America in the last half of the 20th century. He became what is truly embodied in the term Mensch, a complete man.

Besides achieving the respect and love of his congregants and the Christian community of Madison, as well as many others in the State of Wisconsin, honors were bestowed on him as a reflection of what he was and what he meant to the City and the State. He was first recognized in 1967 by a national body, the National Council of Christians and Jews, who bestowed upon him an award for his contributions toward interfaith understanding. In 1971, he was recognized by his co-religionists and was awarded an honorary Doctorate of Divinity by the Hebrew Union College Institute of Religion in Cincinnati. This institution was the first one established in the United States to train Rabbis and later cantors and temple educators in the liberal Reform tradition. In 1973 he was awarded an unprecedented honor. He was the first Jew awarded an Honorary Doctorate by a Catholic College in America. Edgewood College in Madison awarded him an honorary Doctorate of Philosophy, *honoris causa*. His friend Sister Stevie escorted him at the ceremony. This was only the second honorary doctorate ever awarded by the venerable institution.

Further honors followed from the local chapter of the Boy Scouts of America, Hadassah, the largest Jewish women's service organization in America, and in 1973 he was awarded the Sertoma Club Service to Mankind Award.   Finally, in perhaps the greatest academic honor Manfred Swarsensky was to achieve, he was the first clergyman and first non alumnus ever to receive an Honorary Doctorate at the nationally recognized and respected University of Wisconsin, Madison, escorted by his longtime friend and colleague, Menachem Mansoor. He gave a stirring and memorable valedictory.

PART IV –

DECLINING YEARS

1976-80

CHAPTER 11 – PERSONAL STRUGGLES

Retirement

The perception at Temple Beth El that Rabbi's health was deteriorating in the late 60's and early 70's was all too correct. His unremitting angina was causing increasingly severe and persistent pain and it was during these years that esophageal reflux, severe heartburn from achalasia, became evident. This, to, was to become a major persistent problem for Rabbi.

Because of concerns for Rabbi and to lessen his burdens at the temple, first, an Assistant Rabbi, Stephen Barack, was hired. The Assistant Rabbi's primary duties were those of the temple school and adult education. Although very well regarded especially by the young, for understandable reasons Rabbi Barack left to assume his own pulpit after several successful years at Temple Beth El. The Temple board had numerous discussions as to Rabbi's future and the Temple's needs. Both in deference to Rabbi's health and the Temple's desire to attract young families, he was offered retirement with full salary and with the assurance that the parish house was his for as long as he and Ida desired. In 1976 he was offered emeritus status and after some consideration, he accepted. The details of the retirement were shepherded by the then president Marge Tobias. She and her husband Harry were longtime and devoted supporters of the Temple. The other individual involved in Rabbi's retirement and transition to his new status was the long time devoted business professor at the University; treasurer at Beth El, head usher, and venerable greeter, at all high holyday services, Isadore, Is Fine.

The Rabbi had agreed to the retirement initially, but the more he thought about the situation, the more unhappy he became. Especially after becoming aware of the extremely generous contract award to his successor Rabbi Kenneth Roseman, Rabbi felt very badly. By all accounts, Rabbi Swarsensky's compensation was never generous. Nationally rabbinic compensation packages along with other clergy in the mid 1970's, were becoming much more in line with their contemporaries of other callings. By the time Rabbi Roseman was awarded his contract, Rabbi's Swarsensky's salary had not kept up with this trend. Rabbi became unhappier and more agitated relative to the situation, and felt he was being pushed aside. He spoke to many congregants about his unhappiness and voiced his displeasure. He felt he was not being treated with respect. A number of his confidants in the temple agreed that he had not been treated with the respect he deserved. His friend Gordon Sinykin then negotiated a retirement contract to protect Rabbi's interests. This was the first written contract that Rabbi ever had at the temple in the 36 years as its leader. Marge Tobias remembers the time as extremely difficult; although very well intentioned she and the board were excoriated by a number of temple members. In later years, Rabbi thought better of his anger toward Marge and the board and forgave her because he knew, upon reflection, that she was trying to do the right thing for Rabbi and the Temple.

Rabbi Kenneth Roseman, Manfred's successor, was a distinguished scholar and educator. Prior to assuming the Rabbinate in Madison after his ordination in 1966, he had served as assistant, dean, then associate dean, and finally dean, and taught for several years at the Hebrew Union College in Cincinnati. He long had a desire for his own pulpit and Temple Beth El was fortunate enough to attract him to Madison.

The controversy concerning Rabbi Swarsensky's retirement was not of Rabbi Roseman's making, but he was required to navigate the rough waters caused by the tumult. He is said to have done this with kindness and deference to the senior Rabbi, although some dispute this.

Rabbi Roseman's views of his duties were somewhat more circumscribed, according to long time Wisconsin State Journal pundit Bill Wineke, himself an ordained minister. Rabbi Roseman felt his duties should mainly be confined to the temple. Rabbi Roseman was said to be very sensitive to Manfred's feelings and position. Their relationship by all accounts was civil and not collegial. It was very difficult for Rabbi Roseman to follow a legend.

If the retirement after 36 years of the founding Rabbi at Temple Beth El was controversial, there was no controversy about the community's reaction to it. A large organizing committee of many of the most prominent residents of Madison and Wisconsin, including all walks of life, was formed. A tribute dinner was held at the Great Hall of the University of Wisconsin Memorial Union on Lake Mendota on June 13, 1976. So many wanted to attend the dinner that auxiliary rooms had to be employed to accommodate the estimated 1,000 to 1,200 persons in attendance. It became the largest dinner ever to be held at the Memorial Union up to that time. Robert Levine, Reverend Alfred Swan, Senator Gaylord Nelson, Sister Marie Stephen Reges O.P., and Bishop O'Donnell spoke at the dinner. Professor Sam Jones provided musical interludes and Laurence Weinstein announced that a forest of 10,000 trees had been planted in Israel by Rabbi's friends as a tribute. Finally Rabbi responded with a heartfelt personal talk "The Rock From Which You Were Hewn." See Writings.

Many individuals with diverse interests, when queried as to what occupies them after retirement respond, "I'm busier now than before I retired." In Rabbi's case, this was more than true. He was relegated, upon retirement, to a tiny office at Temple Beth El. His copious activities seemed in direct opposition to the lack of space. He said more than once, "It is fortunate that I was not born a woman because I seem incapable of saying no." Shirley Sweet, his long time secretary, recalls having to vacate the office with a rolling cart containing her typewriter and miscellaneous equipment into the adjacent library, when counseling sessions or meeting with even one person became necessary in the tiny space.

In 1977, a year after Rabbi's retirement, Doctor Donald Kahn performed the then unusual operation of coronary bypass involving five heart vessels at the University of Wisconsin Hospital. Rabbi was very grateful that the persistent heart pains that plagued him for almost forty years were gone after the surgery. The in-hospital convalescence was much longer in those days and Rabbi received hundreds of get-well wishes by mail, phone, and telegram. His fellow Rotarians, responding to his wry humor, sent a get-well resolution which was passed by the board, only by a simple majority. Now Rabbi's health improved dramatically and in retirement he was able to pursue other profound interests in books and avocations such as stamp collecting and the genealogy of family names and origins.

When someone accused her husband of being *saintly*, Ida disagreed. He was not a saint she said, smiling all the while. In inquiring why, I was told that he was intolerant of certain things. Several things bothered Manfred, with *phonies* being number one on the list, and number two he was very disappointed in the rather superficial interest in Judaism shown by many of his co-religionists, as previously noted. He had stated more than once that after the last prayer on Yom Kippur he should wish his congregants Merry Christmas and Happy New Year, because he knew he wouldn't see most of then until the Holy Days the next year, as their level of interest and attendance at the temple was limited almost to exclusively to these times. As the years went on, however, there was a resurgence of interest in the Jewish community, in both Judaism and its roots. Rabbi did not live to see this in full blossom, but he would have been very pleased. Rabbi was also very disappointed in some members of the fundamentalist Christian community who in preparing for the hereafter neglected the present and the Christian mandates of doing good on earth. He retained his profound disappointment in the world's reaction and especially the Christian theological community, specifically recalling the lack of response of the Vatican to the holocaust. Many of these matters he only discussed with intimates, but occasionally he felt so strongly that he expressed himself in correspondence to the press. An example was his reaction of pronouncements vis-a-vis the Jews by the President of the Northwestern College, Watertown, Wisconsin in an article published in the Northwestern Lutheran, the official publication of the Wisconsin Evangelical Lutheran Synod, which appears in the Writings. No, Rabbi was not perfect, he was not a saint, but as any biblical scholar knows, neither were Abraham, Isaac, Jacob, the patriarchs, or indeed neither were Joseph and Kings David, Samuel or Solomon. Considering the imperfections, Manfred Swarsensky does qualify as saintly, if not a saint in our time.

Rabbi's improved status of health was not to last. Another type of chest pain from the achalasia, first mild and occasional, became severe and unremitting, finally necessitating another major surgery in early 1981, after becoming so ever present and severe that Rabbi was unable to eat or sleep without significant pain. Marked weight loss and loss of energy followed until the surgery. After the esophageal surgery, it was evident that the disease had caused significant weight loss and had taken a great toll on his appearance. Two older women who had not seen Rabbi in a while declared to him that he "looked like a million dollars." He responded with his always sly sense of humor, "I feel *like a million dollars-after taxes!*" He continued virtually all of his activities after retirement though doing less at the temple. He retained his chaplaincy at all area hospitals, his speeches and sermons throughout the State, and many of his community activities continued unabated.

Hopes for regained health again were dashed a few months after the esophageal surgery when widespread unresectable cancer of the colon was discovered and caused Rabbi's death. He died on November 11, 1981, the 43rd anniversary of Kristalnacht.

The outpouring of grief after Rabbi's death was truly remarkable and appropriate for such a person of high regard. He had relationships with virtually hundreds of people, never forgot a name and had lectured throughout the world. Eulogies and tributes to Rabbi's death poured in. The outpouring of grief at Rabbi's death came from all over the world, as he had lectured and been known widely, as well as universally respected and revered. Eulogies and tributes came from around the world.

CHAPTER 12 -- POSTHUMOUS TRIBUTES AND REMEMBRANCES

At his beloved Temple Beth El, at Rotary, and from the pulpits around the city and in other public gatherings when his death was reported, audible cries and weeping were heard. He had accomplished what few have ever achieved as evidenced by the universal high esteem with which he was held. A private simple graveside family service was held, followed at a later date by a memorial service at Temple Beth El. Numerous newspaper articles appeared attesting to his life and times and accomplishments.

A sermon preached to his congregation at the First United Methodist Church by Reverend Lee C. Moorhead only four days after Rabbi's death began a flood of other tributes some of which are included in the Writings. Among the laudations is a lovely poem by a temple member, Amy Azen. Included here are Amy Azen's Poem and Reverend Moorehead's Eulogy.

Rabbi Swarsensky: In Memoriam 1906-1981

Rabbi, Rabbi...
From you we learned the alphabet of creation,
You were the Great Teacher.
You taught us to transcend divides,
To ascend toward the stars

Rare Singer...
Whose songs were torn from the throat of a nightingale

And transplanted to awakening human hearts.

Great Architect...
Who transformed raw blocks of language
Into cathedrals of thought, temples
Of energized morality.

Lover of Mankind...
Who knew full well
The barbarity and perversity of man,
Yet directed us to build bridges:
You taught that love, not hate,
Is the measure of existence.

Wise Rabbi...
How shall we mourn your passing?
How shall we sustain this immeasurable loss?

We affirm the common core of humanity,
We acknowledge the brotherhood of Christian and Jew,
We accept the challenge to build unshakable bridges
Of love and trust.

Yisgadal Ve'yiskadash Sh'mey Rabbo...
The flesh is extinguished-
But the towering spirit lives on.
It shall illume the path throughout our days.
Uvisman Koreev Ve'imroo Omaine.

Amy Azen

A tribute by Max Gaebler in the November 17th, 1981 issue of the newsletter of the First Unitarian Society and another by Max in a radio talk on November 22 of that year, excerpts of which are reprinted in the introduction; a Madison Magazine article by long time outdoorsman contributor George Vukelich, two tributes by Bill Wineke of the Wisconsin State Journal; a farewell by Mark Scader of Edgewood College, as well as reflections by Edgewood President Sister Alice O'Rourke on the one year anniversary of his death in November of 1982, inaugurating the first memorial lecture series of the Wisconsin Society for Jewish Learning, are examples of tributes to Rabbi Swarsensky. There were eulogies by Hannah Rosenthal and one by Jacob Stockinger of the Capital Times as well as one by Jaquelyn Mitchard of that paper. These are only a few examples of the tributes and eulogies awarded Rabbi.

Posthumous honors followed including the Manfred E. Swarsensky Humanitarian service award given yearly each November on the anniversary of Rabbi's death to the person who exemplified qualities and contributions worthy of Rabbi Swarsensky by Rabbi's beloved downtown Rotary. Also each November Temple Beth El has established the Swarsensky Weekend Lectureship, with several sessions and discussions by nationally known scholars and theologians. The chair of Jewish Life and Thought was established at Edgewood College, shepherded by his long time friend, Sister Stevie. In addition, the chapel of Madison General Hospital, now Meriter, was designated as the Manfred E. Swarsensky Chapel, and finally the Wisconsin Society for Jewish Learning established an annual lectureship.

Eulogy for Rabbi Manfred Swarsensky
By Reverend Lee C. Moorhead
First United Methodist Church, Madison

Early on Tuesday of this past week, a monumental event occurred in the life and history of Madison. In the dark hours of the night the black angel of death drew near and lifted from this earth the saintly soul of Rabbi Manfred Swarsensky. Perhaps few men in the history of this colorful and unique community have been as loved and honored as he. Few have contributed as abundantly and beautifully as he to the moving stream of our humanity. It is likely that never will one like him pass this way again.

Not only enshrined in the heart and memory of Madison, he was a dear and beloved friend of First United Methodist Church. I speak now for my predecessors who have ministered here during the past forty years and for a host of lay admirers who cherished his friendship, his teaching, his leadership, and his prophetic present. I speak especially, too, for many young people of this church who during the last several years sat spellbound during his visits to our confirmation classes. Last year especially was memorable because he spoke twice to our confirmation class. As he spoke I had the feeling that he was giving to these young people a kind of last will and testament. Frail of body, his words often choked by a deepening digestive disorder, he poured forth a stream of intimate detail concerning his early life in Germany, his career as a young rabbi in Berlin, his arrest by the Nazis and his humiliation and ill treatment in concentration camps. He knew that the days of his life were growing fewer, and he wanted these Christian young people to know of his experience and concerns. During the following months I visited him several times in the hospital, talked to him on the phone, exchanged letters, and prayed constantly for his precious soul. And then on Tuesday, he died. Ever since I have felt a great absence in my heart, a deep sorrow in my life.

Yet he is not absent from my memory. Ever since Tuesday morning when I learned of his death I have been absorbed in the meaning, the message and the mission of life. If one such as he may never pass this way again, it behooves us to ponder his treasured wisdom, to savor his compassion and goodness, and to take seriously the scrolls of prophetic warning he has left behind. And we must do these things as Christians, and to do so, as Christians, will be unnerving and unsettling.

-I-

In the past year Rabbi Swarsensky has shared with me two great haunting concerns. One was his fear that this generation would forget the horrors of the Holocaust that blackened and degraded what we call "civilization." Manfred Swarsensky struggled for life during those nightmarish years, suffered under their fiendish fury, became a victim –albeit a survivor –of this incredible wickedness on earth. In the most recent months he was aghast at the monumental efforts raised whether to forget or to declare that these horrors never occurred. Several big attempts have been made to "prove" that these horrors never happened, with one professor at Northwestern University writing a book labeling the Holocaust a hoax. On September 11, 1981, Rabbi Swarsensky wrote me a letter and enclosed an article which he had taken from the Hadassah Magazine. The article was by the great Jewish writer, Elie Wiesel, and it had to do with an event of unspeakable human depravity. On September 29, 1941, thousands of Jews were driven through the main streets of Kiev as Ukrainians looked on. They were being marched by the Nazis, and with the help of Ukrainian police, to a ravine called Babi Yar. There they were machine-gunned and buried in a huge pit. When the mass killing was finished with methodical madness, tens of thousands of human beings had been killed – most of them Jews. Some estimates say 100,000 were savagely slaughtered. In the article that Rabbi Swarsensky sent me, Elie Wiesel, himself a survivor of the Nazi horrors, wrote:

> I returned to Kiev in August 1979. Of course, I
> asked to visit Babi Yar. Since I was on an official
> visit – as the head of the delegation of the
> President's Commission on Holocaust – I obtained
> satisfaction. City officials, followed by television
> cameras and reporters from the local and foreign
> press, accompanied us there. Why not? Now
> they thought they could boast of a monument at
> Babi Yar. In fact, there it is – a monument large
> and grandiose, as only the Soviets are capable of
> producing. Impressive from all points of view,
> except...except the word "Jew" does not appear
> on it anywhere! This monument is supposed to be
> in memory of the Soviet citizens assassinated by

the Fascists...And then (says Elie Wiesel) I lost my temper, as never before. In my address, I said everything that had been weighing on my heart.

In 1965, I stood on this very spot and I felt anger; now it is shame which I feel. I am ashamed for you...You know perfectly well that the men and women who are lying in this grave were killed as Jews! By what right do you deprive them of their identity? They lived as Jews, worked as Jews, dreamed as Jews, and it is as Jews that they were isolated and designated by the executioner; it is as Jews that they were subjected to fear and torture and death. By what right do you now cast them into anonymity? In the name of what do you mutilate their being? Why don't you grant to them the place that, when alive, they claimed in Jewish history? (<u>Hadassah Magazine</u>, Aug./Sept. 1981, p. 15)

-II-

Riveted in my memory is a drama by a German playwright, Rolf Hochhuth, called <u>The Deputy</u>, produced as "the most controversial play of our time" in 1964. The story of the play is based upon a large and substantial judgment of historians that Pope Pius XII did very little to exert his mighty influence against the crimes being committed by Hitler against the Jews. Even noting its fictional character, one is deeply moved and troubled by the anguish of one German Roman Catholic priest, Father Riccardo Fontana, who was so horrified by what he saw happening to the Jews at the hands of the Nazis that he made his way to Rome and demanded an audience with the Pope. There he pleads with the Pope to speak out against these unspeakable horrors. The Pope replies that he has already done much to protect the Jews and that he can do no more. The priest, Riccardo, is appalled by this indifference. In a most telling moment in the drama

Riccardo, while the Pope is signing a proclamation that the priest considers utterly innocuous, takes out the yellow Star of David and pins it to his cassock. When the Pope sees what he has done he is struck dumb. A Cardinal of the court, in breathless fury, orders Riccardo to remove the yellow star. Refusing, Riccardo speaks:

"This star which every Jew must wear as soon as
he is six years old, to show he is an outlaw – I shall
wear it too until…

Then the Pope, quivering with rage, interrupts:

"He will not! We forbid him – forbid – on a cassock
– this…"

The Pope stops, his voice failing him. Then Riccardo speaks, quietly, soberly:

"I will wear this star until Your Holiness proclaims
before the world a curse upon the man who
slaughters Europe's Jews like cattle."
(The Deputy, p. 217, 218)

Many times have I read that passage, but as I re-read it now I think of a great and good man like Rabbi Swarsensky. Our honoring of his memory today will be no more than empty sentimentality if we do not as Christians dedicate our lives to contending against every shred and sentiment of anti-Semitism, in our own hearts and in the hearts of those around us. If we want truly to honor his name, and the names of countless martyrs like him, we too will wear that yellow Star of David in our hearts until the last evil trace of anti-Semitism is washed from our humanity.

-III-

An aspect of this dear man that none of us shall ever be able to forget, therefore, is his endurance of suffering. Our minds are often numbed and paralyzed when we contemplate the intense suffering that seems to fall upon some human beings. Perhaps we don't like to think of it for long, because we fear that it could all happen to us. But here was a man who not only suffered through what he was pleased to hear me call one "a hurricane of horror," but who also was ravaged in his own physical body by repeated maladies. Five year ago he underwent critical open heart surgery. After what seemed like a fine recovery from that he developed a serious malfunction of the esophagus. For a long time he was actually starving to death. Often I wondered if these severe body ailments borne by a man of small physical stature could not be attributed in part at least to the spiritual, physical, mental and emotional abuse he has suffered under Nazi torture. But after the most delicate and critical surgery seemed to give the promise of his recovery from the esophagus malfunction, it was discovered that he was stricken with cancer. During the long years of all of that intense suffering and affliction I am sure that he often felt the anguish and sense of abandonment expressed by Job in the Old Testament. And certainly he must in his own heart have cried out as did our Lord on the cross, speaking as Jesus did the words of the 22nd Psalm: "My God, my God, why hast thou forsaken me? Why art thou so far from helping me, from the words of my groaning? O my God, I cry by day, but thou dost not answer: and by night, but find no rest. Yet thou art holy, enthroned in the praises of Israel."

Obviously there was in this man a grace that enabled him to transcend the hurts, the humiliations, the body afflictions. Several years ago Manfred gave me a record album of a sermon he had delivered to his congregation at the Temple Beth El on Christmas Day, 1970. He had just returned from Berlin where he had been invited to attend the 25th anniversary of the reestablishment of the Jewish Community after the collapse of the Nazi regime. The mayor of Berlin, on behalf of the City, had invited him and several others who at one time had served the Jewish community in various capacities to take part in this historic occasion. As a young rabbi in Berlin he had watched the smoldering ruins of the synagogue he had served, that house of worship having been torched by the Nazis. The house where he had lived had been reduced to rubble. On two nights in November, 1938, the glass window panes in every store owned by Jews in Germany had been shattered. The night in history is now known as "Kristalnacht." Rabbi Swarsensky told our Confirmation Class last February how he had been shoved into a crowded truck and carried off to a hell-hole for assignment to a concentration camp. He remembered that two boys clutched his hand in fear. He had confirmed them in his synagogue. The nightmare of imprisonment followed. I have wondered as he lay dying if he still felt the frightened clutching of these young hands in his; the stomping of the S.S. boots, the clicking of heels; the sight and stench of smoke rising from the gas ovens; the snapping of necks on the Gallows; the taste of corpses in the death camp soup.

On Friday of this week I listened to the impassioned sermon, recorded on these phonograph records, that he has preached on his return from Berlin. He called that sermon "You Can't Go Home Again." In that sermon he told his people:

> Twenty-five years ago I would have said never again
> shall I set foot on that cursed soil. But twenty-five
> years ago no one would have invited me. Nothing,
> of course, is forgotten; nothing, of course, can be
> forgiven. But as a Jew I have no right to push away
> a hand stretched out in reconciliation. Hatred,
> unbending, unending hatred is neither an emotion
> by which I can live or a philosophy by which I want
> my children or my children's children to live.

So Manfred Swarsensky came to our confirmation class and taught us how we can live by the law and the love of Christ. For having known this rabbi neither can we go home again – not home again to the same old selves in which we betray Christ with indifference and ill will.

For some Christians – <u>some</u> Christians, I emphasize – the life of a Jewish man like the rabbi poses a problem. Some cannot believe that such a Jew can find true salvation. Though Rabbi Sawarsensky had more Christian virtue than many of us Christians, he was not a

Christian. He did not acknowledge as do we that Christ is the Messiah. Hence there are certain Christians who say that such a man cannot be received by God in Eternity. Indeed, one highly placed official, the President of a huge Protestant denomination, boldly declared about a year ago that "God does not hear the prayers of a Jew." When I wrote a letter to a newspaper protesting the ugly absurdity of that view, another minister in the community responded in another public letter, not in anger at what the world had done to Jews, but with the judgment that I was scarcely entitled to such an opinion because I had not baptized 2600 people as had the minister who had made the original charge. Manfred wrote me a note thanking me for my letter. No, I have not baptized, and will not baptize 2600 people in this church, but neither will I ever baptize my parishioners with a sense of arrogant and unbiblical superiority over Jews. And if that same point of view that declares that God does not hear the prayers of Jews also means that Jews have no chance of being received by God in Eternity, then I would not want to be received in that kind of Eternity myself. On occasion Manfred Swarsensky enjoined the words of Jesus: "In my Father's house are many mansions. If it were not so, I would have told you." (John 14) I cannot visualize the Eternity Christ has pictured without a mansion for Manfred. Surely the great prophet Isaiah was a comfort to Manfred, as he has been to us this morning as we listened to his words framed in our anthem, "Say to them that are of a fearful heart, Be strong, fear not; behold, your god will come and save you...A highway shall be there, and it shall be called the way of holiness; the redeemed shall walk there; and the ransomed of the Lord shall return with songs and everlasting joy: and sorrow and sighing shall flee away." (Isaiah 35: 3-10, RSV)

About thirty years ago there was an auxiliary Catholic Bishop in Chicago by the name of Bernard J. Sheil. He was a courageous and prophetic man. One night against the objections of his colleagues he went to a hall full of hate to attend a meeting of the so-called Christian front. For 15 tense moments he took the floor and denounced anti-Semitism, white supremacy, and every vile lie that had been bellowed that night by a demagogue. The audience listened with intense hostility. When Bishop Sheil had finished he started slowly to walk down the center aisle. Suddenly there was a scream of rage. An old woman, seething with hatred, stepped out to block his path. She shrieked, "I'm a Catholic, Jew lover! A Bishop! Ha, ha! Rabbi Sheil!" then, completely hysterical, she cleared her throat and spat over one side of the bishop's face. The bishop did not raise his hand to wipe it off. By this time, most of the people were standing on their chairs, roaring with wrath. But the bishop stood silently, and waited. The old woman froze, as did many others. Then she began to shake violently as though a sudden chill had gripped her. The mob of snarling faces became a group of lowered heads. The bishop waited for another moment, then spoke softly. "Rabbi" That is what they called our Lord." He walked out in silence. (from <u>Christian Friends Bulletin</u>, October, 1951, originally printed in THE PROGRESSIVE, Madison, WI.)

For the rest of my life, whenever I confront any kind of evil or hatred, I shall have to remember my dear friend, Rabbi Manfred Swarsensky. I shall never forget the pains that he bore, the suffering he endured. And as I think of him as Rabbi, I shall always be aware that the twelve disciples often referred to the man I call Lord as Rabbi, too. And always as I read the words of the great Prophet of Israel, Isaiah, I shall ponder especially the picture of the Suffering Servant, a word picture summarizing the Ideal Israel, and later used to portray Christ. I can associate this as well with a rabbi who was a dear friend on earth.

> Yet the lord took thought for his tortured servant
> and healed him who had made himself a sacrifice
> for sin; so shall he enjoy long life and see his
> children's children, and in his hand the Lord's
> cause shall prosper. After all his pains he shall be
> bathed in light, after his disgrace he shall be fully
> vindicated; so shall he, my servant, vindicate many,
> himself bearing the penalty of their guilt. (Isaiah
> 53: 10, 11, NEB)

EPILOGUE – THE LIFE WELL LIVED

I realized that in my ardor in presenting Rabbi's life, my approach at times has been openly chauvinistic. I note this, but I do not apologize for it, as before, during Rabbi's life and after, much had been presented on radio, on television, and by the press that has been quite the opposite toward Jews. If I spoke out against anti-Semitic hate mongers and misguided individuals who had continued the 2000 year old tradition of expressing very negative aspects of the Jews and Judaism, a pro Jewish perspective is understandable. Rabbi's life is a story that refutes all the poisonous propaganda hurled against his religion and his co-religionists.

What has one learned from Manfred Swarsensky's life story? It represents triumph over adversity. It represents yet another example of the American Dream, when very humble beginnings and origin as the little Jewish peasant from Pomerania was no bar to the opportunities afforded Manfred Swarsensky, opportunities which are available only to the fullest extent in America as in no other nation. Despite experiences which could have turned Manfred into a scarred and bitter man, he morphed himself into a shining example of forgiveness and into his life's work of *"building bridges."* He was no Pollyanna; he vividly recalled and spoke out against the degradation and victimization which his people had experience for two millennium. His unquestioned love for Judaism, Germany and America were totally requited in a myriad of ways. He was completely surrounded by the love of family, friends, associates, and admirers, yet he felt he did not have a few to share his most deeply felt hopes, aspirations, and ideas. Did anyone believe his self analysis that he was "shy", *"would you believe it!"* It is also a love story and family saga. It is a story of bravery and selflessness. It is the saga of a great theologian who was internally, spiritually driven. He was a teacher of great intellect, who shared his knowledge with many throughout his life. He touched many lives and had warm relationships with theologians both liberal and conservative with nuns, priest, bishops and protestant reverends. He gave his coat to a coatless man on a winter day. He dropped everything to answer a seven-year-old boy's letter. He was a friend to the friendless and companion to survivors of the camps who found the future impossible to cope with. He was kicked out of an association of his peers because of his beliefs and he never wavered in his love of family, his religion, his temple, his origin, his Madison, his Wisconsin, his America in which his resurrection occurred. This was a MENSCH.

Family Photos

Ida Sharon and Gerald Swarsensky

Sharon Swarsensky

Gerald Swarsensky

April 19, 1950

Dear Rabbi Swarsensky:

It is my privilege as president of the American Committee
for the Hebrew University, the Weizmann Institute of Science,
and Technion, to invite you to attend our first dinner and
conference to be held at the Nassau Tavern here in Princeton,
on Wednesday, May 10th.

The occasion takes on added significance because we shall at
the same time commemorate the 25th anniversary of the founding of the Hebrew University.

I can think of no more suitable way of celebrating the 25th
anniversary of the Hebrew University nor of officially launch-
ing the program of the American Committee for U.I.T. than to
meet in good fellowship with men and women who share my heartfelt interest in these three institutions of higher learning
and who wish to join me in the joint effort to advance the
cause of science, technology and mankind's knowledge in Israel.

It will be heartening to learn that you will attend and I look
forward to seeing you here in Princeton on May 10th.

Sincerely yours,

A. Einstein

Albert Einstein

P.S. I have no facilities for taking care of correspondence
here, and I would appreciate your sending the enclosed card
to the office of U.I.T. in New York.

A.E.

Letter to Rabbi Swarsensky from Albert Einstein

Ida and Manfred Swarsensky
with Sharon and Gerald

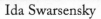

Ida Swarsensky

Manfred as a young boy in Pomerania

Gerald Swarsensky
celebrating his Bar Mitzvah

Ida Weiner, growing
up in Chicago

Manfred Swarsensky
as a young Rabbi

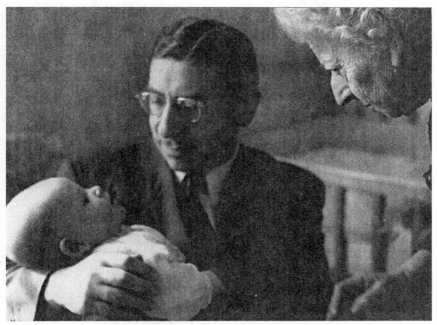

Rabbi Swarsensky holding baby Sharon,
with his mother Louise looking on

Rabbi Swarsensky in his study

Rabbi Swarsensky at the pulpit
in Temple Beth El

For Gerald
Your father gave a
very moving invocation

RF Kennedy

Informal Remarks:

Gaylord Nelson

United States Senator

Wisconsin

Speaker:

Robert F. Kennedy

United States Senator

New York

Gaylord Nelson

Program where Rabbi gave the invocation:
signed by Senators Gaylord Nelson and Robert Kennedy
for son Gerald. Senator Kennedy wrote,
"Your father gave a very moving invocation."

Ida Weiner on her wedding day

WRITINGS

YOU CAN'T GO HOME AGAIN[1]*

*After an absence of 30 years, Rabbi Swarsensky
returned in 1970 to Berlin, the city in which he had
experienced the most creative and most tragic years of his
life. He had been invited, 25 years after the downfall of
the Hitler regime, by the mayor and the senate of Berlin.
During the week-long visits, his lectures and newspaper
interviews advocating the spirit of reconciliation evoked
wide public attention. This somewhat emotional talk
was given extemporaneously before the congregation of
Temple Beth El one day after his return to Madison. It
was recorded by the state radio network.*

Thomas Wolfe was never more correct than when he said: "You
can't go home again." I had occasion to experience this truth in
December, 1970, when, after more than 30 years, I returned to the
city in which I had spent the most formative and creative—but also
the most perilous and tragic—years of my life; the city to which I
came as a young student from the little village in Prussia in which I
was born; the city in which I received my academic and theological
training and served as rabbi of the Jewish community from 1932 to
1939—six years of those years under the Nazi regime.

Physically, I did come home to Berlin but, in a deeper psychological and spiritual sense, I did not come home. I could not come

---

1* Writings so indicated are from *Intimates and Ultimates* published by Edgewood
College in 1981 and reprinted with their permission.

home. In the very city where I knew every important edifice and landmark as well as I do in Madison, I felt like a stranger, a visitor at best. Not only had the passage of years come between the city and me but also the unrelieved memory of the horrors of the past.

"Each time we part," a poet said, "we die a little." I had parted 31 years ago. Indeed, something had died in me. I did not look at the old surroundings with the same eyes and conversely, I felt that the environment did not look at me with the same sense of familiar. The apartment building in which I had lived was gone. Like so much of the city, it had been destroyed by bombs. But a tremendous amount of rebuilding has been completed, most of it in modern architecture. In the neighborhood in which I had lived during my student years all I recognized were the street signs. You can't go home again.

The people, too, have changed. They were still as neat and clean and industrious as always. Signs of the *Wirtschaftswunder* (the economic miracle) are all around. The majority of people are well dressed. The shops are stocked with exquisite merchandise. The industrial output for internal consumption as well as export is high.

Berlin has always had a cosmopolitan flavor. But today it seems as if the nations of the word are having a rendezvous in the former German capital. One can hear a Bable of languages; one can see a diversity of cultures. The streets and the many institutions of learning, notably the campus of the newly-build Free University (in contrast to the old Humbold Universitat Unter den Linden which I attended, now in the East sector of the city) are teeming with students from foreign countries. The first evening while strolling down the fashionable Kufuerstendamm boulevard, I noticed invitations to a 'Black Panthers' meeting: "Down with American Imperialism." Near the headquarters of the American Army of Occupation there was scrawled on the wall *Amens Raus,* meaning "out with the Americans."

However, the majority of the citizens of West Germany, and of West Berlin in particular, do not mind the American military presence at all. On the contrary, the economic boom is due to the priming of the German economy by the Marshall plan. Moreover, the presence of Americans as well as the smaller British and French forces spells military and political security. The Berliners in particular, who live on an island surrounded on all sides by the Soviet-controlled *Deutsch Demokratische Republik,* remember that only the American Airlife saved them from starvation. In commemoration of the American aid, every noon a Freedom Bell rings from the tower of Berlin City Hall. From its steps President Kennedy declared to jubilant Germans, *Ich bin ein Berliner.* The Berliners are even more grateful for the presence of American armed forces because of the fearsome Wall which the Russian-controlled Communist German regime built in 1961 to wall off the East from the West.

In former years, West Berliners were permitted to visit East Berlin at two places after long and cumbersome security checks. I went to the East Berlin mainly to visit the small East Berlin Jewish community of 500 souls and to see the ruins of what once was the largest synagogue with a seating capacity of more than 4,000, to look at the building of my theological alma mater, nowadays part of a hospital complex, and to visit my father's and grandmother's graves. I thanked my lucky stars when at about 6 o'clock in the evening I could return to West Berlin via the Friedrichstrasse checkpoint, for I had a feeling that the second time in my life I had been in a concentration camp.

For a Jewish visitor such as I, deeply interested in Germany's present problems (for it is in Germany, the heartland of Europe, where the future of the great world-wide East-West conflict ill most likely be determined), it is natural to be equally concerned with the Jewish aspect of the visit. Here, too, it is so very true: you can't go home again.

When the plan which I had boarded in Chicago touched down at the Tempelhof Airport, West Berlin's huge airfield, a whole host of memories which for many decades had lain dormant suddenly awoke and leaped into the full light of my consciousness. I could not help but think that it was at the same airport on a cold rainy morning in March of 1939, shortly after I had been released from a concentration camp, my hair shaven like a criminal, that I had boarded a plane to fly to London. Dr. Hertz, the late chief rabbi of the British Empire, had secured a British visa for me which enabled me to leave Germany and to be admitted to England as a visitor. Sneering, bestial-looking S.S. men searched me to see if I had more than the four dollars I was allowed to take along of all my worldly goods.

Now while I was riding from the airport images of years long gone appeared again before my mind's eye. I saw the hundreds and hundreds of children whom I had named, Bar Mitzvahed, and confirmed; the countless happy young couples I had united in marriage; the throngs of the worshippers who week after week filled the large and monumental temples most of which had a seating capacity between 2,000 and 3,000. The last German Kaiser, Wilhelm II, had donated the ornamental wall mosaics to one of these temples. It was at the time of the height of imperial power in 1912, shortly before World War I. It was the period when Jews, inspired by a deep love of the fatherland, felt as secure in their political status in Germany as we feel in this country today. Jews were Germans like the rest of the people. The only different between them and others was their religion.

Such historic recollections were flashing through my mind like pictures on a movie screen as I came again to the city and the land which had seen both the rise and fall of a nation and its culture, both the triumph and the tragedy of its Jewish citizens. Germany's Jews could not possibly believe, any more than any one of us here could, that virtually from one day to the next they would lose their rights as citizens; that they would be reduced to the status of pariahs; that they could be deprived of the sources of their livelihood, their possessions, their freedom; that their lives could be taken away for no other reason than their being Jews; and that overnight the darkest Middle Ages would have returned. Unexpected and unforeseen, the wild fury of a tornado devasted what generations and generations had built.

And so, as I rode through the streets of the city, the memories of those years of horror reawakened within me with full force. Passing the railroad station at Anhalter Bahnhof, I remember that it was to this depot in the dark of the night that Jewish parents—while this was still possible in 1932 and '33—took their young children to put them on trains which would take them via Austria of Italy to Youth Aliyah centers in Palestine which the sainted Henrietta Szold had prepared. (These youngsters of 35 years ago are today among the soldiers protecting and defending Israel. If one knows their childhood memories, one can better understand the source of their valor and resolve: "Never again.")

Yes, so much was rushing through my mind. When we approached the business district of the city, I heard again in my ears the unbelievable crash of thousands of broken windows of the Kristall Nacht when, during the night from November 9 to November 10, 1938, Hitler's S.S. guards smashed every windowpane in stores owned by Jews all over the country. I felt again the indescribable shock of being aroused from sleep at 2 o'clock in the morning during the following night, November 10 to 11, when the telephone rang and the resident custodian of one of the synagogues I served shouted in a tear-choked voice: "Our synagogue is burning!" I arose, ran to the building, and saw how Hitler's henchmen were pouring gasoline over the inside and the outside of the majestic cupola and the walls. They were turning the building into a sea of flames while the police were standing idly by and the firemen were pouring water on adjoin buildings to protect them from the heat of the flames. A fine of several million marks as imposed on Jewish citizens to pay for the cleanup of the debris. In addition, the Nazi government collected from insurance companies. By the morning of November 11, close to 200 synagogues had been burned to the ground.

During the day, mass arrests of Jews took place, filling concentration camps with Jews. Some 10,000 adults were rounded up in Berlin—many thousands more all over the country—and taken in huge police trucks to concentration camps. Driving through the night, two young brothers who had been former students of mine and were sitting next to me on the truck were holding on to me, weeping bitterly. "What will happen to us now?" they asked.

When we arrived at the gate of the inferno hidden in a forest 40 miles outside of Berlin, S.S. men jumped upon us like wild beasts, shouting obscenities, beating old men, breaking people's necks and legs, and driving us through the entrance into the hell hole where a sign greeted us: "There is no God." Yes, there was no God. Where was God? Had He hidden His face? Was He silent as the majority of Berliners, who were either scared, or who indifferently turned away so as not to see, or who stood idly by and as some believe— were silently applauding? Yes, they were all silent: the professors, the intellectuals, the church leaders.

It was left to an uneducated Austrian paper-hanger to carry anti-Jewish theological doctrines to their ultimate consequence, *die Endloesung,* (the final solution). More than 60,000 of the 159,000 Berlin Jews were murdered. Many died of torture and starvation in concentration camps; others perished during transport in railroad cars and from asphyxiation in gas chambers and crematoria. Some few committed suicide. The most fortunate ones escaped and are today scattered all over the world.

Yes, there were decent Christians. There was Prof. Paul Kahle, the world-renowned Orientalist, teaching at the University of Bonn. On the morning after the Kristall Nact the professor and his wife took broom and dust-pan and demonstratively swept the glass in front of Jewish stores. He had to flee to London where he died. There as Prelate Heinrich Gruber who spoke up for Jews and himself had to share their fate in a concentration camp. He survived and was later a star witness at the Eichmann trial in Jerusalem. I sat next to him at the convocation in Berlin last Sunday. I shook the hand of the religious leader who was murdered in a prison shortly before the end of the war. There was Pastor Martin Niemoeller who after years of being deceived by Hitler's siren songs finally recognized the deception of the Fuehrer. Niemoeller also was thrown into a concentration camp. After his release he said: "First they came for the Jews. I did not speak up, because I was not a Jew. Then they came for the leaders of the labor unions. I did not speak up because I did not belong to them. Then they came for intellectuals. I did not speak up because I was not one of them. Then they came for Catholics, and I did not speak up because I was a Protestant. Then they came for me—and by that time no one was left to speak up."

The State of Israel honored those non-Jews whose personal courage will always remain a symbol of human greatness by dedicating a special forest to the "Righteous Among the Nations." Most of tem were little people, working men and housewives. In Berlin along, a thousand Jews were hidden by Christian friends and neighbors at the peril of their own lives.

Back now on the soil of the City of Sorrows—to use Bialik's expression—I could not free myself from the thought that what my eyes had seen in my day was not merely a sudden outburst of cruelty in the middle of 20th century, but rather, after a brief interval, the continuation of an historic pattern which was centuries old. It is often at our own peril that we ignore history, that we forget how infinitely slowly man changes. Throughout the Middle Ages Jews had been treated as property, never as persons. This attitude did not begin with Hitler. The first Jews who lived in Berlin at the beginning of the 14th Century were a gift of the margrave at the municipality.

Jews were living on German soil as early as the Fourth Century CE and in Berlin as early as the year 1300. Jews in Europe were always treated as a commodity and regarded as a source of revenue. If they were useful for the economy, the prince of the state would admit them into territory. If not, they were considered as expendable, expropriated and expelled. This meant that poor Jews had no right, no chance, no place to exist. And the overwhelming majority was poor. A Jew had to be rich to literally buy the right to live. He had to pay what was called *Schutzgeld* (protection money)—in the 17th Century as much as 25,000 guilders. He had to pay when a child got married. He had to pay when a member of his family was buried. He had to pay when the prince needed funds to finance his wars. He had to pay and pay and pay.

But even money did not save him. If things went wrong for the ruler, if the royal subject were dissatisfied, he would divert their wrath towards the Jews. After all, they had it coming. They had committed the unforgivable sin of Deicide. And so for hundreds of years Jews lived in constant fear of the whims of their protectors and of the ire of the mob. If, God forbid, a Jew would be caught in wrongdoing, every single Jew was held accountable for the misdeeds of this one. As late as the middle of the 18th Century a Jew in Berlin, who was caught stealing a chicken was led to the gallows, accompanied by two rabbis, in a public spectacle. Before he was hanged, his tongue was cut out and fastened to his shoulder.

Hitler was no innovator. He was merely a follower. He was a student. He had learned his methods of mental humiliation and physical torture of Jews from the examples of ecclesiastic and civil authorities of centuries past. What his predecessors had done spontaneously, Hitler did systematically on a mass scale, aided by scientists and scientific methods of the 20th Century. Genocide has been reserved for this enlightened 20th Century of ours and for a nation which excelled and still excels in science, in scholarship and in many areas of human culture; a nation where religion was taught—and is still being taught—in public schools four periods a week.

However, the remarkable thing was not the fate that had been visited upon Jews during the Middle Ages and modern times but rather how Jews reacted toward their fate. In spite of torment ad toil, of despoliation and murder, they did not allow themselves to become like their tormentors. They grew inwardly. They lived the life of the spirit. They advanced in learning and scholarship so that, when the sun of freedom began to shine upon them in the 19th and 20th Centuries, they produced giants of minds and heart totally out of proportion to winners (from Einstein to Nelly Sachs, who died last year in exile in Sweden) than their persecutors.

It was in Germany that Judaism experienced its westernization and that Jews went through the process of entering into Western culture and society. It was in Germany that Jewish tradition was first wedded to European Humanism. It was here that modern interpretations of Judaism were born; that the three branches, Orthodoxy, Conservatism, and Reform, formulated their ideologies. It was here that the "Science of Judaism," the scholarly investigation of Judaism, began and became the basis for modern Jewish scholarship. It was here that a Jewish community which is without parallel anywhere in the world.

In the days before Hitler, Berlin with its 159,000 citizens of the Jewish faith was the largest Jewish community in Europe. I shall forever cherish the privilege of having known this community at its height. Strong and proud, reverent of tradition yet modern in the best sense of the word, it was the fifth largest in the world, with monumental cathedral-like synagogues, religious and Hebrew schools, hospitals, old age homes, youth movements, newspapers, theaters, theological seminaries, and secular academies of Jewish learning. It also had organizations for the cultivation of Jewish music, art, and literature.

When I returned my heart ached when I realized that the people I had known were no more, that the synagogues were gone, that the institutions had disappeared. Truly, I did not return home. For home is where there are people you know and love.

After the Sabbath service in Berlin at which I was invited to preach and which was televised by the state T.V. network, a handful of people whom I had not seen for more than 30 years crowded around me to shake my hand or to kiss me—all with tears in their eyes. There were two men whom I had Bar Mitzvahed; there were two women whom I had confirmed when they were 15-year-old girls. One gave me the confirmation picture as a present. There were two couples whose marriage certificate with my signature. It was the strangest, most moving reunion I have ever experienced.

Yes, there are again Jews in Berlin—6,250 of them. In all of Germany there are some 22,000 scattered among some 30 communities. They are natives of virtually all European countries who survived the Holocaust and were stranded in Germany. The resurrection of Jewish life on German soil is a veritable miracle. It was to participate in the 25th anniversary celebration of the reconstruction of the Jewish community in Berlin that the present mayor, on behalf of the senate of the city, had invited a dozen people who were identified with the old Jewish community.

It was an historic event filled with high moments. It was a high moment when I found upon arrival in my hotel room a sign, "Welcome to Berlin,' and a number of books portraying the old and new city in prose and poetry. Shortly thereafter a representative of the mayor's office appeared, offering his services for a pleasant week-long stay.

It was a high moment when on the following day the mayor gave a reception for us at the City Hall, with toast and talks and all the rest.

It was a high moment when a representative of the senate took us on a tour through the city at which we saw part of the old and the new Berlin. Among many places I shall never forget was the horror-filled room at the Ploetzensee Prison where the German officers who had unsuccessfully tried to assassinate Hitler were hanged. (The hooks are still in the ceiling.)

It was a high moment when we, the visitors, presented the mayor of the city and the leaders of the reconstructed Jewish community with a volume *Genewart im Rueckblick* ("The Presence in Retrospect") to which it was my privilege to have contributed a chapter.

On the following Monday morning, Germany's leading newspaper, *Der Tagesspiegel,* published an article headed "It Is Possible To Overcome the Past." Is it? The answer to this question will be given by the generations of the future.

Why did I return to the land which committed the most unspeakable crimes against humanity, to a soil soaked with rivers of Jewish blood?

Twenty-five years ago I would have said: Never again shall I set foot on the cursed soil. But 25 years ago, no one would have invited me. I did go back because 1970 is not 1945. Was it to demonstrate symbolically that the past is forgiven and forgotten? Nothing is forgotten; by human standards there is no forgiveness for mass murder. Ultimately, only the Creator of Man can forgive what His creatures do to fellow creatures. Fratricide is Deicide. The reasons why I accepted the invitation lie not in the realm of the supernatural or metaphysical but solely on the natural plane. They are pragmatic as well as spiritual.

I went, first of all, because I am an American. America has a decided interest in Germany. Germany is the heartland of Europe. When the Nazi regime which Hitler predicted would last for a thousand years collapsed after 12 short but fateful years which shook the world, the United States decided to disarm and to de-Nazify Germany. But, at the same time, it helped rebuild its former enemy. Germany is the natural bulwark against Soviet Union.

I went, in the second place, because I am a Jew. As a Jew, I have no right ever to push away a hand stretched out in reconciliation. I do believe in *Teshuva* (reconciliation) between man and God and between man and his fellowman. I say so every *Yom Kippur*. I believe that is is possible for people to repent and to change. I believe that people who seek to repent should be given a chance to do so. I do not believe that the sins of fathers should be visited upon their children.

In spite of occasional flare-ups of Nazi sentiments, all post-Hitler governments from Adenauer on have tried to make amends. They have supported Israel politically and economically. They have established diplomatic relations with Israel. In 1970 alone, they have sent 3,125 young Germans to visit Israel as exchange students; 1,286 Israelis are presently studying at German universities. German students study Hebrew, Jewish religion, and philosophy. A recent Massada exhibit in Germany attracted many thousands. In addition to government efforts private German organizations (mainly church and youth groups) have gone to Israel on Peace Corps mission to work in Kibbutzim and to help build homes for those who were crippled and maimed in concentration camps. Some Germans have settled permanently in Israel. The first German ambassador to Israel and his family speak Hebrew fluently. They spend their vacation in Israel this year. The German publisher and newspaper czar Axel Springer has given millions for the Hebrew University.

Hatred, unbending, unending hatred is not an emotion by which I can live nor philosophy by which I want my children and children's children to live. Hatred does not open a road to the future of civilization. It does not pave the way toward God's Kingdom, Judaism's hope for peace on earth.

Ultimately, I went back to the scenes of my youth because this journey into the past is a living symbol of the indestructibility of Judaism and the Jewish people. For fifteen hundred years an unredeemed world has been visiting nothing but death and destruction upon our people; yet, in spite of it, we have outlived our tormentors. History has vindicated our undying faith that, as the Prophet said, "not by might and not by power but by God's spirit man prevails."

Life born out of death; fait out of despair; hope out of defeat; the State of Israel risen form the ashes of Auschwitz and the mass graves of Europe; this miracle of resurrection is the mystery of Judaism, the symbol of our historic destiny. As the Psalmist said: "I shall not die but live and proclaim the work of the Lord."

A FATHER'S ETHICAL WILL*

In the Middle Ages it was customary for a Jewish father to write an "Ethical Will" in which he would set forth his hopes for the type of human being his child would become. Some noble examples of these wills are preserved and can be found in libraries. Rabbi Swarsensky tried to revive this ancient custom in his charge to his son Gerald David on the day of his Bar Mitzvah, January 31, 1969.

Gerald could have made things much easier for his father, who for the first time in his life as to double as Father and Rabbi, if he had eloped. But since he decided to celebrate his *Bar Mitzvah* at the Temple, I am well satisfied with his decision. For what would his or any boy's *Bar Mitzvah* be without the company of family and friends?

I deem it a privilege for Gerald to be able to celebrate his Bar Mitzvah in the pleasant and familiar environment of our Temple on this Sabbath which happens to be the Sabbath on which I began my ministry in Madison 29 years go. I am grateful for the large congregation which is present to share in this, my son's celebration, even as I have been sharing the joys and sorrows of our Temple family all these years.

What I can say on this occasion is suggested by the portion which Gerald read from the Torah. "And it shall be, when your son shall ask you in the days to come. What is this? Then you shall say unto him: By strength of hand has the Lord brought us out of Egypt, out of the House of Bondage."

In its original context, this admonition elates to he duty of a father to instruct his son in the mighty acts of God as He liberated Israel from slavery in Egypt at the beginning of its historic career. In a broader sense, the biblical statement bespeaks the duty of a Jewish father to inform his child not only of the one-time event in the days of old, and event which is annually re-enacted at the *Seder*, (the Passover family service), but it refers to the wider parental responsibility to introduce a son into the world of what traditionally is called "our duties in relation to God and in elation to our fellow men" When it comes to the transmission of Judaism, the primary teacher s to be not a hired professional, but the child's father—an ideal no longer real in our world. "And it shall be when our son shall ask you in the days to come: What is this? Then you shall speak unto him."

This I shall do today. In centuries past many Jewish fathers left what was known as an "Ethical Will" to their children. I shall use this device today.

Ethical Wills are part of our literary tradition. They are different from the type of wills and testaments we leave today for those who will come after us. Rather than listing and distributing a person's material assets and properties, they are a distillation of an individual's most important assets: the values which he has accumulated and which he wishes to pass on to those who will follow him.

It is natural for any human being to hope that his life might be extended beyond the limits of his own years and that his tradition would be perpetuated by his children. This hope is part of this-worldly immortality which we aspire to build for ourselves in our own flesh and blood. It does not mean that we parents should expect that our children become what a sociologist called "pleasure-producing machines." What we do have a right to expect, however, is that, notwithstanding the changes of times, those who come after us do not throw away the treasure of the heritage of their fathers and do not break the chain of generations.

I am not different. It is my earnest hope that my son will cherish, cultivate, and live the very ideals and ideas which have meant the most in my life. This is not t say what I want him to be a mere replica of myself. Even if he wanted to, it would be impossible. He was already grown beyond me in physical stature, in his active enthusiasm for sports, in his mechanical skill, and in his knowledge of every latest model of automobile. I would have a difficult time catching up with him in these as in other respects. Indeed, I am not unmindful of generation, yes, the history gap. The world which formed me is no more. The memories of my childhood and youth, dear to my heart, cannot be his. Each individual is cast into a mold which exists only once. Moreover, I know I should have enough humility to heed Longfellow's wise counsel: "Never ask God to make other people like you, for God knows why one person like you is enough."

However, with these reservations, I believe that the fundamental values by which men live are independent of time and space. Among the unchanging values which build a bridge between the generations are these two—Life and History. The former is a universal value; the latter a particularistic one; Judaism, in our case.

Life is the supreme gift which is laid into our cradles as our birthright. It could well have been that we had never seen the light of the sun. But since this privilege was given to us, we should never take what is the greatest of all gifts for granted but rather accept it and live it in the spirit of humility and thanksgiving. The inner misery of man lies in this blindness to the amazing miracle which is life. Rather than living life as a matter or routine, we ought to savor each day on earth. Instead of concluding a day (as we all too often do) in a bitter, disgusted, complaining, self-pitying mood, we should look at each day as an unearned gift from the storehouse of God's grace.

I hope, Gerald, that you will continue my life-log practice of closing each day with prayer, a habit which I have been trying to instill into you ever since you were able to talk. There is nothing superstitious, sanctimonious, or old-fashioned about prayer. Prayer is our humble acknowledgement that we have not made ourselves. It removes from our mind that arrogance which makes us believe that we are the center of the Universe. It attunes our spirit to the World Spirit, to the Ground of all Being we call "God." In a world in which many old forms of piety have vanished, a new piety, a new religious inwardness, a new spiritual attitude toward Life is vital, if man is to live sanely and soundly.

But this is not all. The gift of life, which is so uniquely ours, should evoke within us not only a spirit of perpetual humility and gratitude, but also a never-ending determination to give back to life through active and dedicated service what we receive in such abundant measure from life.

I cannot abide lazy people, be they young or old, who regard work, which is the greatest blessing, as a burden. Work gives structure and purpose to our existence. I disapprove not only of lazy but also of irresponsible people, people who want to receive but not give and who forget that life is duty. Man must give freely and graciously of all that he has—his time, his talent, and his toil. We are but stewards and custodians of what is lent to us. We should never forget Job's elemental insight. "Naked did I come into the world, and naked will I leave it." If we ignore this basic law of life, we are nothing but parasites. Along with the loafer and the hitchhiker, I dislike the anarchist who because of the chaos within himself, tires to throw the world into chaos. Unable to affirm and to build constructively, he takes sadistic delight in tearing down and destroying. Uncritical of himself, he is critical only of others. When I was your age, we learned Greek in School. Among the words of a Greek philosopher which I remember are these: "The undisciplined life is not worth living." A person is mature only if he has learned to lead a disciplined life—to discipline his body, his physical appetites, his mind and his emotions. If he fails to do that, he has progressed little beyond the animal level.

I want you to be in the company of those who do not contribute to the world's problems but rather to their solution. I want you not to be among those who curse the darkness, but among those who light a candle. I want you to be a charitable with your material possessions and understanding of others, even of those with whom you must differ. Always respect what in sacred to them. No human being hast the right to feel superior or to claim to possess all truth. More than anything else, I want you to be compassionate, always feeling the joys and the sorrows of others as your own. The highest ideal for a human being in our tradition is to be a *Mensch*—human and humane. He who fails to be that has missed the mark. The gift of life has been wasted on him.

There are many ways of being human. Our way has been molded by one of the oldest and noblest spiritual traditions—Judaism. A unique religio-historic experience of almost 4,000 years is our heritage. It would be inconceivable for me that a son of mine would not wholeheartedly and unreservedly affirm the prophet Jonah's words: "I am not a Jew and I revere the God of Heaven and Earth." I cannot conceive of anything in this world worth breaking the chain of the 130 generations from Abraham to this day. Our ancestors did not suffer unparalleled pains at the hands of the world's Pagans and our brothers in many countries are not at the mercy of unredeemed savages even at this very hour in order that we may throw one of the greatest heritages of mind and heart and spirit upon the ash heap of history.

Even as it is a privilege to be alive, so it is a privilege to be a Jew, a privilege which we must equally accept in humility and thanksgiving. It is a distinction—and I say this without vain-glory—to be a member of a people that has contributed to the intellectual, moral, social, and spiritual progress of mankind totally out of proportion to its small number.

And let it be added lest we delude ourselves into believing that a new day of universal brotherhood has dawned, when the time is at hand for the past to be buried: Jews will continue to contribute to human advancement only as long as the historic Jewish experience nurtures their concern for man. Those who believe that they can better serve mankind by cutting themselves off from the moorings of Judaism by becoming non-sectarian Americans will find that within a generation of two their descendants will become average, part of nondescript mass of anonymity. Our Jewishness keeps us on our toes. We can never walk on the shady side of life. The force of history propels us toward striving for excellence.

I hope that your Jewishness will be more than a matter of filial or family loyalty even though family loyalty is profoundly cherished value. I trust that your Jewishness will be more than a matter of mere sentimentality, but rather one of conviction and commitment. To this end, I want you to learn and to study Judaism as long as you live. The ignorant Jew cannot be a good Jew. I also want you to belong always to a synagogue, the oldest and most continuous form of organized Jewish life without which Judaism would long since have vanished. The synagogue has handed on the torch of piety, knowledge, and social idealism from generation to generation. I want you to support actively all Jewish organizations which are designed to maintain the fabric of Jewish life in this country and throughout the world even as I urge you to assist all good causes in the general community. Your motto should be Hilltel's words: "Never separate yourself from the life of your community."

Needless to say, it would please me if you would become a rabbi. I already knew tat I wanted to be one when I was your age. But it would not disappoint me if you sought personal fulfillment in a different field. On frequent occasions you have indicated to me that you do not like the many meetings I attend and the fact that I am never at home evenings, and that you see so little of your father. I cannot hold out to you the prospect of a meeting-less existence nor that of a 40-hour week, should you chose your father's profession.

But, more importantly, Judaism is, if one may borrow this term, a layman's religion. Much as Judaism needs rabbis, it needs dedicated laymen even more. All your ancestors, on your mother's as well as on my side, were such dedicated Jewish laymen. There have been no rabbis in my family. Should I be the only one it would make little difference, if only you—no matter where you find your place in life—will follow in the footsteps of your forefathers. Never forget: you are a "son of the Covenant."

And so I say to you, Gerald, on this day, what my father said to me on the day of my *Bar Mitzvah* and what generations of Jewish fathers have said to their songs in the words of the author of Proverbs: "Hear, my son, the instruction of your father, and never forsake the teaching of your mother." Let them be a diadem upon your head to crown your life with all that is good, noble, and holy. "A goodly heritage has been bequeathed to you. Forsake it not! It is a tree of life for those who hold fast to it."

"HE WHO DESTROYS A
SINGLE LIFE..."*

In August, 1970, during nationwide protests against American involvement in the War in Vietnam, Robert Fassnacht, a young researcher at the University of Wisconsin was a victim of the bombing of the UW Mathematical Research Center. This eulogy was given in the presence of his family and colleagues as well as of representatives of the administrations of the University and State and Federal Governments. It was televised by national networks.

We are gathered at this evening hour to express our common grief over the death of an uncommon man who lost his young life under the most uncommon circumstances.

When man stands on the borderline of human existence and senses his utter creatureliness, speech fails and words become brittle. It was in such a moment that the Psalmist said: "When my spirit is overwhelmed within me, lead me to the Rock high than I." Yes, words cannot express the depth of our feelings, compounded of frustration and indignation, of horror and shame. But people who, in whatever befalls them, will not allow the sky already darkened with clouds to become even darker, will also not permit tragedy to embitter their hearts and despair to shatter their spirits.

At this moment of parting from one we all loved, the truth of the words of ancient wisdom comes into full focus: "He who saves a single human life is like one who has saved an entire world: and he who destroys a single human life, is like one who has destroyed an entire world." Each human life is a microcosm, a small world. Each life is precious in God's sight. Each human being is cast into a unique mold which exists only once.

Bob was such a unique person, endowed with extraordinary gifts of mind and even greater gifts of heart. He was a man of culture and nobility of character who was dedicated to scholarly pursuits. He was devoted to the good of his fellow men and to the advancement of the quality of society. He was in love with the quiet beauty of nature and the harmony of music. As once was said of another man: "he lived without display of himself"—quiet, unassuming, genteel. "To do justice, to love kindness, and to walk humbly before God" was the unwritten motto of his life. With him not only an individual has been destroyed but an entire world, a world so full promise and of hope.

Bob's life was a precious treasure most of all for those nearest and dearest to him: for his wife, Stephanie, and his lovely children, Chris, Karen, and Heidi; for his father and his dearly beloved departed mother; and for his sister, Carol. For each of them his life was an entire world.

Buildings criminally laid in ruins can eventually be rebuilt; research wantonly interrupted can someday be resumed; but a life destroyed can never be restored. This is why we, including all of Madison—in fact the entire nation—feel so deeply with all those for whom Bob's life constituted their world. It was a world from which came love and joy, friendship and fellowship, and promise and hope for the days and years to come.

Now all that had been but prologue has become past; all that had been hope has turned into memory. His was a life of great promise. Through his life was incomplete, in our hearts Bob's memory will remain full and fresh. Through his children who were the sunshine of his days, the sun of his life will shine on. In them, his flesh and blood, his immortal spirit will live and grow.

It is to them, yes, to all of us that he leaves a precious legacy. It is a legacy of a spiritual heritage to which history is testimony that ultimately not by violence nor by force but only by God's spirit of compassionate love will man prevail. For we have not come into the world to hurt, to hate, and to hunt but rather to love and to serve and to build and to preserve God's creation. This is our destiny on earth. Everyone's joy is our joy, everyone's sorrow is our sorrow. "Everyone's death diminishes us, because we are involved in mankind. No one should ask for whom the bell tolls. It tolls for you and me."

The senseless sacrifice of a good man should make us dedicated ourselves to guarding the sacred flame of life. May we help complete the still incomplete work of creation by loving peace and pursuing it and trying to build the society which is still our vision.

May we have the inner strength to transmute tragedy into triumph, despair into hope, and death into life. Life is still worth living. America is still worth saving. This country is still mans' last hope on earth.

It is for this hope and this yet-unfulfilled promise that Bob has died. It is the hope for the dawn of that more glorious day of which the poet sand: "The earth on which we live is but a small start in a great Universe, but of it we can make, if we choose, a planet unvexed by hunger and fear, untroubled by hatred and war. Give us O God, the grace to begin this task today so that our children and our children's children may be proud of the name of man."

If this be Bob Fassnacht's legacy for his children—yes for all of God's children—this valiant martyr will not have lived and died in vain.

"THE ROCK WHENCE
YOU WERE HEWN..."*

In July, 1976, Rabbi Swarsensky retired from his congregational duties as rabbi of Temple Beth El, Madison, where he had served for 36 years. A large gathering of his friends, filling the Great Hall and adjoining rooms of the Memorial Union, heard his retirement speech.

"If I had known how pleasant retirement is, I think I never would have gone to work in the first place." These sentiments expressed by Dr. Alfred W. Swan, former minister of Madison's First Congregational Church, at the time of his retirement, echo my own. It is a somewhat strange but, I must admit, pleasant experience to be able to listen to one's eulogy while still alive. May God forgive you for exaggerating my qualities and may He forgive me for liking it. After all, I am not so great that I can afford humility. Let me, therefore, express my deep gratitude to so many of my friends who have planned this singular event.

When I first came to Madison at the beginning of 1940 and asked people: "Who is the most prominent voice in the religious life of this community?" the answer was invariably Dr. Alfred Swan. I was privileged to speak at his retirement banquet. For years we have shared common religious and social ideals. Since our last names begin with the same three letters, Swarsensky always followed Swan on the lists, appeals, and statements, alphabetically as well as ideologically. Concerned about my future, he some time ago asked me: "What are you going to do when you retire?" "I have not even thought about it," I said. "Let's you and I have fun together," he suggested. How can I ignore such a counsel from a wise colleague?

I am grateful, indeed, to all of you who are honoring me by your presence tonight. It warms my heart that the dedication of a forest in the American bicentennial national park of Israel links my name to that Old-New Land, the Holy land, the common cradle of Judaism and Christianity.

The tree is one of the oldest and most universal symbols. It symbolizes the continuity of generations. In ancient times a father would plant a tree at the time a child was born. From the wood of the tree he would later on make the posts of the canopy under which the child would be married. To the Psalmist the word of God is "a tree of life." The Prophet likens the man of faith to a sturdy tree. "Blessed is the man," Jeremiah said, "who trusts in the Lord. He is like a tree planted by the waters which spreads out its roots by the river."

In modern Israel, the tree has become a symbol of life renewed; of a people reborn—a people that, like Antaeus in Greek mythology, has renewed its strength by contact with the life-giving soil of its ancestral land. In our ecology-minded era, which is concerned with the preservation of the essential building blocks of life—soil, water, and air—a forest is a visible manifestation of human efforts to make the barren soil yield fruit and the desert bloom like a rose.

They symbolism of the tree is even more encompassing. Like the tree man, too, needs roots if he is to be strong and vigorous. Elton Trueblood, the noted Quaker philosopher, speaks of our present civilization as a "cut flower civilization." We are only too willing to accept the bouquet, but we have forgotten, yes, we ignore the roots. Whenever man forgets his roots, he becomes unsure of his steps; he grows weak and is in danger of falling apart. In order to endure, society needs roots, particularly in times when the winds of change tempest-like are blowing all around us. The older I have become, the more I have learned to appreciate the roots which have nurtured me.

Permit me to use this occasion to speak about the roots which have sustained me throughout my life. I hope you will forgive me for talking about myself. As you know, great people discuss ideas, average people speak about events, and small people talk about themselves. Three major roots, I believe, have nurtured the tree of my life.

My first and deepest root is my religious faith. It is the root from which have sprung patriarchs and prophets, preachers and psalmists, seers and sages, mystics and martyrs. "The Bible," George Bernard Shaw said, "has remained more up-to-date than the morning paper."

In the darkest moments of my life I have been sustained by faith in God, the Rock of the Ages, the Alpha and Omega of my existence. Even when He seemed to be hiding His Face, I have trusted Him. Without such trust, I would have lost my faith in man and in the worth of life. The moral and social ethos of the biblical tradition has claimed my ultimate loyalty and has fired my unshaken faith that ultimately history is not the making of man's design but the unfolding of God's purposes. He is the ruler yet. Biblical tradition has inspired my belief that man can find his deep fulfillment in this world only as a witness and servant of God, and as a brother showing compassion and loving kindness to his fellow men.

Among my spiritual forebears I number not only the giants of my own faith's tradition but also the towering figures of other faiths and other traditions. Among them are the philosophers and poets of Roman and Greek antiquity who reflected on mysteries of the stars and the soul and who wrote philosophical treatises, epics, tragedies, and poems which uplift mind and heart.

I was fortunate in that as a teen-ager I was exposed to the humanism of classical literature. Latin, Greek, and Hebrew, languages which I learned in high school, are still sweet music to my ears. What little I know and remember I owe to my teachers who forced us unwilling and rebellious boys to memorize the poems of Ovid, the odes of Horace, the epics of Odyssey and the Iliad, the tragedies of Sophocles and Aeschylus, and most of all, the profound wisdom of the 66 books of the Bible. I had no idea how greatly my early exposure to the world of religion and the humanities would assist me in later years. Not only has it broadened my intellectual horizon, but it has also given me inner strength in the darkest hours of my life.

Like countless others in this world, I have known loneliness, homelessness, privation, hunger, imprisonment, and torture. For six years, from 1933 to 1939, I lived in daily fear of violent death. However, in the darkest moments of my life, I have never succumbed to denying God, to despising man or to despairing of life. When I was in prison and concentration camp, the words of Horace were my companion: *Aequam memento rebus in arduis servare mentem* (Under the most arduous circumstances preserve your equanimity). When I saw men pour out their most diabolic venom I thought of the words of Antigone, "not to hate but to love are we born." When it seemed as if God had hidden His Face, I found comfort in Job's assurance, "even though He slay me, yet will I trust in Him."

Western civilization is the product of the confluence of three streams of culture: the heritage of Rome, of Athens, and of Jerusalem. Here are our roots. Here are my roots. These roots thousands of years old, are the tie that binds all of us who have inherited the legacy of the civilization of the West. Here is for all of us, heirs to the Judaeo-Christian tradition, the source of our faith and our culture. Woe unto the generation that does not know its roots. The gravest danger to present-day society is reverting to the moral and spiritual Paganism of our pre-Judaic and pre-Christian pas. Albert Schweitzer once said that in our world it takes ten million laws to put into practice the Ten Commandments. As Matthew Arnold said, "Culture is our only defense against anarchy." More dangerous than an attack from an outside enemy is the peril of moral, social, cultural, and spiritual rootlessness.

The second root of my being is not millennia but centuries old. It lies in the culture of the land where I was born; the land in which for hundreds of years my ancestors lived, died, and lie buried; the

land whose language is my mother tongue and whose music, literature, and art are part of my cultural inheritance. Even today, when
I become excited, my most expressive expletives are in German.
When I sing, I love to sing in German. When I pray—and I have
never started or concluded a day without prayer—I pray in Hebrew
or German. In fact, I still pray the very same prayer my mother
taught me when I was a small child. Goethe's words which my
father gave me on a slip of paper when I left home for college, have
remained my motto throughout my life: *Edel sei der Mensch, hilfreich
und gut...* (Noble should man be, helpful and good), for this alone
distinguishes him from all other creatures. If with all that Hitler destroyed I would have let him also kill the memories of my childhood
and youth and the well-springs of my cultural heritage, I would have
helped him to win a posthumous victory. I could not and I will not
let him destroy my roots.

The third and youngest root of my life is only decades old. I
acquired it only 36 years ago. I say, "acquired,' although, I have often
felt that I was an American long before I came to America because
the spirit of Pilgrim and Puritan, of Jefferson and Lincoln, of Roger
Williams and Thomas Paine has been spirit of my spirit.

It was an unearned privilege that a mere fluke of history—or was
it providence?—brought me to the hospitable shores of this great
land which, as Daniel Moynihan recently said, of all the imperfect
democracies in the world is the most perfect one. America has saved
not only my body but also my soul. It has restored my faith in the
promise of life and in the goodness of people.

It was an equally unmerited privilege to have landed in Madison,
this marvelous city excelling in scenic beauty and cultural riches,
and, most of all, in people who are truly alive and humane. Even if I
tried, I could never list all the wonderful people I have come to know
here, people who in the course of years have become close personal
friends who have trusted me and whom I have come to trust.

I have never suffered the agony typical of clergymen, namely
the agony of undelivered sermons, because there is hardly a town
in the state of Wisconsin in which I have not had the pleasure of

speaking from pulpit and platform. In the land from which I had come, cooperation among faiths was virtually unknown. High walls surrounded the communities of faith. Few dared to look over these walls history had built. And when they did, they never saw individuals but theological abstractions to fit their preconceived ideas, namely: infidels, heretics, and non-believers, rather than people who, though differing in theology, were deserving of respect. Yes, there were exceptions; Niemoeller, Bonhoeffer, Faulhaber, Lilje, Buber, Baeck, Heschel, and others. But their voices were voices in the wilderness which the masses neither heard nor understood. Religion was neither the conscience of the individual nor that of society. As a function of the State, the prophetic voice of religion was muted.

America is different—in this as in other respects. Here we have gradually come to understand that religion, true to its historic roots and to its traditional mission, need not build walls to keep out the stranger; but that it rather ought to build bridges over which to walk to meet our brother. It has fallen to our generation to overcome a dehumanizing past. Malachi's rallying call must at last be heard: "Have we not all one Father, has not one God created us all? Why shall we deal faithlessly brother against brother?" A new form of human existence has developed in our time. Not confrontation in human relations, but dialogue by which we, in Martin Buber's terms, meet others not in an "I-It" but in an "I-Thou" relation; not as objects to be sued and to be manipulated but as persons to be respected and loved. Dialogue is not to convince and to convert but to speak truth in love and to listen with respect to a brother's voice. It is the ability to disagree agreeably. It has been said of those who climb pyramids: The higher they climb, the closer they get. How true of all of us: The higher we climb, the closer we get to one another.

As America stands at the threshold of its third century, our country, yes, the world, is crying for spiritual guidance, and moral instruction. Not the marvels of our scientific and technological achievements, impressive though they are; not the height of our gross national product, vital through it is; nor the power of our armed might, tragically necessary thought it is, will ultimately guarantee our survival; but only the spiritual quality, the moral fiber, and the social dedication of our citizens. The saints of the future will be the men and women who patiently, faithfully, and hopefully will make the America of the future a paradigm of human living and a beacon of hope for the world.

These, then, are the roots of my being; the millennia of my Judaic heritage, the centuries of my European past, and the decades of my American experience.

Over the years I have had many problems, but I have never had the problem of identity. I have always known who I was and have never wanted to be anything but myself. I have suffered many pains but never he pain of boredom and burn out. I have always had more to do than I had time for. Some of my well-meaning friends, worried that I might become bored in retirement or switch to the 40-hour week, have suggested that in order to fill the hours of the day I take up crocheting and needlepoint. I appreciate their concern. However, as long as the Good Lord gives me strength, I shall continue to pursue my chief loves—people and books. In fat, I am so insatiably curious about the future that I would like to make an agreement with the Lord of Life that He deduct one year from my allotted years and, in exchange, permit me to come back to earth one day for the next 365 years. I have a burning desire to know what will become of life on this planet, what will be the future course of history. When David ben-Gurion celebrated his 70th birthday, a well-wisher expressed to him the traditional wish: "May you like Moses be granted a life of 120 years." Whereupon the youthful old pioneer countered: "Who are you to limit my life?

I am grateful beyond expression for the gift of life, this unfathomable gift of divine grace. I have been deeply aware of the fact that the last 36 years of my life have been a special bonus. It, too, could have been in the number of the six million who lost their lives in the European Holocaust. The unusual experience of having been given a second life has profoundly influenced my thinking and living. It has heightened my awareness that life is God's gift to us and that what we do with our life is our gift to God. It has intensified my de-

151

termination to give back to life an infinitesimal part of what I have received so graciously and undeservedly.

I appreciate your kindness; I do not want to be thanked for whatever little I have done. I am here tonight rather t hank you, friends, and co-workers, for the opportunity that you have given me to unfold my interests and concerns in this great and wonderful community. May God's richest blessing abide with us always.

FROM GENERATION
TO GENERATION*

*This chapter is reprinted from Rabbi Swarsensky's book
From Generation to Generation, published in 1955
to mark 300 years of Jewish settlement in the United
States.*

The sense of historic continuity distinguishes man from the animal. The animal exists in the today; man has his being in the threefold time dimension of yesterday, today, and tomorrow. He alone can experience the push of the past, the lift of the preset, and the pull of the future. There are but two types of people who desire to expunge the records of the past—the criminal and the plebeian. The man of true human nobility is neither overawed by the past nor haunted by it. He knows that the past is never dead but lives. The past lives in him. Woven into the fabric of the historic continuum, his life possesses an inexhaustible fountain of inner strength and dignity. His days on earth will not be totally without direction for the future.

Like the Puritan, the Quaker, the Huguenot, and the Catholic, the Jew came to America to find freedom—freedom from persecution by tyrannical governments, freed to work, and freedom to worship God.

Thirty-four years after the Pilgrims had landed at Plymouth Rock, Jews came to this country. The first known Jew to set foot on the soil of North America was Jacob Barismson who came to New Amsterdam from Holland in August, 1654.

In September of the same year, a group of 23 Jews arrived on the St. Charles from Recife (now Pernambuco), Brazil, following the introduction of the dreaded Inquisition by the Portuguese who had taken the country from the tolerant Dutch.

From this handful of Jewish settlers of Manhattan Island 300 years ago has grown the present American Jewish community of some five million people, constituting the largest Jewish community in the world.

The majority of the ancestors of present-day American Jews, however, did not come to America during the 17th and 1th centuries but rather during the 19th and 20th.

First came the Sephardim, Jews those forefathers at one time had lived in Spain and Portugal. They came from South America, Central America, Holland, and the West Indies. Most of the 3,000 Jews living in the colonies, which had a total population of four million at the time of the Declaration f Independence, belonged to the Spanish-Portuguese group. Many of them, importers and ship-owners, brought to the young country a thriving trade with Europe and South America. These immigrants took pride in preserving the Memory of "Golden Age" their forefathers had witnessed in medieval Spain.

Considerably larger than the Sephardic immigration was that of Ashkenazic Jews, Jews from Northern, Central, Eastern, and Southeastern Europe.

The second wave of Jewish immigration to this country consisted of some 300,000 Jews from Germany, who came between 1840, and 1880. They were part of a larger group of five million freedom-loving Germans who had left the fatherland in the wake of the abortive German revolution of 1848 and settled in large numbers in the Middle West as American frontiers advanced westward and southwestward.

These Jewish immigrants, who had been forced into peddling and petty trading in the old country, became middlemen among their former countrymen in the new land. Hard work and thrift enabled many a newcomer to exchange the pack on his back for a horse and wagon and eventually to open stores, small and large. By and large, this group of immigrants quickly became absorbed into the American middle class and integrated with the American culture. Ready to take their place in the life of America, they were equally devoted to their concept of Judaism as a religious heritage. Filled with a yearning for political freedom, they also espoused a liberal philosophy in religion. They established Reform congregations and Sunday schools, founded Jewish fraternal organizations and welfare agencies, and thus became the builders of the American Jewish community. The majority of the 250,000 Jews living in this country about 1880, within a population of some 50 million, were Jews from Central Europe.

The third and largest wave of Jewish immigration came from Eastern and Southeastern Europe between 1880 and 1920. Following the Czarist-inspired pogroms f the '80s, thousands fled Russia to settle on the barren soil of Palestine, but many more turned to America as the Promised Land. Some two million Jews from Russia, Poland, the Baltic countries, Galicia, and Rumania were among the "tired, poor, huddled masses, yearning to breathe free" to whom the Statue of Liberty beckoned as the symbol of hope from a life of freedom and dignity.

Many of them came without their families. As soon as they had saved enough money to pay for steamship tickets, they would send their wives, children, and parents. Eager to transplant the world of the East European *shtetl* (small own) to these shores, they preferred to live in their own neighborhoods. Some turned to peddling as a means of earning a livelihood; others, especially those who settled in large metropolitan centers, became manual laborers and factory workers. The most popular craft was the needle trade. Some of America's most progressive trade unions such as the Amalgamated Clothing Workers and the International Ladies Garment Workers were founded by East European Jewish immigrants. Today more than a half million Jewish workers are affiliated with the AFL and CIO. Unlike their co-religionists from Central Europe, these newcomers who had lived in a culturally and socially self-contained Jewish milieu had a deep attachment to Jewish tradition and folkways. They were enthusiastic in their love of Zion and of Jewish culture. They became the founders of Orthodox congregations, *Talmud Torahs*, (traditional religious schools), and mutual aid societies. At home, they spoke Yiddish and read Yiddish newspapers. The Yiddish press in those days fulfilled the two-fold function of maintaining the immigrant's link with his past and, at the same time, introducing him to the American way of life.

In recent decades, the children and grandchildren of these immigrants have frequently moved into the middle class and taken their place in the trades and professions. Like the descendants of earlier immigrants, they, too, became closely identified with the cultural life of the country. Many of the most active Jewish community leaders are the sons and grandsons of men who studied in East European *Chadarim* (Hebrew schools) and *Yeshivoth* (Talmud schools).

In 1920, shortly before the enactment of the restrictive immigration laws, there were, in a total population of 106,000,000 Americans, about 3,500,000 Jewish Americans.

The ranks of American Jewry were further strengthened by Jews who in the 1930's escaped countries overrun by Hitler's hordes, chiefly Germany and Austria. Special legislation on behalf of D.P.s (Displaced Persons)—survivors of all faiths and nationalities from Nazi gas chambers, concentration, and forced labor camps—enabled approximately 60,000 Jews to enter this country between 1948 and 1953. These Jewish D.P.s—Delayed Pilgrims, as someone suggested interpreting the two letters—were part of more than 300,000 Displaced Persons of all faiths who had either fled Naziism, Fascism, or Communism or refused to return to their Communist-dominated homelands.

Between 1920 and the present, 40 million immigrants of all national, cultural, and religious backgrounds have come to this country. Like most other immigrants, the Jews who crossed the Atlantic came here poor in wordy goods but rich in industry and enterprise. Long experienced in thinking and suffering, they developed a deep attachment to a life guided by reason and inspired by social idealism. Descendants of the people that has been called "the veteran of history," they were convinced that America is different from any other land they have known in their long history of wandering. America, they feel, is home not only in the physical but also the spiritual sense.

It was no accident that our nation's Founding Fathers engraved on the Liberty Bell the biblical verse, "Proclaim liberty throughout the land unto al the inhabitants thereof." (Leviticus 25,10) This very affinity was expressed by Supreme Court Justice Brandeis when he aid: "The ideals of America of the 20th Century have been the ideal so Judaism for 20 centuries." Thus the heirs of the world's oldest monotheistic religion live by the faith that in this free and fair land, "undimmed by human tears," there will yet be realized their millennial hope of the Brotherhood of Man under the Fatherhood of God.

BEYOND AUSCHWITZ—
BUILDING BRIDGES*

This talk was presented at the Church of the Divine Savior (United Methodist), Cleveland, Ohio, at the invitation of its pastor, Dr. Ellsworth Kallas, as part of a series of Lenten lectures in 1980. It was given at a convocation at Luther College, Decorah, Iowa. It was reprinted by **Perspectives**, *Wisconsin Humanities Committee;,* **Aram**, *newsletter of Wisconsin National Guard; and* **Aufbau**, *largest German language newspaper, New York. Senator Proxmire inserted it into the* **Congressional Record**, *United States Senate, on May 18, 1981.*

Speaking about the Holocaust in 1980 may appear to be excavating ancient history. Our attention has become focused upon more recent ominous events which have eclipsed the memory of the years when the hurricane of the Hitler horror struck the world with fear.

There are people today who openly say that they are sick and tired of hearing about the Holocaust. A professor of electronics at Northwestern University even insists that the Holocaust never happened and that it is, as the title of this book says, *The Hoax of the 20th Century.*

Others, notably Dr. Franklin Litttell, professor of church history at Temple University in Philadelphia and one of the world's foremost students of the Holocaust, warn against he temptation to re-

158

press the memory of the Holocaust and to treat it as simply another example of "man's inhumanity to man." Littell sees the Holocaust as an apocalyptic event of eschatological dimensions which was a watershed in human and theological history.

True, there have been orgies of cruelty and mass murder in our century before: the massacre of the Armenians by Turks in World War I; the deportation to Siberia and the slow death of more than 15 million Russian Kulaks; the death of 7 million Ukrainian peasants by starvation in 1931-33; the liquidation of Chinese by Mao; the slaughter of 400,000 Indonesians in 1965; Idi Amin's killings in Uganda; and the large-sale murder in Cambodia. Brutal massacres of innocent civilians by invading armies and by terrorists have darkened the face of the earth. No animal will do to another member of its specials what man is capable of doing to another human being.

And yet, compared with these godless acts of sadism, the Holocaust stands out as an event unparalleled in the annals of history. Never before had there been a program of systematic, government-organized genocide which resulted in the dehumanization, torture, and killing of six million human beings of whom one million were children under 14.

On January 20, 1942, at a high-level conference of the Nazi hierarchy held at Wannsee, fashionable suburb of Berlin, the decision on "the Final Solution" of the so-called "Jewish problem" was made. It was to murder every single Jew. Medieval rulers who put Jews behind ghetto walls said: "the Jew has no right to live among us." The Nazis said: "The Jew has no right live." It was the first time in history that a state had arrogated to itself the right to decide whether or not a whole people had the right to live. Never before had a nation made genocide the fulfillment of an ideology. ("Holocaust" is the Septuagint's translation of the biblical word for "burnt offering," "an offering made by fire.")

The Holocaust has produced an enormous body of historical, sociological, psychological, and theological writing. And yet the more than 6,000 books, essays, articles, and anthologies which have been published will never be able to convey the grim reality of what actually happened during those fateful years between 1933 and 1945. Even the television docu-drama "Holocaust," accurate and moving though it was, could in no way bring to life the actual experience of people living every day for 12 years in fear of violent death.

What normal person could eve imagine that innocent human beings, old men and women and little children, would be dragged from their homes, driven in the dark of the night into the hellholes of concentration camps, stripped naked, lined up in front of trenches they had to dig with their own hands, and shot by firing squads? Others were pushed into box cars without water or food and were shipped to gas chambers to be asphyxiated and incinerated in crematoria. Storm troopers played football with the heads of babies. We can agonize about the death of a single child. The death of one million is an abstraction. A women survivor of Auschwitz, who resettled in Madison after the war as a Displaced Person, had been assigned the task of throwing bodies of people who had been killed by poison gas into the crematoria to be burned. One day she came upon the bodies of her own two young daughters, 12 and 14 years old.

The Holocaust resulted in the extermination of one-third of the Jews in the world as well was in the destruction of 1,500 years of Jewish life and culture in Europe. It was the culmination of 1,900 years of indoctrinating the psyche of Western man with contempt for Jews and Judaism. Hitler was no innovator. He merely exploited and brought to their final conclusion the teachings of ecclesiastical and political leaders before him.

The Holocaust belongs to the past. However, the fundamental questions raised by this outburst of barbarism in the 20th Century have remained unanswered. What are some of these unresolved questions which will and ought to torment the questing human mind for ages to come?

1) How was it possible that the Holocaust did not take place in a remote corner of the earth inhabited by cannibals but in the land of Bach, Beethoven, Mozart, Lessing, Goethe, Schiller, Herder, and Kant? Why did it happen in the midst

of a nation which held a place of preeminence in virtually every field of culture: in science, technology, medicine, art, music, and literature, as well as in philosophy and theology?

2) How does one explain that seemingly civilized people, members of the intelligentsia, including the judiciary and the professors—with notable exceptions—actively supported of silently condoned the most heinous crimes against humanity the world has ever seen? Many even silently applauded, as Dorothy Thompson wrote.

3) Why was it that the churches and their leaders—with notable exceptions—were so ominously silent, some of them only too willing to exchange the God of Sinai and Golgotha for the Pagan gods of blood and soil?

4) Why was it that the greater the fury of persecution, the tighter the nations of the Free World closed their hearts and their gates to those trying to escape? (See Arthur Morse, *Why Six Million Died*, and Bernard Wasserstein, *Britain and the Jews of Europe* 1939-1945, Oxford Univ. Press.)

5) Why was it that even though five million non-Jews, whose martyrdom we honor, also lost their lives in the Holocaust, Jews were singled out as the first and foremost victims of the Nazi assault on humanity?

6) Why does so large a part of mankind wish the death of the Jew and want to make the world *judenrein* (free of Jews), and why is it that there is abroad in some theological circles the belief that Jews deserved the suffering in expiation for the unforgivable sin of Deicide?

But above and beyond these questions which we must confront if we want to come to terms with the Holocaust, there are even more fundamental metaphysical ones which ought to engage our minds and hearts, since they touch ultimate questions of human existence.

What are these questions?

1) Can human beings ever be trusted again after our encounter with the utter human depravity and naked evil of the

Holocaust?

2) Can 19th Century liberal optimism concerning human nature and progress in history still be accepted?

3) Can one ever again believe in God, a God of justice and love? Where was God during the Holocaust?

Indeed, we cannot speak of the Holocaust without coming face-to-face with these questions of ultimate concern. After Auschwitz, the old comfortable ideas by which we have lived no longer seem to make sense, to give meaningful answers, or to offer comfort. Our eyes have seen the "Kingdom of the Night" of which Franz Kafka spoke. We have looked into the abyss of the Gehinom.

It is a total misconception to believe that the Holocaust was merely an encounter between Nazis and Jews and that the rest of mankind had nothing to do with it. To the Rev. Littell the Holocaust is not an event in Jewish history but—to use his words—"an Alpine event in the history of Christendom."

With a profound insight into the nexus of Jewish and universal history, Eli Wiesel, a survivor of the Holocaust and one of its foremost interpreters, recently said: "America is becoming existentially ever more Jewish." What he meant is that the fate of America is resembling ever more the historic fate of the Jewish people, namely: being weak and vulnerable; isolated and despised; surrounded by a growing band of enemies. These enemies, unable to resolve their own domestic problems, brand this nation as the embodiment of all evil and pillory it as scapegoat for all the ills tat beset them. If hitherto survival has been the foremost preoccupation of the Jewish people, today survival has become the most urgent problem of America. In their blind fury, the enemies of America and of the Free World are plotting another "Final Solution," this time with the intent of making the world *America-rein*—free of American spirit and influence.

Not only Jews but everyone living in the Western world today is in the literal sense a survivor of the first Holocaust. The question is: Will we survive another one? Should there ever be another Holocaust, an article of the *New Yorker* recently said, it will be a nuclear

Holocaust. No one will have to leave home to go to war to fight on the foreign battlefield. An atomic Holocaust of the future will find us at home, at our breakfast tables, in the bath, on our way to work— the very places where the Nazi Holocaust found unsuspecting, help- less Jews. Wiesel's statement is more than a metaphor: America is becoming existentially ever more Jewish.

Is the world prepared for a mass descent into the inferno over the entrance of which Dante in the *Diving Comedy* wrote: "Forsake all hope, ye, who enter here"?

It may appear like expecting the millennium, and yet only a spiritual and moral regeneration in the hearts of men can prevent a mass catastrophe. The decisive question before mankind is whether or not it will heed the biblical lessons: "You shall not stand idly by your brother's blood."

It is easy to give up hope and to succumb to cynicism. As a believer, I cannot afford this escape. For 4,000 years Jews have led an existence which has defied logic and natural law. They have lived and survived in spite of everything. The first article of their faith has been *Al Yityaesh* (never despair).

To surrender to despair, to give in to cynicism, are contrary to the entire Jewish attitude toward life. One never ceases to marvel at the sheer endurance displayed by a people that has wandered a long Via Dolorosa with a thorny crown of martyrdom on its head.

Why was it that during the massacres of hundreds of thou- sands during the Crusades, the persecutions of the Black Death, the Chmelnizki uprising, the Czarist pogroms, the torture chambers of Dachau, Birkenau, Majdanek, Auschwitz, and all the other unspeak- able horrors, Jews seldom took their lives as one would logically have expected? Why was it that 37 years ago this month the Jews of the Warsaw ghetto marched to their deaths with the creed of the me- dieval Jewish philosopher-theologian Moses Maimonides on their lips, "I believe with perfect faith in the coming of the Messiah, and even though he tarry, I believe." Why was it that the survivors of the Holocaust did not engage in taking vengeance on their enemies but instead used whatever flicker of energy was left in them toward building a new life in the old land of their ancestral faith or through-out the world? *Lo avda tikvatenu,* (our hope is not yet lost) was tir hymn of faith.

Crucifixion and Resurrection is the perennial theme of Jewish existence, death and rebirth of a people. Jewish suffering can be understood only as vicarious suffering, suffering for he sings of the world. Jewish fate is the barometer of the moral level of the world. By the alchemy of the divine spirit incarnate in man, this uncon-querable people has testified again in our century that tragedy can be transmuted into triumph, despair into hope, and death into life.

Yes, unbelievable though it may seem, even in the land in which "the Final Solution" was conceived, there are Jewish congregations again. Congregations in Western Germany have 22,000 members; the Jewish community of Berlin, with some 6,000 souls, has an ac-tive communal life. And-*mirabile dictum*—only several months ago a new seminary for the training of rabbis, teachers, and community workers was opened in Heidelberg.

Let this be clearly understood: The Holocaust is no proof that the symbiosis of Jews and non-Jews in the world is an impossible ream. The horror of the Hitler era does not prove that Jews were wrong in their aspiration for civic equality. It only proves that Fas-cism and its twin brother, Communism, are dead wrong. Democ-racy is still mankind's and the Jew's last and only hope.

In Germany itself, democracy, which had been unknown in cen-turies past, is beginning to grow only now. The democratic consti-tution of 1949 has created a new climate which has helped in the struggle of a nation—to use the official term—"overcome the past."

This past summer a permanent Holocaust exhibit was opened in Berlin in the building of the old German Reichstag, the former National Parliament. Its purpose is to impress upon generations to come the magnitude of the sins of their fathers. I was present on the occasion and heard high government officials affirm their determination to work for the moral and social regeneration of their nation.

Am I saying that the time has come to forget the Holocaust? Never. To forget would be a sin, a sin against memory, a sin against history, a sin against the dead.

Shall we forgive? I can forgive only wrong done to me personally. The only ones who could forgive, if this were possible, are the six million martyred.

But I can and will stretch out my hand and grasp the hand stretched out to me in reconciliation. I do believe in reconciliation in this as in other situations. The purpose of our Holocaust commemoration is not to sow seeds of animosity against present-day Germany. To hold children accountable for the sins of their fathers is contrary to our moral convictions. Hatred, unending hatred, is not the seed bed from which redemption can grow. The chief task before mankind is still unfinished. Human beings must at long last become human and humane. To endure, mankind needs to build bridges, not walls; bridges between man and man, bridges between faith and faith, bridges between race and race, bridges between nation and nation, and bridges between the creature and his Creator, the Father of us all.

THANKSGIVING—HOLIDAY OR HOLY DAY?*

*Food, fun and football have largely obscured the true
meaning of Thanksgiving. At a time went it is vial
for our nation to revive its fundamental spiritual and
moral values, it is essential that the significance of
Thanksgiving as a holy day rather than a holiday be
restored. In 1967 the Downtown Rotary Club invited
Rabbi Swarsensky to deliver an address on the abiding
meaning of Thanksgiving. The late Henry Reynolds,
well-known Madison businessman and former mayor of
the city, sponsored the original reprint of the address for
Madison Rotarians. In 1981, the rabbi was named an
honorary life-member of the Rotary Club.*

At a time when Thanksgiving has become largely a day for food,
fun, and football, it is well to remember that the Pilgrim Fathers
celebrated Thanksgiving not as a holiday but as a holy day. Steeped
in biblical faith, these sturdy pioneers were conscious of their dependence upon a Power greater than they. Their attitude was all the
more remarkable in view of the hardships and the privations they
had experienced during their first year on American soil.

The world in which the Pilgrims lived is no longer our world.
The 346 years between the Thanksgiving of 1621 and ours today, have
seen undreamed-of changes. The political, economic, and industrial
revolutions which have swept the Western world have changed the
face of this country. The intellectual and scientific revolutions have
changed our outlook on life. To suggest to modern man that he exists, as the Pilgrims believed, by the grace of God, is almost felt to be
an insult to his intelligence. The prevailing secular philosophy of life
sees man as the master and the measure of all things. This changed
attitude explains why it is hard for modern man to be truly grateful.
Gratitude is an emotion born out of man's humble recognition of his

dependence upon forces greater than he: the power of gracious God, the mysterious forces of the Universe, the accumulated wisdom of the ages, the toil of generations past. As the poet George W. Russell said: "A thousand ages toiled for thee." In our time, Thanksgiving is more an occasion for self-praise and self-congratulation than for praising the real Maker and Master of things.

This change in attitude toward life may be inevitable. Its consequences are many and far-reaching. We have come to take Life, including the blessings showered upon us, for granted as if we had a rightful claim to it. Little wonder that the number-one problem of our generation is the problem of the meaninglessness of life.

We are, it is said, alienated from life, estranged from ourselves. Even the affluent society has not answered the problems of a generation that has become increasingly cynical about life. With more to live on than any generation before us, we have less to live for. We have become such a nervous, restless generation that we need pep pills by day and sleeping pills at night. We are so much on edge all the time that even sermons can no longer put us to sleep. Our situation is very like the situation of the man caught in a railroad tunnel. The victim is too far from either end of the tunnel, the home or the hope. He can see neither the light at the beginning of the tunnel nor the light at the end.

This sense of meaninglessness and cynicism is attributable to many causes. Chief among them is our loss of the sense of wonder and awe regarding the amazing phenomenon of life itself. The child learns and feels his way into life by wondering about things which the adult takes for granted. It is the same attitude of questing which makes the scholar, the scientist, the poet, the artist, and the religious person. "To wonder," Plato said, "is the beginning of living and thinking." "Absolutely incredible," writes Kirby Page, "is the way we walk through life, with head down, lowered eyes, and unheeding ears. In the presence of a veritable miracle we stand as unblinking as an old cow in the meadow."

In one of his essays Emerson reminds us that if the stars would appear only one night in a thousand years, we would believe and adore and preserve for generations the remembrance of the city of God which had been shown. But because the stars always shine at night, even when hidden by clouds, most of us rarely give them more than a fleeting glance. In a similar vein, Thoreau said that "if the sight of a flaming maple tree in full color should be seen only once in all time, the memory of it would be handed down by tradition until it became enshrined in the mythology of the race:; or if a man were granted but one unhurried view of the full glory of the sunset in his lifetime, the recollection of it would be treasure all his days. If a husband knew that merely for a single day he would be blessed with the love of his wife and children, how indelibly would that experience be burned into his memory.

A national survey of the personal and social attitude and the aspirations of adolescent girls undertaken by the University of Michigan Institute for Social Research reveals that only one out of five of these girls could recall ever having had an experience that created in her a sense of "wonder or awe." It seems that the deeper man's mind penetrates the mystery of life, the more firmly man believes he has established his dominion over the earth, the more he loses his sense of wonder. If nothing can arouse our sense of wonder and awe, the sense of gratitude is crowded out of our lives. Thanksgiving becomes a mere holiday and loses its spiritually quality. Our generation has a real need for recovering the sense of wonder so as to take the dimness of our souls away.

Among the things we take most the granted are not only the phenomenon of life itself, but our very own existence. As a rule, we grow aware of the unique gift of life only when death shocks us out of the routine of being. It is a very real biological possibility that we would never have seen the light of the world, that we would never have tasted the savor of life. Should we have been asked whether or not we wanted to live, I am convinced that every single one of us would have answered: "Give me life. I would not want to miss this unique experience." So strong is the life instinct within us that most people would bee willing to spend their last nickel just to stay alive another day. If this is indicative of how deeply we cherish life, then it should follow that we do not take life for granted but regard it as the greatest unearned privilege. And even tragedies—and what life has not its share of them—should not mar our appreciation of life nor defeat us as they often do.

It is not surprising to find ingratitude among those who are favored most. The Pilgrims' gratitude arose from the fact that they had little. Gratitude does not depend on how much we have but on our inner attitude. We can be as happy or unhappy as we want to be. Our life can be as interesting or uninteresting as we choose it to be. If our personality is warped, if we are miserable inside, we will see life as a dreary affair. If our attitude is affirmative and appreciative, we will see light and hope in life and say, not only when the going is good, but at all times: "It is good to be alive."

Can we make this affirmation also in regard to living in our time? The Pilgrims' view of history is essentially different from ours. They held the biblical view according to which human history is the unfolding of God's purposes, not of man's design. Today, it seems we are closer to the Greek view of history which sees in the shifting panorama of history the work of the blind, uncontrolled, and uncontrollable forces of a Greek tragedy. This is not surprising. The tensions, the perils, the convulsions of our era are frightening. There are times when we are haunted by the fear that man in his hubris and his fury may blow himself off the globe and write finis under the whole human enterprise. It is tragic indeed that during 92 per cent of all recorded history man has been engaged in fighting wars in one part of the world or the other. War is the murder of brothers.

It is wisely ordained that we cannot choose the time in which we want to live. It would be difficult to select the era into which we would like to be born. I have heard people say that they would like to have lived during the period between 1880 and 1930. This was a time when living was less complex, when Western man was buoyed up with implicit faith in the inevitability of progress, when our country was moving into the position of unchallenged leadership among the nations, when the issues were clearer, and life seemed securer.

But were the issues really clearer? Let me quote a paragraph from an article in *Harper's Weekly:*

**"It is a gloomy moment in history. Not in the
lifetime of most men has there been so much
grave and deep apprehension; never has the
future seemed so incalculable as at this time.
The political cauldron seethes and bubbles with
uncertainty; Russia hangs, as usual, like a cloud,
dark and silent upon the horizon of Europe, while
all the energies, resources, and influences of the
British Empire are sorely tried and are yet to be
tried more sorely, in coping with its disturbed
relations in China. It is a solemn moment, and of
our own troubles no man can see the end."**

This article was written in November, 1857.

A wise man once said: "Never say that the former times were better than yours." A study of history will reveal that with all our tragic involvements from which there are no easy ways out, we cannot overlook the fact that our era is not only full of anxiety but also full of hope. Arnold Toynbee, the British historian, said that our era will be remembered in the annals of history not just for the bitter East-West conflict nor for having produced the atom bomb, but for having made the welfare of all, rather than that of the few, its major concern.

Indeed, one cannot be blind to the enormous advances of our age, not only the expanding frontiers of knowledge but also the growing yearning of men to find ways for peaceful existence and mutual helpfulness. When the history of our time will be written, our age may possibly be called the age of Dialogue. It is easy to grow cynical about the United Nations. But the dialogue which has begun among the nations should neither be minimized nor abandoned in a world which has constantly grown smaller, with everyone being everyone's neighbor, it is indispensable that lines of communications between people be opened and be kept open. "Nothing is more powerful than an idea whose time has come," Victor Hugo said.

We see such dialogue emerging among the religions of the world which, until very recent times, had not been on speaking terms, with each busy confessing the sis of others. This is different now and will hopefully lead to a new era in human relations. We see the beginning of dialogue among the races which up until recently have lived in not-so-splendid isolation.

If some f our contemporaries can only understand that there is not short-cut to the millennium, that force cannot build the Kingdom of Heaven on earth, I am confident that greater Justice will come to those who for so long have been denied a place in the sun. But in this exciting and hopeful age no one can afford the luxury of sitting on he sidelines and letter the world go by. Solon, the Athenian lawgiver, said that justice can be effected only if those who are not wronged feel as deeply as those who are.

Thanksgiving should be a time for remembering the toil and sacrifices that have gone into building this country which has more than any other country in history, in large measures succeeded in finding the necessary balance between freedom and authority, so indispensable for the democratic process.

However, we cannot close our eyes to dangers which bode ill for the health of our society. There is a growing tendency toward acceptance of irresponsibility as a way of life; there is disrespect for honest work and authority. There is an impatience in this "Now Generation," which, raised on instant foods, wants instant solutions to all problems, and is unwilling to postpone pleasures. There is an increasing trend toward making the "Playboy philosophy: of hedonism and pleasure the end-all of life. There is talk that we need a "New Morality" which, in reality, is nothing but the old immorality. There is talk that "God is dad," when in actuality, I am afraid, man is dead. What has died in us are the very spirit and the very values which Thanksgiving represents, namely the consciousness or our dependence upon forces infinitely greater than we and our obligation of a never-ending sense of gratitude to the Giver of Life who in His infinite wisdom has made this beautiful earth a habitation for His creatures. Thanksgiving should remind us that we are indeed a "nation under God" which in its biblical context means "a nation under the judgment of God."

If we could add this spiritual dimension to our lives, Thanksgiving could be for us, as it was for the men of Plymouth Rock, not merely a holiday but a holy day.

THE CLOSING OF THE GATES*

*"The Closing of the Gates" is the theme in prayer,
song, and sermon of the solemn **N'ilah** Service which
concludes the daylong worship of the Day of Atonement.
In this sermon, presented at Waukesha's Temple
Emanu-El in 1979, Rabbi Swarsensky related this
traditional theme to the grandeur of life, the miracle of
its beginning, and the mystery of the closing of its gates.*

In ancient times, when the solemn rites of the Day of Atonement were celebrated in the Temple in Jerusalem, the gates of the
Temple which had been open all day for the worshippers were closed
at the time of the setting of the sun. The holiest of the Holy Days
concluded with *N'ilat Shearim*, (The Closing of the Gates), from
which derives the designation of *N'ilah* for the closing service of
Yom Kippur.

Even in later times when the Temple was no more and the heavy
bronze doors of the Sanctuary no longer had to be closed at the end
of the Day of Atonement, the original prayers of the Temple service
persisted. They have to this day in Jewish services throughout the
world.

Those who will present for the *N'ilah* service will sense the extraordinary mood of solemnity which fills this concluding hour, expressed in words of deeply moving symbolism and in music of a
well-nigh mystical quality. The prayer which expresses most beautifully the mood of this closing service is the plaintive chant: "Open
unto us, o God, the gates of Your mercy before the closing of the

gates. The day is nearly done. The sun is setting. The time is growing late. Let us enter Your gates at last."

The solemn chants of these cadences have an aura of rare spiritual beauty. Above and beyond their original meaning, they are a
symbolic portrayal of what life truly is—an opening of the gates and
a closing of the gates. Life is like the fading day, slowly moving toward the setting of the sun. Some of us are closer to the beginning,
others are closer to the end of the pilgrimage. But a pilgrimage life
is. No one of us will ever travel again the road which lies behind.

The French have a saying which expresses the brief stretch between the opening and the closing of the gates in a different metaphor. Playing on two words, they say: *On sort et crie, on crie et sort*,
(One goes out and cries, one cries and goes out). It is with a cry that
we come into the world, and it is with a cry that we go out of this
world.

On *Yom Kippur* our tradition summons us to reflect, as we rarely
do during the year, on the closing of the gates at the time of the setting of the sun.

The thought that, once life has opened its gates, the day will
surely come when they will also close, may fill us with a sense of
melancholy, even depression. A Talmudic sage counseled against
such mood. We rejoice when a child is born, and we grieve when a
person dies. The opposite, he said, would be more appropriate. The
entrance of a child into life is like a ship setting out on its journey for
an unknown destiny. We have no assurance that the voyage will be
calm or that the ship will reach its destiny and safely return to harbor. Why rejoice in the face of such uncertain prospect, not knowing
whether the journey will be safe, whether the traveler will remain
unharmed by the hazards of the journey? When, on the other hand,
a person has already reached the fullness of the years apportioned to
mortal man and has reached them without harm and hurt, when the
ship has reached port in safety, then is occasion for rejoicing. Ratio-
nally, we may be impressed by this Midrashic simile but psychologically, we will find it difficult to accept its truth.

The consciousness of the inevitability of the closing of the gates of life has at all times filled man with anxiety. It has made him reflect on the swift flight of these earthly days. As a result, a multitude of theories, doctrines, and beliefs as to what lies beyond this life has emerged. We are so constituted that we can neither cognitively think the thought of our own perishability nor emotionally accept its reality. Everything within us revolts against the thought that we, like generations before us, must go the way of all flesh. The illusion that the gates of our life will stay open forever is the greatest, and the most helpful, illusion by which we live. It is doubtful that we could go on from day to day without this illusion which helps us to keep our sanity and maintain what the French call our *elan vital.* We are inclined to deny our finiteness or, at least, to push it out of our consciousness.

Our age has gone even beyond this natural human tendency. Present-day culture, more than any previous one, has placed the accent on the here and now. Emptying the cup of life to the last drop, celebrating life, shouting a resounding Hallelujah to life is the motto of our age. Former cultures exulted in the past. The *aetas aurea* (the Golden Age) has always been seen lying in the past, not in the future, as we like to fancy today.

Whenever the past has been celebrated, old age has been exalted. The oldest of all cultures, that of China, even today gives primacy to the elders. The aged are not put out to pasture to spend what euphemistically is called their "golden years" in old age and nursing homes or in retirement centers away from the pulsating stream of life, but rather continue to live within the full flux of the active life of family and society. In earlier cultures, leadership has always been sought from the older generation, from the Elders and the Presbyters. When Moses needed counsel, he did not turn to Gershom, his son, or to Miriam, his daughter, but to Jethro, his father-in-law. At the latter's suggestions, he formed a "Council of Elders" to advise him. "Ask your fathers, they will tell you; your elders they will advise you," the Lawgiver counseled.

Children, too, throughout the ages have sought advice not from their peers but from their parents. Today, parents are often so confused about values and so unsure about their own standards, that they no longer assert themselves and readily abdicate to the wishes of children. One reason why age is little respected is that age does not respect itself.

The accent on youth has given rise to a rapidly developing gerontophobia, the fear of growing old. This new psychic disease has imperceptibly been creeping into our thinking and been settling in the crevices of our societal existence. It is manifest in our total culture. It has influenced everything, from our tastes n fashions, physical looks, and literature to our economic preferences.

The fear of growing old is rooted in large measure in the fear of losing one's instrumental role in society, which is a more sophisticated term than the cruder "losing one's market value." Man's deepest psychological need is the need to be needed. The Psalmist's supplication is the prayer of all of us: "Cast me not off in the time of old age, when my strength wanes, forsake me not." Man's most tormenting fear is the fear of no longer being needed. This very fear of being thrown on the ash heap of life makes people anxious about their age, self-conscious about the first appearance of grey hair. It makes otherwise honest people conceal, even lie about, their age, rather than rejoice that, like the ship safely returning to port from a long voyage, they have happily traversed the hazardous journey of life.

Acceptance of one's self at whatever age or stage is the chief requisite for mental and emotional health. It is a compliment, not an insult, if somebody says: "You look your age." Each age has its beauty. There is beauty in the angelic face of a baby, in the buoyant ace of the adolescent, in the expressive face of a mature man and woman, even as there s a serene beauty in a face lined with wrinkles and eyes deepened by both worry and wisdom. "Like a candle in a holy place, so is the beauty of an aged face," the poet said.

A person's attitude toward the Closing of the Gates is largely determined by his attitude toward life at the Opening of the Gates. If we ever shouted a Hallelujah at the sight of dawn, we have no reason for breaking out in dirges at the coming of dusk.

Life, this unique experience, so close to us and yet so elusive; this amazing, unfathomable adventure has been rhapsodized by sage and poet as at once the greatest miracle and the deepest mystery. Look at the tiny package of a new-born infant, so wonderfully endowed from the very start with a built-in potential for growing into a thinking and feeling being. All the Nobel prize winners in the world could not fashion a creature as miraculously constructed as a human being. Express it how you will, the fact remains that life is the gift from the hands of a gracious Creator who, as Martin Buber said, can never be defined but can only be addressed in awe and thanksgiving.

If we love the opening of the gates, love it in spite of its pains, its disappointments, and its tragedies, we will not fear the closing of the gates when the day grows shorter and the sun begins to set on the Western horizon.

What we fear, and understandably so, is the gradual withdrawal from life which is our inescapable fate. Withdrawal causes pain.

As a child grows into adulthood, feeling and working his way into the world, he acquires that triumphant feeling of being able to stand on his own feet. Gaining and getting give us a sense of freedom and of mastery over life. However, that sense of victorious conquest which we often experience between 20 and 50 is but a short duration. Hardly have we tasted the sense of freedom and independence which comes with success, when there beckons from afar the prospect of powerlessness, of surrender, and of withdrawal, as the closing time of life draws nigh.

Even the strongest among us cannot escape the sense of ambiguity which is built into the very fabric of existence. The ambiguity of human existence was well expressed by the sage who counseled ever human being to put on slip in each of the two pockets of his coat— one inscribed, "for my sake was the world created;" a second one, "I am but dust and ashes." It is the paradoxical combination of our worth on the one hand and our frailty on the other, which makes us move forward and retreat almost at the same time.

In the 16th Century, Nikolaus Copernicus dazzled the world with the discovery that not the earth but the sun was the center of the Universe. The prevailing theory at the time was that of Ptolemy according to whom the earth was the center of the universe. So startling was the Copernican discovery that it was felt necessary to publish his book with a statement that the theory was only one man's idea. Today, the heliocentric rather than the geocentric theory is accepted without question.

What made man of that century so fearful of giving u the Ptolemaean for the Copernican view of the Universe was not so much theological consideration but rather the natural fear of all human beings, the fear of surrendering their position of centrality. It must have been a psychological shock of gargantuan dimensions which moved people of tat far-off day to the depth of their being when they had to adjust to the idea that the planet on which they were living was but one of many constellations in the vastness of the cosmos. What Copernicus did to is generation, history often does to nations, and life does to all of us.

America is suffering withdrawal pains at present because the world situation is forcing upon us a gradual retreat from our position as the leading nation. It is painful for as proud a nation as our to find itself pushed from its place as the worlds number one super power, as other nations are emerging on the world scene vying the supremacy and a place in the sun.

Withdrawal pains are not limited to nations; they are among the most universal experiences of every living being. Living is a constant retreating from positions we had hardly won. Living is constant giving in and giving up. Life has a way of humbling even the proudest of us. We grow old from the day we are young. We die from the day we are born. We retreat while we are advancing.

Man is born with 20 billion brain cells. Each day we live we lose 10,000 of them. "Each day," the poet said, "we die a little." We retreat, as the vigor of our body and mind diminishes, as our memory grows dimmer, as the past becomes longer and the future shorter.

After a brief advance on the battlefield of life we become soldiers in a retreating army.

The two most important channels through which we establish communication with life are our work and our family. Nothing gives our life more meaning and fulfillment than our work. For some human beings, living is working and working is living. Working is fulfilling one's human potential. It is creative therapy. It gives life structure and purpose. And yet, as surely as the sun sets at eventide, there has to come the time when even the busiest among us has to lay down the book and the spade, the scalpel and the pen, the hammer and the trowel, the plow and the sickle, for the evening time is drawing nigh at the Closing of the Gate. Yes, as our prayerbook so graphically says, "even the place where once we lived and labored knows us no more."

The other of the two poles between which our being moves, is the lives of those who are bound to us by the ties of blood. Our children's and our children's children's existence give our lives not only meaning but also futurity, yes, a sense of this-worldly immortality. And yet, at the very same time our own children are constantly reminding us that life does not stand still and time is marching on, as the author of Ecclesiastes says: "One generation goes and another comes, but the world remains forever."

The Copernican experience of withdrawing is manifest not only in relation to life, to work, and family but also in relation to what often becomes the end-all of our striving, our worldly possessions. It is true, possessions have a tendency to possess us rather than our possessing them. They can corrupt and destroy us; and yet they are indispensable for existence, as well as for the development of character. Man can develop character not only in relation to people but also to things.

Unlike traditions which preach asceticism and self-denial as the epitome of virtuous living, Judaism has never insisted on the mortification of the flesh. One of our sages went so far as to say, "He who denies himself the good things of life is a sinner." However, what is true of life, is also true of our material possessions. Man works in the sweat of his brow to eke out a living, and if he can, to accumulate worldly possessions, only to learn after a few short decades that he has to sit down with an attorney and draw up a will. Whether he is a Rockefeller or a plain, unknown individual, he has to give up the very things for which he had worked hard all his life. When it comes to relinquishing our earthly possessions, we are indeed like a child whose toys are slipping from his little hands while he is falling asleep. When our toys fall from our hands, at the Closing of the Gates we suddenly see life in a different light.

The old comedy "You Can't Take It With You" reveals a serious aspect of human existence. We are not the real owner of whatever we think is ours. We learn that we are but stewards of whatever we possess; our life, our time, our health, our talents, our material possessions.

When the Gates begin to close on us, we also come to the sudden realization of the truth we often spurn: that with all our differences, we are equal as human beings, the prince and the pauper, the rich and the poor, the mighty and the lowly. Essentially we are all poor, we are all weak, we are all lowly when the day is fading and the sun is setting at the time of the Closing of the Gates.

Many answers have been given in response to the oldest of man's quests: What to do with the ineluctable ambiguity of existence? The Epicureans of antiquity said: *Carpe diem*, (Enjoy the day). Life is brief, therefore, enjoy each day to the fullest. The Stoics advocated *Ataraxia*,--no matter what happens, preserve your equanimity; be as calm and unperturbed as Nature which is emotionless. The Cynics espoused the ascetic life—don't let life, with its hustle and bustle, its gaining and getting enslave you. Retain your inner freedom. Leaning on Hellenistic metaphysics, Orthodox Christianity taught that this ephemeral life here and now and this mundane world are not the real life nor the real world. Beyond this life and beyond this world, there is another world, life eternal, the gift of a saving God. Indian Theosophy insists that all existence is illusory. There s not reason, therefore, for man to get agitated about the incongruities of existence. A continuous recycling of souls is evidence of the transitoriness of life.

There is in all of us a little bit of the Epicurean, the Stoic, the Cynic, the Hellenist, and the Indian mystic. We are all gropers for truth, seekers after light. And who will ever know where ultimate truth can be found?

Judaism has never questioned the possibility of an *Olam Habah*, a world beyond this world, a life beyond this life. And yet if we knew for certain what awaits us in an afterlife would it make any difference? Would we live any differently? Man's sanity depends upon his ability to accept the ambiguity of life and the mystery of human existence. In the apocryphal book of Ecclesiasticus it is written: "Seek not to understand what is too difficult for you. Search not for what is hidden from you. Be not over-occupied with what is beyond you." We must accept the fact that we live enveloped in a mystery. But our religion has insisted that the deep dark mystery hich is life, need not dismay us. There is a road, the only road leading out of life's mystery into the brightness of the day, and that is what our tradition calls the *Mitzvah*, (the good deed). Man finds and fulfills himself most completely in what he does.

Mystery and *Mitzvah*, piety and action, are the two poles between which human existence moves. Not the Epicurean's hedonism; not the Stoic's imperturbability; not the Cynic's renunciation of the world; and not the passivity of leaving everything to God; but cooperating, as it were, with God in completing the incomplete work of creation is man's ultimate destiny. In *Maassim Tovim*, (good deeds), we find the highest fulfillment of our humaneness. They are our only positive response to the inevitability of the end of our days at the time of the Closing of the Gates.

Many of us have met noble souls who have lived life to the fullest, because they fulfilled their lives through deeds of loving kindness. I have been fortunate to have known individuals among all groups who made God incarnate in their lives. By the way in which they lived their lives, they enriched the lives of all of us and affected the quality of human existence. Knowing them has strengthened

181

my faith in the inexhaustible potential of goodness in man, a natural goodness, found for the most post not in the proud and the mighty, but in the humble and the lowly.

Today is *Yom Kippur*, a time of reflection upon ultimate questions. Should not every day of our brief earthly pilgrimage be a day for being conscious that there is but one road leading from the impenetrable mystery tht surrounds us at every step; one way to resolving the ambiguity of life of being created in God's image and yet being dust and ashes. And that is acts of love, compassion, and mercy, by which along we give permanence of the transitoriness of existence and the temporariness of all human striving.

If we try to live our lives with such nobility of purpose, then even the closing of the gates at the time of the setting of the sun is not to be feared because it is a triumphant homecoming. It is a grateful celebration that the ship has returned safely and peacefully to the port from which I started a few decades ago on its brief voyage.

Petach lanu shaar b'ayt n'ilat shaar, ki fana yom. Ha-yom yifnay, ha-shemesh yavow v'yifnay, navowah sh'arecha. "Open unto us, O God, the gates of Your mercy before the closing of the gates. The day is nearly done. The sun is setting. The time is growing late. Let us now enter Your Gates."

SEASON OF ILL WILL

Reprints from *The Wisconsin Jewish Chronicle*, December 5, 1969

(Rabbi Swarsensky of Temple Beth El, Madison, is a frequent contributor to The Chronicle. His observations concerning the on-coming Christmas season as it relates to Jews are most interesting and enlightening. Editor.)

The "season of good will"—by which the annual Christmas cel-ebration is heralded by our non-Jewish neighbors—is often turned into a season of ill will so far as we Jews are concerned.

At no time of the year—the season of our High Holy Days not excluded—is the Jew made to feel more Jewishly conscious than at the advent of the annual Christmas tide.

Christmas, celebrating the birth of the Christian Savior—Mes-siah, is next to Easter, commemorating his death and resurrection, the theological foundation of the Christian faith. Despite the fact that the whole drama of Christian belief is set in the context of Jewish history and Palestinian topography; despite the fact that the babe in the manger whose appearance on earth is believed to have brought salvation to mankind, was a Jewish child; and despite the fact that the historic Jesus was born, lived, and died as a Jew, Chris-tian theology severed the Christian drama from its Jewish moorings and turned it into a genuinely non-Jewish and un-Jewish holiday. The belief in an incarnate God whose blood is believed to expiate the sins of mankind is Hellenistic, not Judaic.

This is the reason why at the Christmas season with the overwhelming pervasiveness of the Christian symbols of lights, trees, wreaths, carols, manger scenes, and feigned good will toward mankind, the Jew. While maintaining his respect for his neighbor's religion feels totally isolated and alone. The modern Jew feels eve deeper anguish about the anti-Jewish spirit of large sections of the New Testament Gospels and Epistles than did his believing ancestors who took Christian disdain for Jews and hostility toward Judaism for granted.

He furthermore realized that, in spite of the fact that he lives in a country who Constitution rests upon the principle of the separation of Church and State, this political tenet is widely ignored in practice simply because the United States is a "Christian country"—in the sense that the majority of its citizens are Christians, jus as Israel is a "Jewish country" in so far as the majority of its citizens are members of the Jewish faith.

This is why it is unrealistic to expect Christmas to be ignored in public life. A religious Christian holiday is a legal holiday. To inaugurate the holiday, the President of the United States lights a Christmas tree on the lawn of the White House. The United States Post Office issues a commemorative Christmas stamp. Public places and streets as well as store windows are resplendent with Christmas decorations. The public school which is an integral part of our culture—as some believe, a transmitter of Protestant culture—takes note of the Christmas season in a variety of ways. When December comes, Christian and non-Christian alike, find themselves engulfed by the spirit of the Christmas season. As a citizen of his country, the Jew shares in the rhythm of the season and, in large measure, in the general mood of his environment. As a member of a minority faith, he experiences a sense of differentness; he grows conscious of being, in a sense, an outsider.

To some this situation, which is inescapable, presents a dilemma. To others it is a natural phenomenon of Jewish life, because from the beginning of our history being a Jew has always meant being part of the world and yet being apart from it.

Those who chafe under the dilemma which the Christmas season presents will search for all kinds of "solutions" only to discover that there are none.

Some will insist that the celebration of Christmas outside the Church and the home is "unconstitutional." They will argue that the recognition of the holiday in the public schools violates the constitutional provision of separation of state and church, only to discover that it is only Jews who interpret the first amendment in such a way.

Seemingly everyone has the Christmas spirit except the Jew. At this time of the year he is meant to feel like a stranger in his own beloved land.

LUTHERAN
WRITER RAPPED BY RABBI

Reprinted from *The Wisconsin State Journal*, July 1, 1977.

Rabbi Manfred Swarsensky, rabbi emeritus of Temple Beth El, has accused the president of Northwestern College, Watertown of promoting anti-Semitism in an editorial he wrote for the Northwestern Lutheran, the official journal of the Wisconsin Evangelical Lutheran Synod.

Carleton Toppe, president of the Wisconsin Synod College, a regular editorial write for the Northwestern Lutheran, recently wrote that one reason for the suffering of the Jews over the centuries has been that "as a nation, God's chosen people rejected its Christ."

He warned his fellow Lutherans against persecuting Jews, but added that "the highest love we can show the people of Israel is to endeavor to win them for Christ, to lead them to the heritage of salvation in their messiah and ours."

In an open letter to Toppe, Rabbi Swarsensky said, "I find it impossible to understand how you can reconcile your belief in a God of love, compassion and forgiveness with a God who is a diabolic monster of hatred, cruelty and vengeance when it comes to his relation to the people of the covenant."

He also accused Toppe of promoting a gentle kind of genocide.

"It grieves me to realize that a religious leader in your position is now aware of the fact that your theology concerning Jews represents but another variant of the 'final solution.'

"You want to 'solve the Jewish question' through peaceful means, by conversion. Others have tied to accomplish the same by bloody means. The end result is the same; making the world 'judenrein,' or 'free of Jews,'" Rabbi Swarsensky asserted.

"Do you really believe this is the will og God? Do you truly believe that this is the will of Christ? Do you really regard this the supreme mission of Christendom. Thank God, in my many years of friendship and fraternal cooperation with dedicated Christians I have seen more elevating manifestations of the Christian spirit."

Rabbi Swarsensky also took issue with Toppe's position that the highest love Christian can show Jews is to convert them.

"I must ask you to also understand that this doctrine appears to those who do not accept your position as an expression of theological imperialism," the rabbi said.

"The majority of the world's population is non-Christian (Jews are the smallest group of the world's non-Christians) and this majority is relegated to damnation because it does not accept your theology. To hundreds of millions of people all over the globe this religious triumphalism is theologically non-sensical and morally offensive."

LETTER TO MR. JOHNSON

The identity of Mr. Johnson and his relation to Rabbi is not known.

November 20, 1980

Dear Mr. Johnson:

Please accept my sincere thanks for your thoughtful letter. I appreciate your sensitivity to the persistence of the anti-Jewish feeling in our society. It is usually in times of social upheaval, economic stress, and political tension that anti-Jewishness helps some people find "logical" explanations for prevailing ills and an emotional outlet for their general feeling of discontent.

Since times such as this recur from time to time, anti-Jewishness and all the other anti-feelings persist. Jews are among the oldest scapegoats upon whom to blame social maladies. The Jew who is "crucified" is, as a rule, not the real but a mythical Jew who exists only as a faction in immature, sometimes evil minds. Thus far, intellectual enlightenment and appeal to morality have brought about relatively little change. While this fact is most disappointing to someone like me who was brought up to believe in the advancement of the human mind and in the progress in human goodness, I have to concede that changing human nature is an infinitely slow process. However, while I can understand the cynicism which says that there is no hope for mankind, with its recurrent wars, Holocausts, outbursts of violence, etc., I could not live without a measure of hope nor can I deny the fact that in some areas man has improved.

I can well understand your reaction to Mr. Kazin's speech. I, too, object to his uncalled-for generalization.

It is both incorrect and foolish to think in terms of superiority and inferiority. It would be more accurate to say that human beings are different. Thank God that they are. It would be a drab world indeed if we were all alike.

Although neither the ten to twelve million Jews in the world nor the five million Jews in the United States are not a homogenous whole but rather represent as great a variety of individuals as any other group, it is, nevertheless, correct to state that their long history of almost 4,000 years has created some general characteristics.

Dedication to intellectual pursuits is one of them. Emphasis on learning has its roots in the uniqueness of their religion. Hillel, an older contemporary of Jesus, went so far as to say: "An ignorant (meaning illiterate) person cannot be pious." While 19th Century Hassidism strongly objected to this position, it is, nonetheless, correct that the Jewish religion requires of he humblest member a certain amount of literacy. In this is evident the influence of the much-maligned Pharisees who introduced compulsory education for children (boys) as far back as the second century B.C. (Mohammed) referred to the Jews as "the People of the Book."

I am inclined to believe that this age-old religion-cultural tradition has had an influence on the Jewish psyche even in an essentially secular world such as ours. It explains to a degree the proportionately higher ratio of Jews in academia and of Jewish Nobel Prize winners, a fact which made Father Hessburgh, President of Notre Dame, some years ago, ask the rhetorical question: "Where are our Catholic Einsteins and Rrueds?"

In Eastern European countries a Government *numerous clauses* excluded Jews from attending universities. Between 1850 and 1910 Jews from destitute and politically disenfranchised parents often fulfilled an ambition of their own lives by sending their sons to college. Thus, a relatively higher proportion of Jews attend universities than their number in the general population would suggest.

While this attitude should call for admiration, it often arouses envy on the part of the less successful and becomes a source of anti-Jewish feeling. Human beings often lack the objectivity to realize that society is the loser if there are fewer Salks and Ehrlichs and others whose work benefits humanity.

All this is not to say that Jews are genetically superior. Studies show that any individual or group of individuals is capable of intellectual attainment if it sets its mind to it. College students of all strata of the population can achieve excellence and advance to become successful in the professions, in teaching, and in research. America offers infinitely greater opportunities for persons of limited economic and social backgrounds to rise than almost any other country in the world – and that includes women who at one time traditionally were kept from moving into fields reserved for men.

Again, individuals who are satisfied with a life centered on the satisfaction of their carnal appetites and who lack higher motivations – and we know next to nothing about stimulating motivation will look with envy at their more successful contemporaries. If the latter are fellow Christians, they will accept it more or less as a matter of fact; if they happen to be Jews, they will often express their envy in anti-Jewish pronouncements and, if they have the opportunity, eliminate "the Jewish competition." There is a Latin proverb: "If duo faciunt idem, non est idem," "If two do the same thing, it is not the same."

A number of years ago a student at a local high school asked the teacher: "Why did Hitler kill the Jews?" Her answer: "They were too smart." On the basis of this "logic" all people who are "too smart" should be killed. Such, indeed, is the attitude of a great many primitive people. Anti-intellectualism leads to immoral behavior and eventually an impoverishment of human society.

With human nature ever change? Since it has in many respect, I have not given up for a better future.

With kind regards, I am
Cordially,

LETTER TO A MADISON CLERGYMAN[2]

I was saddened to learn that the teaching in your Sunday School that "the Jews killed Christ" has led to the harassment of Jewish children by students attending your church school.

While this fact is shocking to Jewish children and their parents, it is nothing new to me since I am thoroughly familiar with Christian teachings.

The purpose of my writing is not to ask you to teach anything which is contrary to your belief in the inerrancy of the literal account of the Gospels.

However, I regard it my responsibility to call your attention to the incontrovertible fact that the teaching of the above doctrine has had the most tragic consequences for the Jewish people from the times of the Crusades and the Inquisition to the Holocaust in our century.

I am referring to such recognized studies by Christian theologians as The Anguish of the Jews, by Father Edward Flannery; The Crucifixion of the Jews, by Dr. Franklin Littell, professor of Church History at Temple University; Faith and Fratricide and the Theological Roots of Anti-Semitism, by Dr. Rosemary Radferd Ruether, professor of Applied Theology at Garrett-Evangelical Theological Seminary. These and other Christian theologians have recognized the inescapable fact that because of the teaching of the Church that "the Jews killed Christ" believing as well as unbelieving Christians

---

2 When and where this open letter appeared is unknown.

for nineteen hundred years have used this as a theological alibi for murdering Jews. In his book Dr. Littell calls attention to the fact that it was not Pagans but baptized Christians in Hitler's Germany ho tortured, slaughtered, and incinerated six million European Jews of whom one million were children.

As the French professor, Jules Isaac, in his book, <u>The Teaching of Contempt</u>, points out, it is impossible to teach contempt for people century after century without reaping evil results. Impressionable young minds as well as uncritical adults who hear from the pulpit and in classroom that "the Jews kill Christ" will of necessity associate any person of Jewish faith with the alleged "Christ Killers" of nineteen hundred years ago. They cannot help but accept the church teaching that the descendants of those who committed "the unforgivable sins of deicide" deserve the worst fate. I am referring to what among others the Church Father Chrysostomus and the Reformer Martin Luther have said on this subject.

Personally, I have never been able to understand how a human being can kill God. More importantly, if "the Jews" in the second half of the first century sentenced Jesus, a fellow Jew, for blasphemy it was their right to do so, jus as it is the sovereign right of American Courts of Law to sit in judgement over any fellow American who, they believe, violates an American law. In reality, however, it was not "the Jews" (a term made popular by the Gospel of John) i.e. the entire Jewish people who rejected Jesus' claim to messiahship but only some sudducean priests. The latter were frightened by the claim of a fellow Jew to be "the Kind of the Jews" at a time when Rome which was occupying Palestine tolerated "no Kind but Caesar." Scholarly research has established that it was the Roman procurator, with the consent of some members of the Sanhedrin, who sentenced the gentle Rabbi of Nazareth to the shameful death on the cross, a cruel Roman way of administering the death sentence. The ironically intended inscription on the cross, "INRI", "iesus Nazarenus Rex Iudaeorum," "Jesus of Nazareth, Kind of the Jews" gives the reason why Jesus was crucified.

According to Christian theology Jesus had to die in order to save mankind from its sins. It is not the living Jesus but the crucified Christ who brought salvation. Thus, had Jesus lived out his life like any other human being there would be no salvation. His death was indispensible to divine salvation. Accordingly, whoever crucified him was an instrument of God and, rather than cursed, should be praised.

However, the concern of this letter is primarily not with historical or doctrinal aspects but rather with the practical consequences of the teaching that "the Jews killed Christ." Even if "they" had, it would be contrary to all codes of morality to blame children "for the sins of their fathers." Who would think of holding present-day Greeks accountable because "the Greeks killed Socrates." Would anyone hold the present generation of Germans and their descendants accountable for all eternity for the crimes of their forefathers during the Nazi era? Only in the case of Jews are the normal ethical standards set aside. Why? Why, in God's name, should the descendants of the very people which gave Christendom its Holy Scripture, its moral code, yes, the foundation of its religion be punished for "the sin of deicide" they did not commit in the first place? How can such a doctrine be reconciled wit the profession of Christian forgiveness and love which is to extend even to enemies?

Most certainly, Jews are not enemies of Christians but, as the medieval Jewish philosopher, Moses Maimonides, said, "co-workers in the building of God's Kingdom on Earth." It is high time that we unite at long last as God's witnesses and servants in the building of His Kingdom.

THE HEART OF THE MATTER

*Given at Downtown Rotary on May 7, 1977 after
his recovery from multiple vessel bypass surgery at the
University of Wisconsin Hospital. This is an abstracted
version.*

To be able to attend Rotary again makes this a Red Letter Day
for me. On this occasion I want to express to you my heartfelt thanks
for your concern and good wishes for me. The thoughts of good
friends are a source of encouragement for which I am deeply grateful. In the hundred of get-well cards I received there was one which
I particularly appreciated. It said: "The Board of our organization
voted at its meeting last night 9 to 8 to wish you a speedy recovery."
With such over-whelming support how can one not get well.

Today I am here in response to an invitation which I received
from President Owen and the program committee to tell you how it
was. I am glad that I am alive to tell the story.

When you go to the shopping centers on Madison's East and
West sides, particularly on day of inclement weather, you see members of a new fraternity which in recent years has come into being, "Brothers" yes, even some "sisters," under the Skin," individuals
engaged in their daily ritual of walking up and down the shopping
malls. The credo of these peripatetics is: "Do not interrupt – walking." This growing brotherhood is made up of individuals who have
undergone heart surgery and who have been advised by their doctors
to walk – walk – walk. Some who at one time worked for a living
now walk for a living. His special group is part of the even larger

more conspicuous brotherhood of the growing number of joggers who faithfully puff their way through our streets while others go to the University's Natatorium for daily or weekly exercise. All of them have one common goal, namely, to regain strength after heart surgery or to help prevent the hazards of cardio-vascular trouble.

Heart disease has grown into a foremost health problem in our society. Americans have twice as many heart attacks as people in other countries. Are they to be found in the way we live, or are they based on genetic inheritance? In Finland heart disease is virtually unknown. The same is true of Crete and Southern Italy inspite of the high cholesterol level of Mediterranean food. A Winston Churchill could smoke long black cigars non-stop and drink to his heart's content all his life and live to 91. Some individuals can eat all the eggs and cheese, the good fatty German Leberwurst and all the other high cholesterol foods without any adverse effect; others seem to get high cholesterol from drinking water.

While our understanding of the causes of heart disease is still rather limited, it is remarkable, nay miraculous, what medical science and technology have accomplished in recent years to prolong he life of people suffering from cardiac trouble. It all began with Dr. Christan Barnard of South Africa and Dr. De Bakey of Houston, the fathers of heart transplant surgery. Drs. Lepley and Johnson of St. Luke's Hospital in Milwaukee, have been chief pioneers in cardiac bypass surgery.

Three of our four local hospitals are equipped for this highly complicated kind of procedure. In 1976 one of them did more heart surgery cases than appendectomies. Over a year ago we where at Rotary heard the personal testimonial of Pres. John Weaver. He told us that the very first coronary artery bypass in the world was done in 1966 by an assistant professor at the University of Michigan Medical School, Dr. Donald R. Kahn, who six years ago was persuaded to come to the University of Wisconsin Hospital and who is now chairman of Division of Thoracic and Cardio-vascular Surgery. The coronary bypass operation is today the foremost life-saving heart operation in the world. 70,000 coronary bypass operations are now being performed in the United States annually.

Today, I am here to give still another testimonial. My open heart surgery for five artery bypasses was done at University Hospitals on January 11ᵗʰ, exactly four months ago. During the nine hours of surgery from 7:00 a.m. to 4:00 p.m. a battery of physicians, medical technologists and nurses worked on me to repair my clogged arteries. They sawed the breastbone down the center to expose the heart, took a vein from the leg to be implanted into the heart's surface to carry blood which will bypass the diseased heart and narrowed coronary arteries, and put the heart and lungs to rest while their functions were being taken over by a heart-lung machine. Thanks to anesthesia and high potency drugs have no recollection whatsoever of the surgery, of being in he intensive care nit after surgery, nor of the 18 days in the hospital, except for the last four days. In a sense, I was not there, i.e., consciously. I cannot even recall what happened to me from December of last year on. It began when Dr. Rowe, one of the country's foremost experts on heart catherization, recommended bypass surgery after he had found that my arteries were 90% clogged. This meant that I would have little change to go on working by living on nitroglycerine pills as I had for so many years. Even today, four months to the day, my short-term memory has not come back. Some to whom I have mentioned this disconcerting experience of not being able to remember, have consoled me by saying that they forget even without ever having had heart surgery.

But this amnesia seems to be Nature's merciful way of making otherwise agonizing experiences bearable. Who would like to remember the sigh of myriads of tubes connected to his body. Not only do I not recall anything that was done with and for me but I also do not have the slightest idea of how physicians, ordinary mortals, can do what they do. For the layman it is all beyond comprehension. We are living in an age of scientific and technological miracles. No wonder at the ancients regarded physicians as miracle workers and magicians.

No human being can go through an extraordinary experience in his life without reflecting upon its deeper implications. I still recall my very first class in philosophy as a freshman at the University of Berlin in the fall of 1925. The professor introduced us to the world of philosophy by distinguishing between what he called "the naïve realist" (who takes life and whatever pertains to life for granted) and the philosopher who searches for deeper dimensions. Reality is not just that which appears to our naked eye on the surface. Reality has a way of transcending itself, point beyond itself. SO have human experiences. So has Life. It is for its transcending meaning that we must look to become more fully attuned to the miracle and the mystery of Life.

Can we discern some transcending meaning in a physical ordeal of the type of surgery which brings us close to the valley of the shadow?

We are so constituted that we learn most by contrast and experience. After I had lived six years under the Nazi regime in daily fear of violent death, I came to cherish the freedom of this greatest of all countries in the world more than if I had never known its opposite. When in the summer of 1939 I arrived in Chicago with four dollars in my pocket and for months had to look – not by choice but by pure necessity – for drugstores where a bowl of soup was five rther htan ten cents, I came to identify with the poor and hungry in the world more than if I had never gone through this experience. Nothing in life becomes real until it becomes personal.

It is the same with trouble, physical or otherwise. To be sure, we do not look for trouble. We do not seek pain. We try to escape it. And yet, no matter how hard we may try, we cannot. Pain seems to have a definite function in the total economy of our lives.

Bodily pain is a warning signal that something has gone wrong. Without this signal we would not go to see a doctor. Pain makes us aware of our creatureliness. When we are in good health, we do not appreciate the incredible gifts of body and mind. We are not even conscious of the fact that we have a head and a heart, a pair of eyes and legs, or nay of the organs which keep us going from day to day, making our existence possible. It is only when we have a headache that we suddenly realize we have a ahead, when our teeth hurt that we have teeth, when we have heart trouble that we have a heart. Until such time, we have been "naïve realists,' taking the most miraculous for granted, as if it had to be so. Furthermore, pain makes us conscious not only of our creatureliness, but also of our common humanity, so that ultimately and hopefully nothing human remains alien to us. Man who is often unbelievably cruel would be infinitely more cruel were it not for the fact that he experiences trouble and pain. Well being has a tendency to make us self-centered, even arrogant; pain and suffering humbles us, making us realize that all people in the world are bound together into one universal bond of humanity. Much as we shun pain, its discipline has an obvious function in the total scheme of human existence.

During the months of my slow recovery I had ample time for the reflection toward which we are less inclined amidst an active and busy life.

I say "reflection." I am using the word deliberately so as to differentiate it from "analysis." In an age of scientific materialism we are less and less aware of the inherent limitations of the human mind. We have acquired the tendency to analyze everyone and everything. For mortal man to try to analyze the mysteries of life is like for an ant crawling on the ground to try to analyze the human enterprise. It is a common experience that too much analysis leads to paralysis. The mysteries of life cannot be analyzed; they can only be accepted with humility and awe. They cannot be expressed in rational language but can only be alluded to in poetry, in music and dance, in sacrament and symbol. "The most beautiful thing we can experience is the mysterious," Einstein once said. "He to whom this emotion is a stranger, who can no longer pause to wonder and stand rapt in awe, is as good as dead...To know that what is impenetrable to us really exists, manifesting itself as the highest wisdom and the most radiant beauty which our dull faculties can comprehend only in their most primitive forms – this knowledge, this feeling, is at the center of true religiousness."

I am saying this because when we speak of "Life" we are dealing with a mystery – in fact, the deepest of all mysteries before which even the wisest are without knowledge.

Once we see and experience Life for what it really is, our whole attitude toward life, toward people, toward ourselves will of necessity undergo a decided change. Instead of fretting and complaining about all the little things that do not go according to our wishes, each day that we wake up with renovated power, that we can do our work and that we can fulfill our human potential, ought to be a day of thanksgiving. In short, the realization that for a little while we share in the privilege of living ad in the mystery of existence will give our life a new direction and quality. It will impel us to try to give back to life what we have so graciously received. Life is God's gift to us, what we do with our life, is our gift to Him.

The same change of attitude will also come from the realization of the brevity of earthly existence. Naturally, when you undergo surgery which bring you close to the gates of death you cannot help but reflect on the precariousness of human existence. Life is precarious from the moment we are born. We never know which day will be our last day or how much of this amazing life experience is left. It is true that we all live by the greatest and most helpful of all illusions, the illusion that our life will go on forever. There is no limit to our thirst for life. Yet, when you get to be seventy you know that most of your earthly life span is over. It is the brevity of our days which make them so very precious.

There is nothing morbid in thinking about the brevity of our earthly pilgrimage. "We cannot live fully until we have faced our finiteness" says Elizabeth Kubler Ross, one of the leading thanatologists. Thinking about the end of earthly days should most certainly not be a constant preoccupation – which would be a sick obsession. But reflecting at times on our true human situation even before we have come to the threshold of the allotted three score years and ten, is healthy. It can remove from our spirit the natural fear of the Unkonwn. Socrates said that Death is either a permanent sleep of the entrance into a different possibly higher form of existence. Whichever it is, the ancient sage added, there is no reason to live in dread of what lies beyond.

Confronting our finiteness can also give us a proper perspective of life. While it is true, as Kierkegaard said, that life must be lived forward but can be understood only backward it is equally true that life an be understood and appreciated best not from its beginning at birth but from the vantage point of its consummation in death. Since our lives are woven into an infinite stream of eternity, Spinoza was right when he said that life ought to be viewed "de specie ae- ternitatis," "From the aspect of eternity." "Look at the palm of your hands," our Latin teacher in High School said "the lines in your palm form two capital m's, standing for "Memento Mori," "remem- ber that your are mortal." The certainty that our earthly days are few and fleeting should not dismay us but teach us "wisdom," as the Psalmists said: "Teach us to number our days that we may acquire a heart of wisdom."

What is this wisdom? It is the wisdom that comes from a bal- anced view of life which accepts its beauty and grandeur but also its agony and pain, the latter being the price we have to pay for the privilege of being alive. It is the wisdom that makes us conscious of the ambivalence of existence which is to say that we ought to be in the world but not to be totally of the world. Yes, we must be in the world. This is the only Life we know and love. We ought to take it seriously, do our duties, strive unceasingly to leave this world a better place than we found it. Parasites only accept and exploit. Human beings find their destiny in a synthesis of working and witnessing, in serving and loving, as Freud and others before him have said.

There are cultures which belittle and deprecate man's involve- ment in life. They regard escape from the prison house of existence as man's highest goal. These cultures are for the most part backward and their people appear to be miserable. Western culture has a posi- tive attitude toward material achievement and intellectual progress. Yet, at the same time, or better, because of our life-affirming philoso- phy we ought to be on guard that this life does not absorb us totally, does not swallow us up, does not enslave us, does not blind us in our awareness of what is of ultimate importance. Success, accomplishment, name, fame are important for our self-fulfillment but they are not the ultimate. With all of our involvement in life, we ought to retain what Nietzsche called "the pathos of distance." We do need distance toward life, toward the world, toward people, and most of all, toward ourselves. To be in the world and yet not be to be of the world is the secret of balanced and creative living. It is "the heart of wisdom" of which the Biblical poet spoke.

Thoughts such as these were going through my mind, not so much during my hospital stay when the hope of going home and returning to my usual activities as fast as possible absorbed much of my thinking, but rather during the months of my slow convalescence.

Being laid up in the hospital has its compensations. It affords you time to think; it makes you meet wonderful people, doctors and nurses; it renews friendships, and most of all, it makes you well. But it is no fun to be recycled. It disrupts your life. For the money it costs, you could have taken two trips around the world. It makes your wife nervous and keeps her busier than ever (I was afraid I would have to negotiate a new labor contract with my wife for fear that a government agency would sue me for exploitation of woman's labor.) On top of it, you literally lose your pants. (There must be a less inglorious way of losing thirty pounds.) In addition, you are the recipient of all kinds of ideas. Someone suggested that my surgery depressed the Stock Market for on January 11, the day of my surgery, the Dow Jones Industrial average dropped 10.22 points. You would be surprised at how much gratuitous advice you receive when you are sick from such well-meaning people as psychiatrists, marriage counselors, estate planners, weight watchers, salesmen of cemetery lots, and purveyors of schemes of salvation – from Positive Thinkers to Meditation Societies. I even received a letter from a Milwaukean, now a student at the world headquarters of the Maharishi Yogi in Switzerland urging me to contact the local branch office for spiritual counseling.

A well-meaning elderly lady suggested that for purposes of filling my time and maintaining my mental health I should take up crocheting and needlepoint. Even the local Telephone Company seemed to have been eager to help me in my recovery. For reasons totally unknown to me – I have always paid my bills – they omitted my name and phone number from the new directory. I do appreciate all the advice and help offered to me from so many quarters. Hen you are flat on your back, you cannot afford to reject any assistance. And yet, having myself practiced medicine without a license and psychiatry without a couch for 45 years, as most clergymen do, I realized that ultimately it is only Mother Nature and Father Time, these gifts of divine grace, which can heal and help. I have placed my trust in them in the past and shall continue to do so in the future.

"More than anything," the author of Proverbs said, "guard your heart for from it go out the issues of Life." The heart which we have to guard is not only the physical heart, the motor of the spirit, which gives life quality, meaning, purpose, and mobility. The Prophets of old exhorted men to give up the old heart of stone and to seek a "new heart" of flesh because only a new heart could possibly change the world by building, as they said, a new heaven and a new earth. Many years ago, an elderly lady, in fact the mother of a fellow Rotarian, showed me a little slip of paper which she carried in her purse bearing this quotation. It is plan but much to the point: "We go through this world only once. Every little kindness we can do, let us do it now, for we shall not come this way again." This is the heart of the matter.

THE ECUMENICAL COUNCIL
AND THE JEWS

Given before final approval of the Encyclical in 1965.
This is an abstracted version. Errors and abbreviations
are exact copy of this draft from the Swarsensky
Archives.

I wish that this lecture on "The Ecumenical Council and the Jews" which I have been asked to give, be presented by a Christina theologian. A Jew, no matter how hard he tried, will find it well-nigh impossible to discuss this problem as Livy, the Roman historian he would write Roman history, "sine ira et studio," dispatsionately. While for a believing Christian the subject is primarily one of theology, for the Jew it is one that involves literally life and death. It is humanly impossibly to take the rational detached attitude of a scholar when your very existence is involved.

On the other hand, I would not want my presentation to be or to be understood as a philippiea against Catholic Church or a polemic against Christian doctrine. Aside from the fact that some of my best friends are Christian, there is too much of sublime value in Christianity which I reverence. Moreover, I conour with the position expressed in our century by the J. theologian Frans Rosenzweig in his major philosophical work "Star of Redemption" that both J. and Ch. have their distinct and necessary place in the divine economy, or as the J. philosopher Moses Maimonides in the 12 c., who said that both, J. & Chr. are stepping stones leading up to the kingdom of the

Messiah. I deem it necessary to make this prefactory statement to that the intent of this discussion which is didactic, rather than polemic, not be misconstrued.

Why should Jews be interested in an Ecumenical Council of the Church of Rome?

As citizens of a one-world community, we are vitally interested in what our neighbors no matter how far away they live, think and do for everyone is our neighbor. As members of a community of faith, we are deeply concerned how adherents of other religions about God, life, Eternity and death, man and society. As Jews we have a direct interest, yes a measure of curiosity as to what the spokesmen of a tradition with which we share historic and religious heritage, have to say about us.

And indeed, Vatican KI, as the Ecumenical Council is known, had in addition to many other things, also something to say about Jews.

It is said in draft, consisting of six paragraphs from which I quote the following most significant portions:

> "Since the spiritual patrimony common to Chr. and
> Jews is of such magnitude, this sacred synod wants
> to support a recommend their mutual knowledge
> and respect a knowledge and respect that are the
> fruit, above all, of biblical and theological studies as
> well as of fraternal dialogues. Moreover, this synod,
> in her rejection of injustice of whatever kind and
> wherever inflicted upon men, remains mindful of
> that common patrimony and so deplores, indeed
> condemns, hatred and persecution of Jews, whether
> they arose in former or in our own days.
> May, then, all see to it that in this catechetical work
> or in their preaching of the world of God they do
> not teach anything that could give rise to hatred or
> contempt of Jews in hearts of Christians.

May they never present the Jewish people as one
rejected, cursed or guilty of deicide.
What happened to Christ in His Passion cannot be
attributed to the whole people then alive, much less
to those of today. Besides, the Church held & holds
that Christ underwent his Passion in death freely
because of the sins of all men & out of infinite love."
The draft concludes:
"The Church awaits that day known to God alone,
on which "all people will address the Lord in a
single voice & serve Him should to shoulder."

This document was approved on November 20, 1964, the last day
of the third session of the Ecumenical Council in Rome by a vote of
1,651 of the church Fathers in favor, 242 in favor with reservations
99 against, and 4 abstaining.

In its condemnation of anti-Semitism, in his rejection of the
doctrine of the J. people as one that is cursed and guilty of deicide,
the declaration by the high legislation and representative Council of
the Catholic Church marks a turning point in history attitudes of
some 1500 years.

This declaration which will be presented for the final vote when
the Vatican Council reconvenes for its fourth session in Sept. of this
year, has in itself a checkered history. The genesis of this draft declaration is recounted in detail by a Catholic author who observed
the often dramatic developments in St. Peter's as well as behind and
inside the Vatican walls. You may read this account in the January
issue of <u>Commentary Magazine</u>.

But even more important than the five year old history of this
document in the 1,500 year old history which gave birth to this declaration on the Christian attitude toward Jews and Judaism.

A great many Jews are abysmally ignorant on the official Christian attitude toward Jews and Judaism. They see what often mani-
fests itself as anti-Jewish sentiments, or anti-Semitism, as a matter
of prejudice which is based on the universal dislike of the unlike.

Consequently, they believe that better acquaintance of the inter-faith amity, appeals to brotherly sentiments members of the majority and minority group would eventually eliminate ill will, acrimony, prejudice.

Due to this rather naïve, superficial view which sees the problem in sociological and psychological categories, it is not understood that the problem is essentially theological. It, therefore can neither be undersottd nor resolved by applying common secular categories. It can be comprehended and resolved, if at all, only by viewing it as a theological proposition.

What then is the traditional theological view of Christianity toward Jews and Judaism?

In answering this question, it is important to understand that the attitude of the Church to other non-Christian religions, such as Buddhism, Hinduism, Confucianism, is fundamentally different from that of Judaism. To the former, Christianity has no organic historic relation. The Church can therefore be more relaxed, more tolerant in her attitude.

Not so to Jud. Both stem from the same spiritual root. To Hindus and Buddists, Pope Pius XI could never have said "Spiritual we are but all Semites, not Muslims and Hindus." "Jews & Jud. hold a definite and unique place in Christian theology.

The Church views the J. people as the people whom God had chosen to make known His will to all mankind. But this sublime status which the J. people held in the divine scheme, since the days of Abraham, God removed from them with the coming of Christ. The divine sonship was not transferred from the J. people to Christ, who, because what Israel was to be – God's only begotten Son.

Israel's choseness was merely in preparing the way for Christ. With the advent of Christ, the ancient Covenant was abrogated to be replaced by the New Covenant. The Church became the chosen people of God, the new, the true Israel.

The Jews should have been the first to accept the New Cov. but, instead, they repudiated it, they rejected their own Messiah, they put the Savior to death, they crucified the son of God.

By committing this unforgivable sin they incurred divine punishment. They were rejected as the people of God, dispersed among the nations. Their suffering, their homelessness, their persecution is deserved. It is in expiation of the unforgivable sin of having rejected and killed the God-man Christ.

This guilt rests not only on the Jewish people who lived in the days of Christ but upon all Jews for all times. Only their conversion at the end of time will bring them peace at last. The presence of Jews and Jud., after the coming of Christ is an anachronism in history and an affront to God.

As the Bible History for use in Catholic schools in the U.S. first copyrighted in 1881 reads on p. 208:

> "For 1800 years has the blood of Christ been upon
> the Jews, driven from Judea – without country,
> without home – strangers among stranger – hated,
> yet feared – have they wandered from nation to
> nation, bearing with them the visible sign of God's
> curse. Like Cain, marked with a mysterious sign,
> they shall continue to wander till the end of the
> world."

A more recently revised version of the same paragraph reads:

> "For 1800 years the Jews for the most part have
> refused to accept Jesus as the Christ. Yet the
> abundant graces He won for all men will be theirs
> as soon as the J. attain to real faith in Jesus. St. Paul
> tells us that the Jews are still the chosen people of
> God, and that as soon as their unbelief gives place to
> belief in Jesus, they will enter into all the privileges
> of the Kingdom of Christ."

It is correct that these doctrines – including that of Deicison have never been made of Dogma of the Church; yet, the impact of these theological vies has been profound and lasting, never he less. They determined the fate of the Jews for 1500 years.

The secular powers incorporated the teachings of the church into legislation which was directed toward humiliating the Jews, treating him as social outcasts, segregating him from the general populace behind Ghetto walls, depriving him of the normal ways of earning a livelihood by forbidding him to own land, join the gilds, and forcing him into occupation no one else watned, making his life one of constant harassment and insecurity, robbing him of his meager possessions, and expelling him from country after country and confronting him again and again with the alternative of conversion or death.

"If there are ranks in suffering, writes the 19th c. historian, Leopold Zuns, "Israel takes precedence of all the nations – if the duration of sorrows and the duration of sorrows and the patience with which they are borne ennoble, the Jews are among the aristocracy of every land – if a literature is called rich in the possession of a few classical tragedies, what shall we say to a National Tragedy lasting fifteen hundred ears, in which the poets and actors were also the heroes." (Syn. Poesie)

It was only in Christian countries and under Christian ruler that life of Jews was a veritable nightmare. In Muslim countries and under Muslim rulers a symbiosis took place which resulted in cultural cross-fertilization as attested by the so-called Golden age in Span which knew no Inquisitions, no auto-der-fes, no persecution, no expulsion, no bloodshed.

The teachings of the Church concerning Jews & Jud. did something else which has its reverberations to this day, long since after the medieval Christian state has given way to the modern secular state: These teachings have poisoned the psychological bloodstream of Western man to a degree that even the non-believing Christian, the Gentile, whose thinking is secular rater than religious, is infected with a attitude toward the Jews which reflects not merely the universal dislike of the unlike, the psychological basis of the common phenomenon we call "prejudice" but rather an attitude which is utterly unique n te realm of psychology because it is a strange admixture of antipathy, xenophobia.

Anyone interested in this psychological phenomenon which, to my knowledge, is without parallel in history.

As Father Cavanaugh pointed out in a recent issue of the Catholic Sunday Visitor, the church came to forget that Jesus was a Jew, that his mother was a Jew, that the apostles were Jews; that the crowd that shouted Hosianna was made up only of Jews; that Martha and Mary Magdalene, and Nicodemus who wept when he went via doloras to Calvary were Jews; that those who stood silently by his tomb, were all Jews. In the popular mind, the only Jews was Judas Ischar the betrayer. The Church came to present the Jews as enemies of Christ; Jud. as a religion of vengeance the Pharasees as hypocrites, as worship of dead letter of stern law, Jews were money changers whom Jesus threw out of the Temple; merciless people like the Levite in the store of the good Samaritan.

The J. became a theological abstraction; he was no longer human. And so the medieval mind could explain the altogether non-human nature of the Jew in only one manner: The Jew must be a creature of the Devil, the minion of Satan, the anti-christ.

This concept goes back to John who in the 8th chapter (verses 44) presents Christ addressing Jews "If God were your father you would love me. But ye are of your father, the Devil." or the 3rd chapter of the Book of Revelations which refers to the Jews as "the synagogue of Satan."

While Christ is portrayed as blond, blue-eyed, Arayan, Satan is depicted with Semitoic features, warthy, hooked-nosed, curly haired.

A vast literature grew up which supplanted the real Jew with the theological image of the Jew.

Canon Law and Liturgy, the writings of the Church fathers and Semons in Churches portrayed the Jew as a vile creature. Med. mystery, miracle, and morality plays, legends, poems, folk tales, even the writings of Chaucer, Shakespeare, Byron, Dickens, Thackery, Proust,

T.S. Elliot – not to forget the Oberammorgan passion play – perpetuated the theological image of the J. with the result that the popular mind became poisoned with what amounted to a "Pious Hatred" unequalled in its ferocity.

As a result, the often repeated term "Christian love" had a strange, ring to J. ears. It appeared as love that knew one exception: the Jew. And the Jew grew weary of being loved to death. The Jew had a strange feeling when he heard about Christian forgiveness. It excluded one alledged guilt: deicide, the sin that could not be forgiven.

Moreover, to this day, the Jew has never been able to understand what "Deicide" is. How can man kill God?

But assuming that his forefathers did kill the God, man-christ, was this not part of the Providence of God?

Had Jesus lived out his lifelike any other Jew and died like any other man, mankind would have no salvation, no atonement, no everlasting life. In order to fulfill his mission as vicarious sacrifice for man's sins, he had to die. He blood, his death atones, not his life. Were then the Jews not merely instruments of God's will. Was Christ death not a necessary part of the history of salvation? Rather than cursing the Jews, should they not be thanked for having allowed themselves to be used in the divine plan of salvation? Jews have never been able to resolve this seeming contradiction in Christian theology.

But the truth of the matter is that the J. really did not kill Jesus. Did all the 4 million Jews then living in Judaea and in the lands of the Diaspora take part in the Cruxifixion? Did they take a vote whether Jesus be put to death or not? Did all the Jews living in Judea, or even in Jerusalem know what was going on in the capital city that Passover week? "Jewry was never involved since Jewry knew nothing about it," writes Barbares Ward Jackson in an article "Rooting out the Fatal Myths pub. in <u>London Observer</u>, (Aug. 11 & 18, 1963).

If a Jewish court of Law sentenced another Jew, that would have been part of its jurisdiction as is an American court as much legal authority to sentence another American who has been a judge guilty.

However, from the point of view of J. law there was no legal ground for Jesus being sentenced to death. It was unfortunate, yes, tragic, that he died innocently at the hands of the Roman forces of occupation authorities who regarded him a rebel against the Empire who claimed to be King, misunderstanding his claim that he was the "King, Messiah, as having political implications thus nailing him to the cross, a Roman, not a Jewish way of execution, mocking him as Kin by pulling a crown on his head, a purple mantle over his shoulders and placing the inscription on the cross, "Jesus, Nazarenus, Rex Judaeorus, Jesus of Nazareth, King of the Jews." The socalled J. part in Jesus death lies in the cooperation of a few J. leaders, possibly Saddurean priests with the dominant power of imperial Rome.

But all this I know, has no bearing on the problem which is theologically lodge in the realm of rather than history.

To the popular mind, the Jew is the enemy of Christ therefore "God hates you," St. Chrysostomos said, and therefore men must hate the Jew too.

Owing to the influence of this teaching, the very word "Jew" has become in the Christian world not just the designation of someone who adheres to another religion but rather an epithet of apprebrium, word of contempt even to this day when I am told that a recent teen-age fad of students in Madison schools call anyone they dislike, "a Jew."

This opprobrious use of the word "Jew" began in the 2nd half of the 5th c. when the <u>Codea Theoldosianus</u> first give it the connotation of contempt it has retained in the Western world.

This use of the term Jew as meaning Jews of all times, past, present and future, established the principle of corporate responsibility or association by guilt. It was not only the Jews living at the time of the crucifixion who bear a holy guilt but Jews for all times, even those yet unborn.

But why did the Church not preach genocide in retaliation for deicide? Why were not all Jews murdered? Since they murdered the song of God?

Hundred of thousands were. For the masses who did not know and understood the subtleties of theology, this was the consistent reaction to the teachings and preaching to which they had been exposed.

The truth is that the church as such never tought extermination of Jews. It was not infrequent that Popes interceded on behalf of Jews who would appeal to the Pope when the masses reacted with violence toward inflammatory sermons of the lower clergy.

Why could Jews appeal to the highest ecclesiastic authority and often be assured of protection from the mob? The answer lies again in theological concept, the "Privilege of Cain." Cain murdered his brother Abel. His punishment is not to be murdered but to become a homeless wanderer upon the face of the earth.

Not death but a life of humiliation & contempt is the punishment for deicide. The Jew must live, not because he deserves mercy, but rather because as a harassed peopoe his continued existence is a living witness to the fate that awaits those rejected the Christ.

To the popular mind, the suffering of the Jew, homelessness his persecution are fully deserved. Under a picture in a religion magazine showing Jews fleeing for their lives during a program I read these words: "This is what happens to those who deny Christ."

As Father George Tavard, the Catholic theologian, has written (The Church, the layman and the Modern man, pp. 79-80):

> "To the mind of anti-Semitic bigots (the idea that
> the Jews are cursed because their ancestors crucified
> the Lord) explains a good deal of history. God
> would periodically "visit" the murderers of Christ
> and incite them to penance through persecution.
> All the anti-Semitic excesses of times past and
> present can thus be cheaply excused. They are freely
> granted the blessings of Providence..."

Even Luther, who in other respects broke with the religion heritage of the past, did not alter the traditional attitude toward Jews and Judaism.

"Verily," he said, a hopeless, wicked, venomous and devilish thing is the existence of these Jews, who for 1400 years have been & still are our past, our misfortune, our torment. They are just devils and nothing more. And then he goes on the recommend that their Synagogue be destroyed, their property be taken and they expelled from the country.

What Luther had recommended – scholars say out of anger he because the Jews did not flock to his reformation faith – Hitler did. He burned their Synagogues, he robbed their property – he expelled them from their homes and murdered as many as he could get hold of – 6 million – close to 40% of all the Jews in the world.

Hitler was not a believing Christian, he was a Pagan. I doubt whether he had ever read the Gospel of John, the church fathers, the scholastics nor Luther's writing; and yet he was infected to the degree of an obsession with the poison of the general conception of the Jew, and he knew that he could rely upon finding a responsive echo in the conscious and sub-conscious mind of millions of Europeans, not only Germans. Thus, he drew the ultimate and inescapable consequences of 1500 years of teaching of contempt and hatred of the Jew.

The Church had said, "The Jew has no right to live among us." Hitler simplified this statement: "The Jew has no right to live." "I have been attacked," he said, "because of the way I treat Jews. For 1500 years the Catholic Church has considered Jews as pernicious, has relegated them to ghettos, understood what Jews were...I join myself to what was done for 1500 years...I am perhaps rendering the greatest service to Christianity."

When cattle care filled with Jews were rolling over the railroad tracks of Europe to extermination camps and crematoria furnaces of Auschwitz & Dachau were belching with the smoke arising from asphyxiated and burned J. bodies – the blood brothers of Christ – the world majority of church leaders, both Catholic and Lutheran, remained silent because they were not certain in their minds and hearts that Hitler was not right in what he wrote in "Me in Kampf" "I believe today that my conduct is in accordance with the will of the Almighty Creator. In standing guard against the Jews, I am defending the handiwork of the Lord."

Cardinal Bea declared on the floor of the Vatican Council, "that the Nazi atrocities would have been almost impossible if some of the claims of Nazi propaganda did not have an unfortunate affect even on faithful Catholics; the more so, since the arguments advanced by that propaganda often enough…was drawn from the New Testament and from the history of the Church."

The Rev. James O'gara, editor of the Catholic weekly, <u>Commonweal</u> wrote, "The Nazies' attack was carried out in a climate of opinion prepared by the fact of centuries of hostility to the J. people. It is this teaching of contempt that is at fault, and it is this cancer that we must root out of we are to call ourselves Christians."

Dorothy Thompson, said it in simpler newspaper language: "Hitler could not have executed his diabolic plan, had the world not stood idly by and silently applauded."

When the ware was over – 20 years ago this week – and the conquerion armies of General Eisenhower and Zukov broke open the iron gate to the Concentration and Extermination Camps, when the world stood aghast before the incredible results of 1500 years of teaching a dangerous theological myth, thousands upon thousands of skeletons of starved, maimed, murdered, still unburied J. bodies whose only crime had been that the blood of Christ had been running in their veins, some Jews felt: This was it, we have nothing to lose any more. The time for being polite is over. There is a time to be silent and a time to speak as the author of Ecclesiastes said. The Time to speak and to speak up has come.

In the wake of the holocaust, J. efforts were directed towards rebuilding J. life chiefly in the old-new land of Israel, where Jews have given the only dignified response to death and destruction – by creating one place on earth where the building life, new life by the homeless Jew can rest his weary feet and re-create his bruised soul

– thus writing finds under the tragic chapter of enforced homeless-ness, and destroying the cruel myth of Abasver.

But there were also others who were thinking about the deeper causes of the re-current Jewish martyrology.

One such individual was the author of the seven fol. "Cours d Historire", the renowned French historian, Jules Isaac. He was a Jew, but, like many others one who had never thought took deeply about J. life and destiny. However, when his wife and his children, were deported and gassed at Auschwitz like hundreds of thousands of other French Jews, this learned gentlemen, then well over 70, be-gan to read everything that could provide a possible clue to the ques-tion that tormented him unceasingly. How could human beings, members of a nation known for its civilization in which religion and state were unified, yes, religion taught in public schools, turn into beasts like the Nazies?

Prof. Isaac, at the age of 85 – he died 2 years ago – gave the answer in two books: "Jesus et Israel," "Jesus and Israel" and more important, the second one, "L'enseignment du mepris," "The Teach-ing of Contempt." In his studies, Isaac discovered what other Jews had known long before him but never dared to say, probably for fear of repercussions, that what he called the teaching of contempt of Jews on the part of Church, namely that they were collectively ac-cursed for the crime of deicide and that it was God's will that they suffer and be a homeless wanderer on the face of the earth, was the ultimate cause for the poisoned mind of believing and even no-mind Christians toward Jews and Judaism.

In 1947, he organized a conference in Switzerland made up of concerned Jews and Christians at which the participants drew up a ten point – statement concerning the Christian attitude toward Jews.

With the zeal of a neophyte the old man pursed his goal. In 1949, he was granted an audience with Pop Pius XII in which he asked that certain offensive phrases concerning the Jews in Catholic prayers be changed. The Pontiff refused the change the actual word-ing a few months before he died on June 3rd, but consented that new less an offensive translation be made. In 1963 John XXXIII angrily interrupted the Good Friday service at St. Peters when the Sistine Choir changed the old offensive version and had the Choir repeat the prayer "De Perfidis Judaeis: with the offensive phrases omitted.

On June 13, 1960, three years before this incident, so characteristic of the sainted Pontiff, John XXIII one of the great and noble spirits of the throne of St. Peter, Isaac had met the Pope and submitted to him a voluminous dossier on Jewish – Christian relations. The Pope studied it and was deeply impressed with the spirit in which and the purpose for which it was presented. He beseeched the Pope to appoint a special commission to deal with the question of Jews and Jud. The Pope responded to this request of the aged J. Scholar. The Pope himself in his 70's, <u>instructed</u> another aged gentleman, the German Jesuit, August Cardinal Bea, to study the documents presented by Isaac and to draw up a document "De Habitudine Catholicorum Ad non-Catholicos et Maxime Judaeos" "Concerning the Attitude of Catholics towards non-Catholics and especially toward Jews."

The document on the Jews was presented in the closing days of the 2nd session of the Ec. C., on November 8, 1962.

Essentially it contained 3 points:

1) The church has its roots in the Covenant made by God with Abraham and his descendants. A deep bond binds the Church to the people of the Bible.

2) The Jews are not a cursed people, nor should be called Deicides, God-killers or held accountable for the crucifixion of Christ. Responsibilities for his death falls not on all Jews living then and much less on the Jewish people today, responsibility falls rather on all sinful mankind – a statement first made at the Church Council in Trent in 1545/63., and regarded by some Catholic theologians as the official position of the Church.

3) Hatred and persecution of Jews in ancient times and in our time must be condemned. Better understanding and esteem should be promoted between Catholics and Jews.

After three days of debate, the discussion on the statement was postponed. No action was taken when the Vatican Council adjourned in December 4, 1963.

The schma was attacked no only on the theological but also on political grounds, as diplomatly dangerous.

Even in the days of Pope John, Nasser and the heads of other Arab governments had registered their protest against all of Cardinal Beas' proposals. Contributions from Cairo and like-minded sources in Italy, and Spain has financed the publication of an Anti-Semitic book "Plot against the Church" which was distributed among the Church Fathers. A document friendly toward Jews may lead to Vatican recognition of Israel. Cardinal Bea countered such attacks by reiterating that whatever document be drawn u, would be strictly theological not political in character. Pope Paul, to dispel any such fear on the part of the Arab world, on his visit to Jordan and Israel took pains to avoid the impression that he recognized the political state of Israel. He visited the Holy land, entering it as a Pilgrim by special, unofficial route, not used by foreign diplomats.

When the Council reconvened for its third session, there was a debate on the revised text lasting two days. Sept. 28 & 29 of last year. Prior to the debate, 170 American Bishops had met and unanimously decided o actively press for an improved declaration by reintroducing deleted passages and by deleting those, not in the spirit of their position. They delegated as their spokesmen, Aux. Bishop Leven of San Antonio, Arch. Bishop O'Boyle of Washington, Cardinals Cushing, of Boston, Ritter of St. Louis and the late Card. Meyer of Chicago and many others.

In the meantime, Nasser had sent his ambassador to Rome to see the Pope. Pres. Sukarno of Indoeasia who received by the Pope informed him that, f the document of Jews was passed, all Vatican diplomatic missions in Arab countries would be closed.

One may wonder what would happened without the massive support and the moral indignation, the spiritual fervor and the eloquence of the American Prelates.

2500 Fathers of the church listened when Cardinal Clashing booming voice known to millions of American form Pres. Kennedy's funeral service echoed through the basilica of St. Peter. "We must condemm," the Cardinal declared, "every attempt to justify hatred and persecutions as Christian actions. We have all seen in our time the evil fruit of such attempts. Neither Christian theology nor historic reason implies hatred, iniquities or persecution of Jews. We should really think whether it would not be just to confess humbly before the world that Christians have often failed to live up to Christ in their relations with the Jews. In this age of ours, how many Jews have suffered and died because of indifference because of silence... If not many Christian voices were lifted in recent years against this great injustice, let our voices humbly cry out now."

On November 20 of last year, the last day of the third session of the Ec. C. 89% of the Fathers of the Church assembled n Rome, gave overwhelming approval to a third draft drawn up as was the first one of a year ago, by Cardinal Bea and his secretariat.

When the text of this document was published in the secular press, many newspapers accounts carried the heading, "Jews Exonerated of Deicide Charge." The Christian Century reacted differently.

"The document tells Catholics that they should "not impute to the J. of our time what which was perpetrated in the Passion of Christ." "This is scarcely adequate apology," write the Protestant indenominal weekly – "certainly it is not adequate atonement for the crimes Christians have committed against Jews and defended with the charge that Jews are God-killers – Sept. 23, 1964

...The Christian sin against the Jews remains until Christian bodies repent publicly for the atrocities which Christians in all ages have committed against Jews and which they have justified with the historically false and brutal charge that Jews deserve such treatment because they "killed God. Let them so act that headlines read "Christians Repent of Sin Charges against Jews."

"Catholics have nothing to forgive" – wrote Edward M. Keating, publisher and editor of RAMPARTS, a Catholic layman's journal, "instead Catholics should seek forgiveness for 2000 years of anti-Semitism."

The British archbishop Heenan expressed himself in commenting on the declaration of the Vatican Council he said in a sermon in Westminster Cathedral: "What the Ec. Cl. Had in mind was moral reparation to the J. People."

No one felt more deeply that the church, not the Jews were on trial in Rom, than Pope John himself. Had he lived for the final promulgation of this codument he would have instructed all priests from all the pulpits throughout the world to offer on a fixed day the following prayer which, according to the Catholic author of the Commentary article to which I alluded earlier, he composed three months before his death:

"We are conscious today that many, many centuries
of blindness have cloaked our eyes so that we can
no longer either see the beauty of Thy chosen
people nor recognize in their faces the features of
our priviledge brethren. We realize that the mark
of Cain stands upon our forheads. Across the
centuries our brother Abel has lain in the blood
which he drew or shed the tears we caused by
forgetting Thy Love. Forgive us for the curse we
falsely attached to their name as Jews. Forgive us
for crucifying Thee a second time in their flesh. For
we knew not what we did."

219

With this declaration marked a turning point in the history of Christian-Jewish relations. Will, the words with which Pop John XXIII opened the Ecumenical Council, become a living reality, that "divine Providence is leading us to a new order of human relations?"

The Sperry Center at the non-denominational ProDeo University for Social Studies in Rome is engaged in a project of surveying religious textbooks for prejudicial reference to Jews and other non-Catholics. The project has the approval of the Pope.

The Center's research is similar to studies initiated by the American Jewish Committee at St. Louis University and Yale Divinity School in this Country.

The real question is whether the popular mind will gradually be cleansed from notion of the past. Will Christianity eventually give up its ambivalence to Jews and Jud. Will Jews have to continue to cring in fear the moment of reference is made in sermons and speeches and catechetical instruction toward the Jews of Jesus times of today. Will Jews be able to freely and fully and happily appreciate the sublime elements in the Christian faith which was almost 2000 years have brought inspiration and solace to millions of Christians who have found and are finding still in this presumably post-Christian era a satisfying answer to the ultimate questions a man will ask forever about God and man, about life and death.

We must also be mindful of what cannot be expected, neither today, nor tomorrow or ever. We cannot expect, Christianity to amend the text of the New Testament by excising anti-Jewish passages in the Gospels and Epistles.

Jews do not change the text of the Old Testament either. Those of us who are liberal simply ignorethe portions of the Bible which we feel are but of historic significance but have no relevance for us today.

We also cannot expect Christianity to surrender its hope for the ultimate conversion of Jews. Msgr. John Oesterriecher, the head of the Institute of Judaea-Christian Studies, expressed the official Christian position correctly when he said in his work. "The Apostolate to the Jews" "Whether we will or no, we are missionaries at all times…we will win the Jews if we move on the height to which we are call." (Vol. 6, no 4, pp. 82 FF)

That the church entertains and will continue to entertain even after the schema is promulgated, this her eschatological hope should be neither a cause of surprise nor of resentment to Jews. Christianity surrendered her desire to bring the good news of the Gospel to all the world – including Jews – it would surrender what it considers its divine mission. This Jews must understand is not a matter of good will that are promoted of Brotherhood week meetings but a matter of ultimate and unalterable theological commitment to a super natural mandate. Believing Jews can expect any such change of the Christian posture no more than Christian and other non-Jews can expect Jews to abandon their messianic hope that "The Lord shall be king over all the earth; in that day the Lord shall be one and His name shall be one." (Zech. 14:9/ 16)

But these theological differences need, not be the cause of antagonism distrust. They can and must be made part of the new Dialogue between Catholic Christians and non-Catholic Christians as well as non-Catholic Christians, of which are schema speaks. Dialogue implies to learn from each other, to respect each others convictions and to speak whatever we consider the truth in love.

The desire to speak truth, as I see it, in love compels me to state that I do not contend that the teaching of the Church concerning Jews is the sole cause of what is commonly called "Anti-sem."

So-called "Anti-Semitism" has essentially three roots: 1) psychological 2) economic 3) theological; on the psycholical plane it is caused by the universal human trait of the dislike of the unlike on the economic level it is caused by the universal human trait of envy of the gifted. On the theological plane it is caused by the religious image Christianity has curated of the Jews as part of its theology, and the charge of the Jew as a Deicide people to be held accountable for all times for the death of Christ.

If now, the highest authorities of the church of Rome, through the official declaration designed to change this age-old image, to view the Jew not as theological abstraction but as men, members of the Community of the Covenant with the religious desting, a religious etos, different from that of Christianity, and yet, valid and essence in the divine Providence, there is hope that together we may realize our common vision of that world in which men will at long last live as brothers.

GROWING OLD
WITHOUT BEING OLD

From the Wisconsin State Journal November 23, 1975.

After Rabbi Manfred Swarsensky of Temple Beth El recently addressed the Downtown Rotary Club, advising "Never Grow Old," The State Journal received many requests to publish his talk. Here it is, slightly condensed.

There are three ages in the life of man: youth, middle age and "how well you look."

Age is something we usually observe only in others rarely in ourselves.

We push the thought of our own growing old out of our mind. The deliberate building of a psychological darn against the onrushing flood of years is part of the greatest – and most helpful – illusion by which we live, the illusion that our life will go on forever.

The resistance to growing old is born out of the anxiety over the finiteness of our human existence. What has been a universal experience of man in all ages, is compounded in our age.

Our culture is town between the Greek and the Biblical attitudes toward age. Biblical faith holds that a society which respects its elders possesses stability. The Hebrews accorded highest honor to the aged. The Greeks worshipped youth.

Western technological civilization places a high premium o youth, infinitely higher than any previous civilization. While of late, society has begun to focus increasing concern on its senior citizens, we, nevertheless, idolize the young, the young executive, the young college president, the young teacher, the young doctor.

Prejudice exists

The prejudice against older people which exists in our economic life also prevails in our social life. The more urbanized our society has become, the more isolated from the mainstream of society have older people become.

It is an accepted fact of modern life that aged parents do not live with their married children. If they can no longer maintain their own homes or apartments, they have to live in the company of other aged in retirement homes or in homes for the aged.

Most older people today would not even want to live with their married sons and daughters. An occasional visit, not extended too long, is felt to be the best way to maintain tension-free relations.

Aging means losses

When one's life partner has passed on and when children have moved away and established their own families, loneliness becomes a heavy burden.

There is no denying aging means suffering losses. What are these major losses? There is the loss of bodily vigor and mental faculties.

We lose our instrumental role in life. Man's greatest need is the need to be needed. We simply are no longer needed as we were before, either in our jobs or in our families.

We lose prestige and dignity. It has been said that people die of loss of dignity as often as they die of medical causes.

We lose close ties with loved ones. The number of our friends and contemporaries is constantly diminishing. We already know more people who are dead than are living. We attend more funerals than weddings.

As a result, we are in danger of losing the sense of purpose in life and, wit it, the sense of futurity. We have nothing to look forward to.

It is often an unwarranted euphemism to call old age "the sunshine years of life." For all too many there is little sunshine in the declining years of life.

The losses we suffer with aging often create in older people a veritable gerontophobia, a fear of aging. The prospect that he sun of life is setting strikes fear in the human heart. The knowledge that we must withdraw from the arena of active life fills our hearts with melancholy. No wonder that the ancient Greeks envied their gods who, according to their mythological belief, were endowed with eternal youth.

Throughout the ages, man has used all kinds of devices to retard aging and to recapture youth.

Life expectancy rising

Because of society's growing concern for the aging, government has begun to play an ever increasing role in the care of the elderly.

In 1971, I was privileged to attend the second White House Conference on Aging in Washington as one of the Wisconsin's 36 delegates appointed by the governor.

The purpose of the White House Conference was to recommend to the government legislation on behalf of our aged population. In preparation, the state delegation had met for months to present its own legislative proposals. We took ours along to Washington in a small volume titled "Wisconsin Elderly Speak to Their Nation."

Family responsibility

It is my personal belief that the primary responsibility for caring for the aged does not lie with the government but rather the family of the aged.

While government has a definite responsibility for the welfare of our elderly citizens, the sons and daughters of aging parents should not be permitted to abandon responsibility for those who have given them the best that anyone can give, life and love. It is an old story that so very often one father and one mother can care for 10 children, but that ten children cannot care for one aged father or mother.

The needs of older people are not necessarily financial. Social security, pension plans, and Medicare have in large measure begun to take care of these needs. The needs of older people are far more often social, psychological, and spiritual. Erich Fromm lists five psychological needs as basic: 1) The need for a sense of identity; 2) The need for relatedness and belonging; 3) The need for rootedness; 4) The need for a frame of reference to organize our life; 5) The need for transcendence of our time-limited existence.

While these are the needs of human beings at all stages of life they are more especially the needs of older people. And the satisfaction of these needs can certainly not be relegated to government of any outside agency. They are part of the interplay of the individual and his family as well as that of his cultural and religious community.

The second exception I had to take to some of the speakers at the White House Conference on Aging was their insistence that, when the delegates return to their home communities, they should concentrate their energies on changing the total national attitude which regards the ageing as second-class citizens.

Changing attitudes

I hear just a little too much about changing attitudes. Everyone wants to change someone else's attitude. When I started out in my career, also 45 years ago, I wanted to change the attitude of the whole world. For the last 35 years I have been trying to change the attitude of my present congregation. Since I have not succeeded, thus far, I have now come to the point where I realize that there is only one person whose attitude I might possibly change – that is myself – and that too is difficult enough.

The only one who can possibly change the attitude toward aging, are the aging themselves. The real question is: how do older people accept the fact of getting old. In all the circumstances of life, not what we experience is decisive, but how we relate ourselves toward what we experience.

Our attitude toward growing old depends in large measure upon our general attitude toward life. A person who has been a misanthrope all his life will be the same self-centered miserable person in old age. Conversely, an individual who has lived life with zest, with openness to new ideas, with dedication to ideals and with concern for people, who has learned to transcend his own life, will carry the same love of life unto the advancing years without bewailing his lot and pitying himself.

Life is supreme gift

Life is the supreme gift bestowed upon us by the Creator. If we truly appreciate this fact, if we are mindful that life is a sacred and revocable trust to which the Giver of Life retains the title, if we realize that the brevity of this trust makes it all the more precious then aging is neither a calamity nor a tragedy or a disease but a natural process in the cosmic economy in which even death has its purpose as a great and final home-coming.

The kind of philosophy of life we evolve during our formative years determines our attitude toward life in our advancing years.

There is a serene beauty in old age. I like beards on grandfathers (not grandsons). I like the sight of little old grandmothers, bowed by the burden of age, with knobby knuckles on their fingers, signs of a whole lifetime of work. And what is work? It is our passport toward life.

Yes, aging necessitates retiring from active work. Depending upon the type of our work and our attitude toward work, retirement from active work, be it mandatory or voluntary, is for some a great liberation, for others a traumatic experience, adding to the many withdrawal pains which come with aging.

Marvin Zolot, M.D

Mandatory retirement

The senior-citizen lobby, supported by the American Medical Assn., finds mandatory retirement at 65 socially unwise and physically and psychologically unhealthful. Studies prove that older workers are often more productive than young ones, have a lower absenteeism rate and show more positive work attitudes.

Retirement form active work, which has to come for everyone, need not be retirement from life. Retiring, yes, but retiring from what to what, that is the question.

Some of my friends have suggested to me that, in preparation for retirement, I take up hobbies. When I ask them what they have in mind, one suggested knitting, another recommended needle point, a third one basket weaving. I have not yet come to a definite decision.

Only this I do know that if a human being wants to save himself from inner and outer corrosion, he must remain active as long as this is physically possible.

At Lincoln Center in New York, a university called "College at 60" has been set up for older people who wish to continue keeping their minds active. The Attic Angels Assn. in our community is sponsoring a wonderful project for the Continuing Education for the Elderly open also to people in local nursing homes. The youngest member attending the classes on world history, music, and art is 76, the oldest is 93.

In Madison, the University, the Extension Division, the Area Technical College as well as many churches offer splendid opportunities for continuing intellectual and spiritual growth.

Studies which have been made show that people who remain active, who keep up an interest in the affairs of the world, of their country and community, who give of their time and energy to organizations and outside concerns, in short, who care about life and people, actually live longer.

True, our longevity depends in large measure on whether or not we have been careful in the selection of our ancestors.

Some of the world's greatest minds have contributed to the enrichment of our culture in their seventies, eighties and even nineties. Plato did his best teaching after 60, Socrates gave the world its wisest philosophy in his seventies. Webster worked on his monumental dictionary when he was between seventy and eighty. Goethe wrote his "Faust" when he was 82. Verdi composed "Ave Maria" at 86. Commander Vanderbilt added another hundred million to his enormous fortune when he was between 73 and 75. We may think of men in our generation: Winston Churchill, Albert Schweitzer, Martin Buber, Pope John XXIII.

These and others made their greatest contributions toward life long after they had reached the threshold of Biblical age.

One does not have to be a genius to discover the secret of never growing old. Growing old without being old is accessible to anyone.

Alone but not lonely

Years ago, I learned a lesson from an old lady at the Dane County Home in Verona. She died at 92. One day when I called on her in that little cubby hole in which she lived, which she gave me claustrophobia, she said to me in the course our conversation: "I am alone, but I am not lonely. I have spiritual resources."

How true. Aloneness, which is inevitable as we grow old, does not have to be loneliness, especially not if we have spiritual resources. Spiritual resources drive loneliness away.

Our spiritual resources consist of the totality of the knowledge, the interests, the concerns, the ideas, the aspirations which we have accumulated throughout our entire lifetime. All of life is a preparation for growing old. No one grows old; we are old only if we stop growing.

Age breeds beauty

I once heard Frank Lloyd Wright say: "The older I grow the more beautiful the world becomes." If a person can say this, rather than become bitter, cynical, and hostile toward the world and toward younger people, as older people often do, then he has emptied the cup of life to its fullest. Old age should give our lives greater serenity and "a heart of wisdom."

It is the time when our attitude toward the miraculous fact of being alive should be determined more than ever before by the three great indispensible H's of life – humility, humanity, and humor.

I like the story of the rich old uncle who in his way also set an example of never growing old. He had died childless. His nieces and nephews had gathered at the lawyer's office for the opening of the will in expectation of generous legacies.

When the long expected moment came, the attorney opened the large envelope, pulled out the document and read the uncle's last will and testament: "Being of sound mind and body, I spent it all."

JUDAISM IN THE SECULAR AGE

Keynote Address
By Dr. Manfred Swarsensky, Rabbi
Temple Beth El, Madison, Wisconsin
Convention, Midwest Federation of Temple Sisterhoods
Madison, Wisconsin
March 25, 1968

Jews today constitute six-thousandth of one percent of the world's population. However, the impact which they individually and collectively have made and are making upon human society is totally out of proportion to their infinitesimally small number. It is no vainglory to say that the Jewish people is one of the most gifted people that has ever appeared in the arena of human history. Its disappearance would be an incalculable loss to humanity.

The Jews are not only one of the smallest but also one of the oldest people in the world. Next to the Chinese, the Jews have the longest and most continuous history, spanning almost 4,000 years.

Judaism was born in antiquity in protest to the world-view and the life style of idolatrous Paganism. Judaism still conceives its destiny as witness against idolatry in all its countless manifestations.

Judaism gave birth to two world religions, Christianity and Islam. As a Protestant theologian recently said: "Judaism is the Start of Redemption, Christianity is the rays of that start reaching out to a Pagan world."

Jews have lived in virtually all lands of the Western World and the Middle East. For less than one third of its history, the Jewish people lived in a land of its own. Two-thirds of its historic career unfolded itself in the Diaspora. Judaism can exist and flourish wherever Jews affirm their faithfulness to the Covenant of Abraham, in Israel as well as in the lands of the dispersion.

The nations in whose orbit Jews have lived have been Pagan, Muslim and, for the longest part, Christian. Because of Christianity's built-in anti-Jewish posture, the symbiosis with Christian nations has been marred by successions of oppression, expulsion and murder, reaching a climax in the 20th Century with the systematic annihilation of one third of the Jewish people.

The rebirth of a Jewish nation in its historic homeland is living testimony to the unbroken Jewish will to live.

While Jews have been scattered over many lands, there always emerge a center of Jewish gravity. The vital, creative center of Jewish life and culture shifted with the shifting fortunes of the Jewish people. Today, the center of Jewish gravity, which until the first part of the 20th Century was in Europe, lies in the United States and Israel.

Despite their existence as a small minority in a – for the most part – hostile world, the Jews have demonstrated not only a remarkable capacity for adapting themselves to their political and cultural environment but also an equally astounding capacity for preserving and deepening their spiritual and cultural heritage. Jews are master bridge-builders and synthesizers. By some mysterious alchemy of the spirit they have worked out a veritable miracle: acculturation without assimilation. They have been in the world without being of the world.

Jews have survived political Empires from Haman to Hadrian to Hitler. Judaism has emerged unscathed from the cultural impact of Hellenism and Aristotelianism, Renaissance and Humanism, the Enlightenment and the Industrial Revolution. The revolutions in human thought set off by Copernicus, Rousseau, Darwin, Marx, Freud, and Einstein did not shake Judaism as much as they did the predominant Christian culture which only grudgingly made concessions to movements which tended to undermine its metaphysical and theological world-view.

It is only now, in the second part of the 20th Century at a time when the Jewish people has just emerged from the greatest holocaust in its entire history, that we are confronted with a threat to our spiritual survival. This threat does not come from anything hostile but rather from a friendly and benign force: the secularization of human life and thinking and the Open Society which is the result of the enlargement of modern man's freedom.

Up until modern times, that is until the era of Enlightenment, Jews existed in a closed society and Judaism was accepted as a supernatural world-view. The society in which Jews lived was the self-contained autonomous community. Even the Ghetto was not necessarily a way of existence forced upon Jews by a hostile world but in many instances freely chosen as a way of communal Jewish living. Jews conceived of themselves as a nation in exile, a nation living in expectation of redemption through the advent of the Messiah who in God's own time would gather the exiles into their ancestral land.

What kept the Jews sane and inwardly secure during the insane and insecure Middle Ages was not a liberal faith in progress, nor the hope that Christianity might relent in its hostility and mankind grow more humane, but rather a faith that God would keep His Covenant with Israel if Israel would be faithful to its covenantal pledge to God. Suffering, which to us has often had a demoralizing effect and which seems to prove that there is no God or that God is hiding His face, was to Jews in centuries past proof of the very opposite, namely that Israel's woes were "yisurim shel ahavah," "chastisements of love." Unlike us, who in the face of Jewish misfortune and tragedy are tempted to look enviously at the seemingly good fortune of non-Jews, the Jew of the past found nothing in the world around him that attracted him to the degree that he desired to embrace it. And even, if he personally should never live to see the consummation of ultimate hope for the end of Golus, he was sustained by the certainty that a just God could be depended upon to balance the scales in "the world to come." I have often wondered how our ancestors who for well-nigh 1500 years lived an existence so insecure that it is difficult for us to fathom, could maintain their sanity. The answer is easily found: They lived by a God-centered faith strong enough to move mountains.

I am not saying this for the sake of idealizing the past. I am painting this picture only for the purpose of contrast in order to bring our own situation today into sharper focus.

Wherein lies the radical difference between the Jewish past and the present? The freedom for which Western man has struggled during the past 200 years, and which is now his possession, has shattered the strong hold of the closed community and the fortress of a supernatural faith which had made Jewish life and religion impregnable. Secularism and the Open Society have created unprecedented problems for all Western society, particularly the Jew.

From the days in the 18th Century when our forebears emerged from the pariah status to which Medieval Society had relegated them to this day, we have struggled for a world hospitable to us. Jewish organizations have labored arduously for a society which opened its doors to admit the Jews to full political, social, and economic equality. Gaining acceptance into fraternities and sororities and admission to the executive suite and social club had become a major project of the Jewish community. An exorbitant amount of energy has been expended on the goal of breaking down the walls of segregation. Negroes have just begun to fight this battle which for them presents infinitely greater odds. If Jews are increasingly accepted as members of once exclusive social clubs, if Jewish college students are admitted to general fraternities and sororities, if quotas in medical schools have virtually been eliminated, and if instead of five Jewish professors on the faculty of the University of Wisconsin twenty-five years ago there are now between 150 and 200 – with Jewish deans and members of the Board of Regents – then we cannot but say: "Temporar mutantur et nos mutamur in illis," "Times change and we change with them."

The closed society of the past has in large measure given way to the open society of toda. We Jews are among the beneficiaries of this evolution. We would not want to go back to the closed society of the past with all the disabilities and indignities which is once brought to our people.

We are also the beneficiaries of a second phenomenon which followed in the wake of the era of Enlightenment with over increasing speed: the secularization of our culture. Without the secularization of culture there would today be no political democracy, no science and technology, no capitalism, and no religious freedom.

Christianity, especially in its Catholic form, has most tenaciously opposed the secularization of culture because it presented the most serious threat to the Catholic world-view. Hence, its opposition to the Reformation and Humanism, the Copernican and Darwinian view, Democracy and Socialism, Rationalism and Individualism, as well as the philosophical Positivism and Freudian psychology. Its present battle against birth control and abortion is the last bastion in its century-long battle against the all-encompassing secularization of thought and life. The more ready acceptance of the secularization of culture on the part of Protestantism and Judaism as compared to Catholicism has resulted to the socially relatively more progressive spirit in predominantly Protestant countries as well as in the comparatively larger number of Protestants and Jews engaged in scientific pursuits. Characteristics of this phenomenon was Notre Dame President Theodore Hessburgh's rhetorical question: "Where are our Catholic Einsteins, Salks, and Oppenheimers?" The answer is obvious: The supernatural Catholic world-view for along time conditioned Catholics against entering fields that require research unhampered by dogmatic theological systems.

The best known analyst of the secularization of society and culture is Harvey Cox, Professor of Church and Society in the Harvard Divinity School. In his book, THE SECULAR CITY, a best seller for a long time, he proclaims the good news that Western man has entered "The Secular City," leaving behind the City of God, the sacral society of the past. Secularization occurs when man turns his attention away from worlds beyond and toward this world and this time. It is the process by which man emancipates himself, his culture, his values, and his life form the sanction of a supernaturally revealed religion and makes himself, his reason, his will, and his society the ultimate source of his values. Secularism makes man rather than God the measure of all things.

The de-sacralization of life and thought is the hallmark of our era. Early man lived in a sacralized cosmos; modern man, living in an urban industrialized society, exists in a desacralized cosmos which does not seem to leave room for God. Man no longer feels that he is in need of God to satisfy his needs since he himself has the power for which he once thought he depended upon a cosmic Power. The new secularism insists that the age of religion and metaphysics is gone and that man must derive his standards not from any source outside himself but rather from the source of his own freedom and responsibility. The new secular spirit is not anti-religious in the traditional sense. It rater by-passes and ignores religion. Secularization has accomplished what fire and chain could not: It has convinced the believer that he could be wrong and persuaded the devotee that there are more important things than dying for the faith. Religion is still here, but not as a compelling world view or a divinely felt source to validate our values; religion is rather a hobby, for some, for others a mark of national or ethnic identification, for still others an aesthetic delight. For fewer and fewer does it provide an inclusive and commanding system of personal and cosmic values and explanations. The gods of traditional religion play no significant role in the public life of secular metropolis.

When it comes to morality, man in the Secular City looks less and less to religious sanctions for ethical norms. The old "Thou shalt" and "Thou shalt not" no longer speak to the conscience of secular man.

The process of secularization rolls on, and if e are to understand ad communicate with our present age, we must learn to love it in its unremitting secularity.

These are some of the basic ideas in Cox's deep searching study, THE SECULAR CITY.

If his analysis is correct – and I believe that it is in its essentials – if it is true that the secularization of culture is the major factor determining the ethos of our society, then the question arises: How does this universal phenomenon of present-day culture affect Jews and Judaism.

The secularization of culture and the open society which is its fruit have presented us as Jews with seemingly unresolvable paradox. On the one hand, we have welcomed the advent of the new secular world view and the open society because of the enlargement of freedom which they have afforded us as individuals. On the other hand, we have grown apprehensive as we realize the effect which the process of secularization and the open society are bound to have upon the Jewish community and upon Judaism.

Like the world situation, the present Jewish situation is unprecedented; the new problems which confront us are unparalleled. We have entered a new era, the secular era in our nearly 4,000 year-old history. The past seems to have few answers for the new situation into which we have been catapulted. We are bewildered. We are perplexed.

When I cited Prof. Cox's interpretation of the Secular Age, I believe all of us felt that almost everything he said of the Christian situation applies, mutis mutandis, to the Jewish situation as well; in some respects, less, in others, more.

The modern American Jew, I believe, is secular man par excellence. As a predominantly middle class urban dweller, his life style and his values are those of the Secular City – pragmatically oriented – intellectually sophisticated – cynical toward traditional systems. He, too, wastes "little time thinking about 'ultimates' or 'religious questions.'" His religion, while nominally Judaism, is in reality a variant of secular liberalism. While not attracted to Christian metaphysics and mythology, he feels increasingly uncomfortable within the Jewish orbit; it is not so much "the people of Israel" as "the God of Israel" that causes him intellectually and emotional discomfort; and often, also, his seemingly enforced membership in "the people of Israel."

Like for most inhabitants of the Secular City, so also for its Jewish denizens, the God of his fathers – the God of Abraham, Isaac, and Jacob – has died long ago. Worship has little or no meaning; even though congregational affiliation has increased, membership has become more a matter of belonging than believing, of identification rather than identity. Worship is the weakest of the activities of Synagogue. To 85% of our embers it would make no difference if the doors of the Temple were kept closed from the Memorial Service on Yom Kippur afternoon to the ROs Hashanah eve service of the following year. Synagogues, like hospitals, must be available in case of emergencies or special needs such as Bar Mitzvahs, weddings and Yahrzeits, but even these occasions are more a matter of religious convention than of religious experience.

I do not say this critically but in full understanding of the fact that once the God=consciousness has dropped out of our lives, everything changes. We no longer feel personally addressed by Prayerbook and Bible. We no longer feel the compulsion to relate our lives to any source beyond ourselves. We no longer feel a need for the Synagogue even in the crisis situation of lour lives. Life itself, deep miracle that it is, is no longer regarded a gift of Grace to be celebrated in thanksgiving. Death, deep mystery that it is, is experience in totally naturalistic terms. Thus fewer people feel an inner urge to say Kaddish for departed parents. Piety has become an obsolete experience. Even the word has dropped out of our vocabulary. The secular spirit which has invaded our culture has also taken hold of the Synagogue. We retain the symbols, the ceremonies, and e language of tradition but the spirit seems to have died. Even if our lips move, our heart remains unmoved.

Are we whose Judaism is Synagogue-centered essentially different in our Weltanschanung from those to whom the Synagogue is on the periphery of their Jewish life or not within the circumference of their life at all. Are we more deeply committed to social action programs than the un-synagogued because we have a Social Action Center in Washington and pass resolutions at our Biennials. Is our personal and civic ethic – whether in human relations or sex, whether in our political, social, or business life – Jewish or rather secular middle class? The revolt on the part of our most sensitive youth is often directed against these ver bourgeois values of their elders.

Parents often wonder about the seemingly wide gap between the generations, the crisis in discipline. What we euphemistically call "the generation gap" is in reality merely an index of the from generation t generation increasing penetration of life by the secular spirit. Our children are different from us not in kind but only in degree. We must understand the dilemma of our young people as they leave their home for the college community. Parents, rabbis, and synagogues expect them to remain loyal to Jewish tradition and to maintain Jewish contracts. The University community suggests to them the very opposite: to examine critically whatever they have been taught, to broaden their intellectual experiences and their social contacts, and to look at parents, family, and religious tradition though the lenses of psychology and sociology. It does not take them too long to find out what is wrong with the values and attitudes they have been taught.

The impact of "the Secular City" upon our young people finds its most drastic and dramatic manifestation in the one phenomenon that touches the life nerve of Judaism and the heart strings of Jewish parents more than anything, the growing phenomenon of young Jewish people marrying outside of their own faith community.

We Jews are not the only ones who are confronted with this problem. Forty per cent of all American Catholics marry spouses who are not born Catholics. The extent of Jewish-Christian intermarriage in this country is not accurately known. The Chief Rabbi of Great Britain recently said that thirty per cent of all Jewish college students in England intermarry. The percentage of intermarriage in this category is equally high, f not higher, in this country. Jewish parents often wring their hands in desperation: "Wherein have I failed?" Such self-reproach is unjustified. Since Jews and Christians now live side by side in the Secular City, young people follow the inner dynamics created by the Open Society and by the secularization of our culture. The walls which once separated people are down, and so are the inhibitions of former times. In high school and college, in library and laboratory, in office and in resort hotel, young people meet. And human beings chose a mate from among whom they meet. According to the Government statistics American G.I.s during and after World War II married girls from sixty –one different countries throughout the world. I read of Jewish parents living in a small American community with hardly any Jewish contacts for their daughters. Concerned about their choice of future spouses, the parents sent them to Israel. One married a Christian newspaper correspondent from Greta Britain; the other a Muslim student at the Hebrew University of Jerusalem. According to the Israeli news columnist, American-born Carl Alpert, marriages between Israeli girls and Muslim men have steadily been on the rise despite the legal-religious and technical difficulties involved. Even in Israel the society is an open one. Would that young people listen to the rule, "He who would not be suitable as a mate is not suitable as a date." A recent study made at one of the major Universities in this country seems to indicate that strong parental disapproval as well as maximal Jewish social contact, do make a difference in young people's marital choice. Yet, it is equally true that fewer young people heed their parents' voice.

Our arguments against intermarriage are either sentimental or sociological: Do you want to break your parents' heart? Do you want your grandmother to turn over in her grave? And this, after all we have done for you. Marriage itself requires a difficult adjustment. Why look for additional problems. There is only one authentic argument: Do you want to abandon "the Covenant?" Do you want to throw away 4,000 years of the most noble history? Do you want to cut off your roots for the sake of what you call "love?" But even the latter argument will not impress a young person whose mind is formed by the secular age and whose life style is molded by the open society-particularly not at eighteen, nineteen, and twenty when biology is stronger than theology.

Having sketched the contours of the social and cultural milieu in which we live and in which our children are growing up, the question before us is: How shall we respond to the age of Secularism in which Jews and Judaism find themselves today?

Essentially, we have this option: We can react with anger and with tears as we see old worlds crumble and ancient landmarks being removed. A recent report from Vatican City stated that Pope Paul broke down and wept during an audience at which he recounted reports of disloyalty and disobedience to the Church in Latin America. The bitterness in his heart, the Pontif explained, stemmed from the chronicles of indiscipline and lack of obedience and of filial love received daily by various offices of the Holy See.

We, too, have reason to week as we witness the disintegration of Jewish life, the attrition of time-honored Jewish values, the evaporation of once strong Jewish loyalties. And yet, we do not want to break forth in elegies. Nor do we want to become angry Jews. This is generally the attitude of our Orthodox brethren. Forced by the trends of time into a position of constant retreat, they have in large measure become angry Jews or made desperate attempts to insulate themselves from the currents of the time.

As liberal Jews, we cannot adopt such a policy. We do not want to be Jews by resentment. We do not wish to surrender the benefits of enlarged freedom which the secular age has brought to us as well as to all of Western society. We do not wish to revert to the closed society of the Middle Ages, to the status of the Jews as that of a "despised people" and to the status of Judaism as that of a "despised faith." We know that we cannot share in the benefits of the political, cultural, and economic freedom of the Open Society and adhere to a philosophy of Judaism that prevailed in the Ghettos of Central Europe or the Shtetle of Eastern Europe. We cannot have it both ways, enjoy the benefits of a free and Open Society and not pay a price. At the same time, we cannot close our eyes to the perils inherent in the new secular age. Franz Rosenzweig, renowned Jewish thinker, epitomized our situation when he spoke of it as one of "beloved jeopardy." Secularism has placed Judaism, like other religious traditions, in jeopardy. This "beloved jeopardy" is the source of our ambivalence, the source of our hope as well as the source of our anxiety.

Wherein lies our hope and wherein our anxiety in the secular age? Our hope is grounded in the fact that Judaism by its very nature is prepared for existence in a secular age, certainly better prepared than Christianity.

In the first place, the distinction between the secular and the sacred is essentially alien to Judaism. This dualism is typically Christian, an inheritance from Platonic and Hellenistic thought patterns within Christianity. Judaism does no more countenance a dichotomy between the temporal and the spiritual, the secular and the sacred than between religion and life. Biblical Hebrew does not even have a word for "Religion." To us, the mundane and the sacral are one. Religion is co-terminous with life, and life is the domain in which the spirit of religion has to operate. The doctor who restores health to the human body. The psychotherapist who reintegrates a personality estranged from itself, the civil rights leader who heals the wounds of the broken social organism, the labor board member who mediates between parties at odds with each other, the United Nations peace maker who puts an end to hostilities between warring nations – in short, whoever devotes himself to the supreme task of making life a domain of the divine)"Kiddush Ha-chayim,") – is doing God's work as much and often even more so than the professional custodian of the sacred: the priest, the minister, or the rabbi. From the Jewish vantage point the hope of mankind lies in the expanding company of those who do the work of God even though they may not be conscious of it.

It is because of the unity rather than the duality of the sacred and secular that authentic Jewish leadership is "religious" as well as "secular." It is not merely synagogues that represent Jewish concerns but the multitude of Jewish organizations that make up the fabric of Jewish life from Welfare Federations to Civil Defense Agencies, synagogues as well as Jewish community centers.

We are prepared for the secular age, in the second place, because Judaism is no mere religious denomination (as is Christianity) but both a faith and a community, a unity of faith and fold. Judaism knows no heresy trials. Spinoza's case notwithstanding, we do not excommunicate one who does not subscribe to Maimonides' or any one else's "Articles of Faith." According to Halacha a Jew is and remains a Jew if he is born of a Jewish mother or adopted the Jewish faith or according to our liberal standards, as long as he has not adopted another faith. Many religion-less Jews discovered "the mystic tie that binds" in last year's Israeli crisis as they did in the days of Auschwitz.

As a community of faith and folk, Judaism does not depend upon a systematic theology including a clearly defined concept of God. It is commonly acknowledged that Judaism has doctrines but no dogmas in the Christian sense of the term. It is no accident that the High Priest of the Protestant "God is Dead" theology concede that the question of whether God is dead of not is of no vial concern to Judaism. Unlike Christianity, Judaism does not rise or fall with a dogmatic theology. To us, God is no object of metaphysical speculation but a matter of one's total attitude toward life. The Hebrew term "to know God" does not mean to know His essence – how could finite man know the Infinite? – but to do His will. To do His will means to love God and His creatures. To love God means to love life, to have a trusting attitude toward life (Emuna); life is good, despite all the experiences to the contrary. To the Jew, not doubting or denying this or that doctrine about God but despairing of life is blasphemy. Even Freud admitted that "Jews are animated by a special trust in life." "Religious people call it trust in God," he writes in Moses and Monotheism. From the day when our spiritual ancestor Jacob became an "Israel" to this day, the Jew has wrestled with God and throughout the ages has remained "God's most loyal opposition." Job's cry has been the Jewish credo: "Even though He slay me, yet will I trust in Him."

We are prepared for the Secular Age, in the third place, because for us religion is a matter of social rather than personal salvation. Among the revolutionary changes of our era is the growing acceptance by the Christian Church, yes by the world, of the Jewish position that "the road to holiness must go through action."

Time was – and this trend is far from being obsolete – when the dominant religion depreciated this life here and now in favor of the real life of spiritual bliss in the world to come. The social woes, the frustrations, the dislocations of human society never troubled the Christian conscience as much as ours. "The Jewish people were way ahead of us in their concern for social justice," the wife of a Presidential candidate said the other day in this city.

Today, we hear at long last non-Jewish voices proclaim what Judaism has affirmed for thousand of years, namely that not only the individual but also society is in need of redemption. Christendom has begun to discover the sacredness of the "secular" world. "The Church is tossed into the steam of life." (Teilard de Chardin, Jesuit philosopher). "The sin of the Churches is that it has taken us this long to get involved and concerned with social problems." (Gerald Kennedy, Methodist Bishop). "Religion is where the action is." (Hans Kung, Swiss theologian). "Organized religion's exclusive concern with personal salvation and its disconcern with social salvation, its traditional indifference toward social justice are God's judgment on the Church. The earthquake of Secularism has shaken all of us out of hiddenness and complacency." (Father Erich Kellner, Paulus Society). The Secular Age has forced Christians to discover the world, as it were. In its growing recognition of the need for social redemption Christendom is moving in the direction of Judaism. Judaism is not unprepared for the Secular Age. In many respects the new age heralds the long delayed vindication of Judaism. This is the ground of our hope.

However, our hope, as all human hope, is not without its anxiety. Our anxiety stems from the fact that the new freedom which is the gift of the secular age also contains seeds of destruction. Freedom is the source of man's grandeur; it is also the source of man's corruption.

We cannot be blind to the fact that the secular spirit with all its grandeur has also spawned new idolatries: Pragmatism, Scientism, and Hedonism. These idols have become man's Gods in the secular age.

The perils to the Jew inherent in this new idolatry were eloquently stated by the late Rabbi Abba Hillel Silver: "What we Jews should fear most is the rise of a generation of prosperous Jews who have no spiritual anchorage, a generation of clever, restless Jews of quick ferment and high voltage, rooted in no religious tradition, reverent to no moral code, ignorant of all Jewish learning and held to no social responsibility by inner spiritual restraint, who will range and bluster all over the American scene from business to the professions, from politics to government, from literature to art. Such floating mines are a danger to any people, but particularly to us."

The rise of this generation is not in the distant future. It is already here. It is most certainly not confined to Jews. But here we are concerned only with Jews.

It is becoming ever more evident that the division of Jews into Orthodox, Conservative, and Reform has become obsolete. Since we all live in the same intellectual, social, and spiritual climate of our secular culture, the erstwhile differences between Jews in worldview, life style, belief and observance have lost their meaning. If they exist, they are difference of degree, not of essence, differences of sentiment, not of philosophy.

In reality, new divisions among us have been emerging which are far more accurate descriptions of the real situation. Jews today fall essentially into these three categories 1) Pagans 2) Secularists 3) Traditionalists.

The term Pagan was originally synonymous with Gentile. Gentile did not mean Christian. Here is nothing to attract Jews to Christian metaphysics and mythology, especially not at a time when Christians themselves have begun to de-mythologize their faith. Also, in the Secular City there is not longer a practical advantage in embracing the majority faith as was the case in the days when the State was a Christian State. However, Jews are attracted by the Pagan spirit within modern secular culture. Their religion is Hedonism, a life who essence and goal is pleasure-seeking and the satisfaction of physical appetites – nothing else. They have fallen victim to the modern malaise of materiosclerosis. They are void of all Jewish wisdom. They have no commitment to Jewish values. They want to be free of the burden of the "Ol Malcut Shamayim," the "yoke of the Kingdom" – as Pagans always do. They want to be "kegoyim." They want to vanish as Jews. And they do. Every year, some 90,000 Negroes pass into the stream of the white society. Similarly, an unknown number of Jews pass into the homogenized mass of the nondescript who are anchored in no tradition. Since their values are antithetical to those of normative Judaism, there can be no dialogue between hem and us. We are talking different languages. We are living in different worlds. They create for themselves a problem of personal identity, as one of their spokesmen said: "What have I in common with Jews, I have hardly anything in common with myself." They are lost to us. They are probably lost to themselves. The world is full of lost souls. Society is full of lost Jews. They have sold themselves to the idols of a Pagan world. Jewish tradition calls this type "Epikoros," a term which denotes hedonistic philosophy of life and the resultant denial of the basic principles and values of Judaism. Pagan Jews deserve our pity, not our scorn.

The second group in this emerging stratification of American Jews is the new breed of "secular Jews." Secular Jews are not a totally new phenomenon in Jewish history. Today they abound in the ranks of so-called intellectuals and academicians.

For the secular Jew, the God of his fathers, the God of Abraham, Isaac, and Jacob has died long ago. Worship is a totally meaningless activity. He has no need for the Synagogue, neither its ministrations nor its fellowship. He is anti-synagogue, anti-religious, and anticlerical. He despises rabbis. He feels intellectually superior. He is often in rebellion against the world of his immigrant parents. He is unhappy, yes, resentful that the American ethos almost forces him to join a synagogue if he wants to identify Jewishly or if he wants to have his children receive a Jewish education. If he is interested in Jewish education for his children – and some Secularists are – he will engage a student to teach his children Hebrew. In larger cities he will band together with others to have his children taught a so-called cultural, religion-free Judaism. He is blind o the elemental fact that his "cut-flower Judaism" can neither survive nor be transmitted to future generations. One cannot expect children to acquire the Jewish ethos or what some call Jewish culture, by cutting off the root which is Religion. A religiousless Judaism is bound o wither away like a flower that has no roots and is not watered. Unless he is a Zionist, the secular Jew will contribute if at all, but miserly or reluctantly to philanthropic Jewish causes since he has an ambivalent feeling about Jewish survival and separatism. As a rule, he is a "universalists." To be concerned about Jews and Judaism is parochial. His "universalism" makes him insensitive to specific Jewish needs. In Israel's six-day war Jewish adherents of the New Left exhibited greater concern of the national and social aspirations of Arab nations that for the life and death struggle of the Jews in Israel.

I am taking pains to describe this new reed of secular Jew because, living as I do in a college community, I see the ascendancy of this type. He should be a profound concern of ours because e constitutes a reservoir of intellectual excellence. In many instances he has retained the Messianic fervor of Jewish tradition which drives him into the ranks of those who struggle for social justice. To lose him would be an infinitely greater detriment than losing the Jewish Pagan. The Pagan is a victim of Hedonism. The Secularist is the victim of hazy universalism and cold scientism, the deification of science, one of the gravest perils of our time. The growing understanding of the secrets of the universe should make man humble before the miracle and mystery of creation. Too often they evoke the opposite, man's sinful pride of intellectuality. So insecure is modern man with all his vaunted knowledge that he covers up his insecurity by playing God.

The exposure of the Jewish college student is predominantly to Jewish secularists. He absorbs a philosophy which suggests that the educated person must divest himself of all parochial, particularistic, anachronistic, atavistic loyalties. And Jewish identity is seen as one such loyalty of which to rid oneself.

While there can be no dialogue with Pagans, dialogue with the secular Jew is possible and necessary. Winning him to total Jewish commitment is the particular mission of Reform Judaism today. Of all Jewish groups we understand him best, we can best talk his language. We are liberal; so is he. But as religious-oriented Jews, we also see the danger of scientism, philosophical positivism, and universalism continuously evaporating the substance of religious tradition leaving modern man – and particularly our young generation – morally and culturally naked and estranged to himself.

Where do we come in? The third category of Jews today, who are neither Pagans nor avowed Secularists, I would like to call "Traditionalists." To me this term is not synonymous with "Orthodox" but rather descriptive of those Jews who seek their center of Jewish gravity in the Synagogue. The Synagogue in a secular age is placed into a position in which it has to justify its continued existence. We can no longer rely upon the momentum of the past.

If the Synagogue – and that includes Synagogues of all Jewish branches – has a reason for being, it must stand today, as it has at all times, for a total, undivided Judaism of God, Torah, and Israel – no matter how differently interpreted. We cannot divorce fold from faith and substitute a vague Jewishness which is often nothing more than a kind of sentimental tribalism for a Judaism based upon principle, conviction, and commitment.

If our membership in a Synagogue has any meaning at all, we cannot permit the Pagan and secular spirit to erode the ethos of Judaism nor can we allow its spirit to invade the Synagogue. We must stand for something. We must expect discipline. We must have the courage to be different, lest we lose our soul and the soul of Judaism.

More precisely, first of all, the time has come for adopting a totally new attitude toward worship. Worship, "Avoda," is still the heart of Judaism, as stated, incidentally, in the constitution setting forth the purpose of our congregations. If we continue to belittle the significance of worship, we will soon see all spiritual inwardness drained out of Judaism. If we continue to follow present-day patterns, Judaism will be the only religion in which an individual can be a "good Jew" without being religious. Even psychology concurs with Biblical insight that "man does not live by bread along." Judaism has always regarded worship as "Chova" the obligation of a human being. And that it is still today. The question is not whether we like the sermon, the choir, the prayerbook, the rabbi or the people next us in the pew. Worship is not to be enjoyed. It is not entertainment. It is the corporate expression of the recognition of our creatureliness and the celebration of our grateful acknowledgement of the ineffable privilege of being alive. "Lo hametim yehallelu yah," "The dead do not praise God – only the living." The greatest words that can come from the lips of any mortal is "Barechu et Adonai Hamevorach," "Praise to be Him to Whom alone praise is due." This attitude has to be built into the fabric of one's life from childhood on like other attitudes which become habits. If we have to decide each week at 7 o'clock on Friday whether to go to Temple or not, forget it. You know what the answer will be: the dinner party, the T.V. show, the basketball game are far more enticing. Worship is one purpose only – to have time, time for God in order to give back to Him a modicum of that which He has given to His creatures as our only real possession: Time. The emptiness of our Synagogues is not a sign of our intellectual and psychological scruples as to the realness of God and of our inability to pray, it is rather symptomatic of the resistance on the part of the Pagan and secularist within us to hallow time and life, or, if you will, to say a weekly "Thank you" for the privilege of life. The skepticism of contemporary man is not as we often believe about God, but about man. It is the humanity of man and the meaningfulness of life that are no longer self-evident in an age which is tormented by a feeling that man is depraved and that life is absurd. Jewish worship can help us restore our faith in man and in life.

In the second place, the Synagogue must justify its existence in secular age by transmitting the treasures of the Jewish spirit from generation to generation. Judaism without "Torah" in the broadest sense has lost its soul. And Jewish education is not for children only,

In an age of knowledge explosion, Jewish education must meet the highest standards of education. Twenty-five years ago, I would have opposed Jewish Day Schools for the usual reasons given by Jewish liberals. Today, I would support Jewish Day Schools under Reform auspices not for all our children, to be sure, but for some in larger cities because I have become convinced that without the training of an elite prepared for leadership, we cannot survive in the secular age.

In an age in which Yiddish is vanishing as the second language and as a culture vehicle for Jews, Hebrew and Hebraic culture must become the second language and culture of the modern Jew. The very richness of the Jew lies in his rootage in two cultures rather than one. In Madison and Milwaukee, in Minneapolis and Chicago we are fortunate in having Departments of Hebrew and Semitic Studies at our respective universities. Our best students should spend at least a year at the Hebrew University of Jerusalem.

"Chibbat Zion," "Love of Zion," should be an integral part of our love for "Kelal Yisrael." I often fear that our children, growing up in the secular climate, will become Jewish "America Firsters," people who feel no sense of fraternal responsibility to Israel and World Jewry. As Jews we are members of one large family, "Keneset Israel." It is tragic that in this day of material affluence Hillel Foundations all over and other Jewish needs. Modern Israel has done more for us than we have done for it. The Synagogue must constantly nourish the love of and concern for the whole House of Israel.

In the third place, the Synagogue in the secular age must be a powerhouse of concern for the moral and social ills that plague society, The Christian world is only now beginning to discover the world, to discover what Judaism has known for thousands of years: that not only the individual but also society is in need of redemption. I do not say that our congregations should turn into Social Action Committees. I do say that we of all people have a Jewish mandate to be champions of justice. We cannot relinquish this Prophetic mandate to secularists; nor shall we impose upon ourselves second-class citizenship by remaining silent when the world is burning for fear we migh invite the wrath of the Pagans by standing up and speaking out.

Torah – Avodah – Gemilut Chassadim have been the three pillars upon which Judaism has rested and upon which Judaism will rest if it is too play a vital role in our lives and in the life of society.

But the ultimate test of Judaism's relevance lies today, as at all times, in the manner in which it influences the moral quality of our won persona lives. It is no accident that the Jewish home has been called "Mikdash Katan," "the small sanctuary." It is no accident that the Jewish family, its purity, its cohesiveness and stability, has preserved Judaism throughout all the storms and stresses of our history.

Never – and I mean never – in our entire history have we been confronted with such frightening prospects of the moral and social disintegration of the Jewish family as we are today. Even our detractors have admired the stability of Jewish family life. Promiscuity was unknown. Undisciplined anti-social behavior of the young was unheard of. Jews were hardly ever found in correctional and penal institutions. We were immune to the evils of alcoholism and drug addiction. "Jews", Freud said, "are masters of instinctual renunciation." We no longer are. The Pagan spirit of Total permissiveness – everyone doing what is right in his own eyes – has entered Jacob's tents. The more the Jew has emancipated himself from the Synagogue, its values and disciplines, the weaker his moral fiber has become. Better educated, more money, ampler opportunities, greater freedom – but more divorces, more delinquency, and more moral and mental breakdowns. Judaism can have no truce with so-called "Situation Ethics" nor with the "New Morality" which is neither new nor moral but nothing but the old Pagan Immorality against which already Abraham, our father, protested when he followed the call of the Invisible God.

It is to His call, the call of an authentic, historic, living Judaism to which we must open ourselves in order to save ourselves and society from the very perils which beset modern life: spiritual nomadism, moral nihilism, and philosophical cynicism.

The Secular Age presents Judaism with a new challenge. History has placed before us a new opportunity to bring our message of salvation – and I mean "salvation" in its most original sense as "healing" – to an ailing world. As a veteran of history, who has weathered the storms of history and survived the rise and fall of nations, the birth and death of ideologies, Judaism is prepared and possibly predestined to make the sun of righteousness rise with healing in its wings.

But to this task we must become inwardly attuned. We must undergo in the most literal sense a conversion to Judaism. Merely being born a Jew is not enough. Judaism must be a matter of experience, conviction, and commitment; or it is nothing. We must again learn the Jewish art of being <u>in</u> the world without being totally <u>of</u> the world, the art of integration without assimilation. Vis a vis the "beloved jeopardy" of our existence, we must have the courage of speaking our "yes" to the secular world where it brings blessings and equally powerful "no" where we see its danger signals. At a time when the humanity of man is not longer self evident, Judaism is still the best and the easiest way of being human. We must freely and joyously choose this way if we are to remain faithful to our unchanging destiny of being God's witnesses and servants.

INTEGRATION
WITHOUT ASSIMILATION

Note: Where and when this address was given is not known.

Man derives his identity from identifying himself with the totality of the focus, visible and invisible, that have made him. The Jew learn to understand himself as he accepts his singular place in history as well as his peculiar heritage of mind and heart and spirit which is so unique that, unable to fathom its uniqueness, men have spoken of Judaism as a mystery.

As yet, this is precisely our perennial Jewish situation and our half-chosen destiny: we want to be accepted as individuals, and yet, at the same time, we want to preserve our separathess as a group. We want to mingle freely without neighbors in school, college, and community and yet maintain our Jewish identity.

Is such an attitude "narrow," "Parochia," "atavistic?" To some of us, particularly younger Jews, this may seem so. Judaism, however, has a history of deliberate self-segregation. It is not true that Jewish separateness is solely due to enforced segregation.

Jews themselves have always wanted to be <u>part of</u> the world and yet <u>apart from it</u>.

To modern ears the word "segregation" has an ominous sound. We smell the air of Harlem and Watts; we see the Ghettos of ancient Rome and Warsaw. But we forget that there are two types of segregation: voluntary and enforced. It is the evil of forced segregation against which we protest. Voluntary segregation need not be an evil.

All human associations are based on commonality of ideas and interest, on likeness of back ground on similarities of values. In order to preserve its religio-historic identity, the Jewish people, like any other group, needs some measure of voluntary segregation. We may differ as to the degree, we may differ as to the means, but we cannot differ as to the need and the principle. The principle does not imply hostility toward of a feeling of superiority over others. It is rather an indispensable means for self-preservation. The modern Jew in particular who is in danger of losing himself in the anonymity of his environment and become a non-descript, non-sectarian American must build for himself his own Jewish milieu within the larger non-Jewish milieu. This is the reason why Jewish education in home and Synagogue is so vital, why the maintenance of Jewish organizations is so important.

It is still the role of the Jew today, as it has always been, to be in the world and yet not to be of the world, to be part of the world and yet to be apart from it.

Rabbi Manfred Swarsensky